ISNM

INTERNATIONAL SERIES OF NUMERICAL MATHEMATICS
INTERNATIONALE SCHRIFTENREIHE ZUR NUMERISCHEN MATHEMATIK
SERIE INTERNATIONALE D'ANALYSE NUMERIQUE

Vol. 48

Constructive Methods for Nonlinear Boundary Value Problems and Nonlinear Oscillations

Conference at the Oberwolfach Mathematical Research Institute, Black Forest, November 19–25, 1978

Edited by
J. Albrecht, Clausthal, L. Collatz, Hamburg, K. Kirchgässner, Stuttgart

1979
BIRKHÄUSER VERLAG
BASEL, BOSTON, STUTTGART

CIP-Kurztitelaufnahme der Deutschen Bibliothek

Constructive methods for nonlinear boundary value problems and nonlinear oscillations:
conference at the Oberwolfach Mathemat. Research Inst., Black Forest, November 19–25, 1978/ ed. by J. Albrecht ... - Basel, Boston, Stuttgart: Birkhäuser, 1979.
(International series of numerical mathematics; Vol. 48)
ISBN 3-7643-1098-7
NE: Albrecht, Julius [Hrsg.]; Mathematisches Forschungsinstitut ‹Oberwolfach›

ISBN 3-7643-1098-7
Printed in Switzerland

PREFACE

The conference 'Constructive Methods for Nonlinear Boundary Value Problems and Nonlinear Oscillations' (Konstruktive Methoden bei nichtlinearen Randwertaufgaben und nichtlinearen Schwingungen), organized by the editors of this proceedings volume, took place at the Mathematischen Forschungsinstitut Oberwolfach from November 19–25, 1978.

The main theme of the conference was analytical and numerical procedures for the solution of nonlinear boundary value problems, whereby emphasis was placed on branching problems and their application to nonlinear oscillations. Some problems treated were: Nonlinear wave propagation, nonlinear boundary value problems for the determination of plasma flows and their numerical treatment, numerical procedures for the solution of secondary bifurcation problems, solution of oscillation equations of a chain with a 'hard theorem' on implicit functions.

The response was particularly large, the participants numbering almost beyond the capacity of the Oberwolfach Institute and the varied possibilities for meetings which the Oberwolfach Institute offers were used to the benefit of this conference. We would particularly like to thank the director of the Institute, Professor Dr. Barner, and Birkhäuser Verlag for the cooperation in the production of this book.

J. Albrecht, Clausthal
L. Collatz, Hamburg
K. Kirchgässner, Stuttgart

Contents

Beyn, W.-J.:
On the convergence of the finite difference method for nonlinear ordinary boundary value problems 9
Cryer, C. W. and H. Fetter:
The numerical solution of axisymmetric free boundary porous flow well problems using variational inequalities 20
Georg, K.:
An iteration method for solving nonlinear Eigenvalue problems .. 38
Hackl, H., Hj. Wacker, W. Zulehner:
Aufwandsoptimale Schrittweitensteuerung bei Einbettungsmethoden 48
Joubert, G.:
Explicit hermitian methods for the numerical solution of parabolic partial differential equations 68
Klein, P. P.:
Zur Einschliessung des betragskleinsten Eigenwertes bei Eigenwertaufgaben mit gewöhnlichen Differentialgleichungen vierter Ordnung 85
Mawhin, J.:
Periodic solutions of nonlinear dispersive wave equations 102
Rautmann, R.:
Eine Fehlerschranke für Galerkinapproximation lokaler Navier-Stokes-Lösungen 110
Reissig, R.:
Continua of periodic solutions of the Liénard equation 126
Scheurle, J.:
Über die Konstruktion invarianter Tori, welche von einer stationären Grundlösung eines reversiblen dynamischen Systems abzweigen 134
Schmitt, B.:
Deux méthodes numériques simples dans le domaine des oscillations non linéaires 145
Schumacher, K.:
Obere Schranken für die Ausbreitungsgeschwindigkeit bei parabolischen Funktionaldifferentialgleichungen 150
Seydel, R.:
Numerical computation of primary bifurcation points in ordinary differential equations 161

Sprekels, J. and H. Voss:
Bounds for the critical value of a nonlinear circular membrane under normal pressure 170
Weber, H.:
Numerische Behandlung von Verzweigungsproblemen bei gewöhnlichen Randwertaufgaben 176

ON THE CONVERGENCE OF THE FINITE DIFFERENCE METHOD FOR NONLINEAR ORDINARY BOUNDARY VALUE PROBLEMS

Wolf-Jürgen Beyn

There are well known conditions which finite difference equations approximating a linear ordinary boundary value problem have to satisfy in order to guarantee consistency and stability of the method and hence convergence of the finite difference solutions. Furthermore, under analogous assumptions a local convergence theorem holds in the non-linear case. In this paper we give two global versions of this local result, one which yields a global stability inequality for the finite difference equations and another one which shows that the number of solutions is the same for the difference equations as for the boundary value problem. Our results are illustrated by two examples.

1. Introduction

Let us consider a nonlinear boundary value problem of order k

(1) $D^k u + f(\cdot, u, \ldots, D^{k-1}u) = 0$ in $[0,1]$, $Ru = d \in \mathbb{R}^k$

where f and its partial derivatives $D_{j+1}f\,(j=1,\ldots,k)$ are continuous in $[0,1] \times \mathbb{R}^k$, $u \in C^k[0,1]$ and Ru is of the form

$$Ru = \left\{ \sum_{j=1}^{k} (a_{ij} u^{(j-1)}(0) + b_{ij} u^{(j-1)}(1)) : \; i=1,\ldots,k \right\} \in \mathbb{R}^k .$$

We will treat a general class of finte difference equations for (1) which can be written as follows

(2) $T_h u_h := p_k^h E^{-k_1} \Delta^k u_h + M_h f(\cdot, D_h^0 u_h, \ldots, D_h^{k-1}) = 0,\ R_h u_h = d,$

where $u_h \in U_h$ is the unknown grid function and U_h is the space of real valued functions on the grid $J_h = \{0,h,2h,\ldots,1-h,1\}$ $(h = n^{-1}, n \in \mathbb{N})$. $T_h u_h$ is an element of U_h', the space of grid functions on $J_h' = \{k_1 h, (k_1+1)h, \ldots, 1-k_2 h\}$ where $k_1, k_2 \in \mathbb{N}$ and $k_1 + k_2 = k$. Furthermore, we have used in (2) the translation operators E^m (defined by $E^m u_h(x) = u_h(x+mh)$, $x + mh \in \text{domain}(u_h), m \in \mathbb{Z}$) and the divided differences Δ^m (defined by $\Delta^m u_h(x) = (E-I)^m u_h(x)$, $x + jh \in \text{domain}(u_h)$ for $j=0,\ldots,m$, $m \in \mathbb{N}$).
The operators $p_k^h : U_h' \to U_h', D_h^j : U_h \to U_h$ $(j=0,\ldots,k-1)$, $M_h : U_h \to U_h'$ and $R_h : U_h \to \mathbb{R}^k$ in (2) are assumed to be linear. By their use we are able to consider difference formulas of higher order as well as Hermitian expressions ([5] III, §2).
For linear boundary value problems (1) a theory of convergence of the finite difference solutions with respect to different norms has been developed in [7 , 9] (see also [2 , 16]). Following the simplified approach of [2] we will call (2) a linear scheme for (1) if some conditions of consistency and stability are satisfied for p_k^h, D_h^j, M_h and R_h. In the linear case these conditions imply convergence of the finite difference solutions. In the nonlinear case a local theorem of convergence follows for isolated solutions of (1). This local result appears in various abstract versions in the literature [1 , 8 , 13, 14, 15]. The main drawback of this theorem is that it yields existence and uniqueness of a solution of (2) in a small neighbourhood of

the exact solution of (1) which is just to be computed. By using some global information on the equation (1) we give two theorems in section 3 which determine the number of solutions and show the stability behaviour of the difference equations (2) in the whole space U_h.
These results will be applied to two examples. In particular, we will show that some "parasitic" solutions, which have been found in [3] for a certain finite difference equation at a fixed mesh parameter h, have to disappear as h tends to zero.

2. Linear Schemes

We introduce some further notation. Let $[u]_h \in U_h$ and $[u]'_h \in U'_h$ denote the restrictions of a function $u \in C[0,1]$ to the meshes J_h and J'_h resp.. Furthermore, we will use the norms

$$\|u_h\|_j = \sum_{i=0}^{j} \mathrm{Max}\{|\Delta^i u_h(x)| : x=0,h,\dots,1-ih\}, \quad u_h \in U_h.$$

$\| \ \|_0$ will also denote the maximum norm in U'_h and $\mathbb{R}^k$.

DEFINITION

The difference equations (2) are called a linear scheme for (1) if the following assumptions hold:

(i) D^j_h is uniformly $\| \ \|_j$-bounded, i.e. for some constant $C > 0$, $\|D^j_h u_h\|_0 \leq C\|u_h\|_j$ for all $u_h \in U_h$ and for all h $(j=0,\dots,k-1)$, and D^j_h is consistent with D^j, i.e.

$$\|D^j_h[u]_h - [D^j u]_h\|_0 \to 0 \text{ as } h \to 0, \text{ for all }$$
$$u \in C^j[0,1] \quad (j=0,\dots,k-1).$$

(ii) M_h is uniformly $\| \|_0$-bounded (cf. (i)) and consistent with I, i.e.

$$\|M_h[u]_h - [u]'_h\|_0 \to 0 \text{ as } h \to 0, \text{ for all } u \in C[0,1].$$

(iii) R_h is uniformly $\| \|_{k-1}$-bounded and consistent with R, i.e.

$$\|R_h[u]_h - Ru\|_0 \to 0 \text{ as } h \to 0, \text{ for all } u \in C^{k-1}[0,1].$$

(iv) p_k^h is consistent with I, i.e.

$$\|p_k^h[u]'_h - [u]'_h\|_0 \to 0 \text{ as } h \to 0, \text{ for all } u \in C[0,1],$$

and p_k^h satisfies the root conditions (see [2]).

Conditions (i)-(iv) are satisfied for nearly every reasonable difference approximation to (1), the only nontrivial assumptions being the root conditions in (iv). These have been verified in [2] for a large class of difference methods including those which can be composed of formulas from [5 , Appendix]. Now the following local result is well known, it can easily be derived from the abstract theorem [15, §3(14)] (see [1 , 8 , 13, 14, 16] for related results) and from the linear theory [2].

THEOREM 1

Let $\bar{u} \in C^k[0,1]$ be an isolated solution of (1), which means that the linearization at $\bar{u}$

$$\left(D^k + \sum_{j=0}^{k-1} D_{j+2} f(\cdot,\bar{u},\ldots,\bar{u}^{(k-1)})D^j, R\right) : C^k[0,1] \to C[0,1] \times \mathbb{R}^k$$

is invertible.

Then for each linear scheme (2) there exists an $h_0 > 0$ and a $\rho > 0$ such that (2) has a unique solution $\bar{u}_h$ in the ball $K_\rho = \{u_h \in U_h : \|[\bar{u}]_h - u_h\|_k \leq \rho\}$ for all $h \leq h_0$. Moreover, for all $u_h, v_h \in K_\rho$ and $h \leq h_0$ the stability inequality

(3) $\|u_h - v_h\|_k \leq C(\|T_h u_h - T_h v_h\|_0 + \|R_h(u_h - v_h)\|_0)$

holds and $\|[\bar{u}]_h - \bar{u}_h\|_k \to 0$ as $h \to 0$.

We note that the assumption on the linearization at $\bar{u}$ can be weakened by a condition on the Leray Schauder index at $\bar{u}$ [15, §3(43)]. Since the center $[\bar{u}]_h$ and the radius ρ of K_ρ are unknown a priori, theorem 1 doesn't give much information on the numerical solution of (2). This, of course, is natural under the weak assumption of an isolated solution.

3. Two Global Results

In our first global theorem the assumption on the linearization at the solution $\bar{u}$ is extended to the whole space $C^k[0,1]$.

THEOREM 2

Assume that for some $K_j, K^j \in C[0,1]$ $(j=0,\ldots,k-1)$ we have

(4) $K_j(x) \leq D_{j+2}f(x,y) \leq K^j(x)$ for all $x \in [0,1]$ and $y \in \mathbb{R}^k$.

Let there exist an $\varepsilon > 0$ such that the linear pairs $\left(D^k + \sum_{j=0}^{k-1} p_j D^j, R\right)$ are invertible on $C[0,1] \times \mathbb{R}^k$ for all coefficients $p_j \in C[0,1]$ satisfying $K_j(x) - \varepsilon \leq p_j(x) \leq K^j(x) + \varepsilon$ $(x \in [0,1],\ j=0,\ldots,k-1)$. Then the boundary value problem (1) has a unique solution $\bar{u} \in C^k[0,1]$. Moreover, for each linear scheme, for which M_h is represented by a nonnegative band matrix of a band width independent of h, there exists an $h_0 > 0$ such that (2) has a unique solution $\bar{u}_h$ for all $h \leq h_0$. Finally, $\|[\bar{u}]_h - \bar{u}_h\|_k \to 0$ as $h \to 0$, and the stability inequality (3) is valid for all $u_h, v_h \in U_h$ and $h \leq h_0$.

Instead of going into the rather lengthy proof, which will be given elsewhere, we consider two examples.

Example 1

(5) $u'' + \lambda e^u = 0$ in $[0,1]$, $u(0) = u(1) = 0$.

This problem has a unique solution if $\lambda \leq 0$, two solutions if $0 < \lambda < \lambda^*$ (λ^* a certain critical parameter), a unique solution if $\lambda = \lambda^*$ and no solutions if $\lambda > \lambda^*$ (see [6 , 10] and the references given therein). In case $\lambda \leq 0$ the problem (5) has only nonpositive solutions and it is a standard procedure (cf. [12]) to replace e^u in this case by

$$f(u) = \begin{cases} e^u, & \text{if } u \leq 0 \\ 1 + u, & \text{if } u > 0. \end{cases}$$

Assumption (4) is then satisfied for f with $K^0(x) = K^1(x) = K_1(x) = 0$, $K_0(x) = \lambda$ and it is easily seen by monotonicity arguments (cf. [11]) that for some $\varepsilon > 0$ the equation $u'' + p_1 u' + p_0 u = 0$ in $[0,1]$, $u(0) = u(1) = 0$, has only the trivial solution provided $|p_1(x)| \leq \varepsilon$ and $\lambda - \varepsilon \leq p_0(x) \leq \varepsilon$ ($x \in [0,1]$). Hence any linear scheme (2) applied to (5) with the modified nonlinearity has a unique solution for sufficiently small h which converges to the unique solution of (5). We refer to [4] for a totality of linear schemes. Note that the monotonicity methods of [4] also provide results on the difference equations at definite values of h.

Example 2 (cf. [3] and the references therein)

(6) $u'' + \lambda \sin u = 0$ in $[0,1]$, $u(0) = u(1) = 0$ $(\lambda \geq 0)$.

In case $\lambda < \pi^2$, theorem 2 can be applied with $K^1(x) = K_1(x) = 0$, $K_0(x) = -\lambda$, $K^0(x) = \lambda$ $(x \in [0,1])$, so that every linear scheme (2) applied to (6) has only the trivial solution if h is small enough.

But again, as in example 1, we cannot deal with the case of several solutions which in example 2 occurs as λ exceeds π^2. This problem is covered by the following theorem.

THEOREM 3

Suppose that (1) has exactly N solutions $\bar{u}_i$ $(i=1,\ldots,N)$ in $C^k[0,1]$ which are isolated in the sense of theorem 1. Assume further that for some $p_j \in C[0,1]$ $(j=0,\ldots,k-1)$ we have $f(x,y) = \sum_{j=0}^{k-1} p_j(x) y_{j+1} + g(x,y)$ $(x \in [0,1], y \in \mathbb{R}^k)$, where $\left(D^k + \sum_j p_j D^j, R\right)$ is invertible and g is sublinear, i.e.

(7) $$|g(x,y)| \left(\sum_{j=1}^{k} |y_j| \right)^{-1} \to 0 \text{ uniformly in } x \in [0,1]$$

$$\text{as } \sum_{j=1}^{k} |y_j| \to \infty.$$

Then each linear scheme (2) has exactly N solutions $\bar{u}_{ih}$ $(i=1,\ldots,N)$ in U_h for h sufficiently small and these satisfy

(8) $\|\bar{u}_{ih} - [\bar{u}_i]_h\|_k \to 0$ as $h \to 0$ $(i=1,\ldots,N)$.

The existence of the solutions $\bar{u}_{ih}$ is guaranteed by theorem 1 whereas the nonexistence of further solutions follows from a compactness argument. It shows that any sequence of possible solutions u_h of (2) has a subsequence which converges to a solution of (1) in the sense of (8) so that the local uniqueness result of theorem 1 applies.
In case $N = 1$ this underlying idea is already contained in an abstract theorem of Vainikko [15, §3(27)]. Note, however, that this argument is valid for arbitrary $N \in \mathbb{N}$ and even in the case $N = 0$, if "N solutions" are interpreted as "no solutions".
Let us reconsider example 2. If $n^2\pi^2 < \lambda < (n+1)^2\pi^2$ for some $n \in \mathbb{N}$, then (6) has $2n + 1$ distinct solutions which we assume to be isolated (we still have no complete proof of this). Since $\sin u$ is sublinear theorem 3 shows that any linear scheme (2) applied to (6) also has $2n + 1$ solutions for sufficiently small h. In [3] some additional solutions to these have been discovered for a certain linear scheme applied to (6) at a fixed value of h. Our theorem then shows that these solutions have to disappear as h tends to zero.
Due to the strong nonlinearity e^u, theorem 3 does obviously not apply to our example 1 in case $\lambda > 0$. However, in some cases it is possible to derive a priori estimates for all solutions of a superlinear boundary value problem (cf. [6] section 4).
For example, in the case of (5) we can proceed as follows. For any solution u of (5) we have $u(x) > 0$, $u''(x) < 0$ $(0 < x < 1)$. Hence u has a unique maximum $M = u(x_0)$. Since

$w(x) = u(2x_0 - x)$ satisfies $w(x_0) = M, w'(x_0) = 0$ and the same differential equation as u we obtain $x_0 = 1/2$. Consequently, $-u''(x) > \lambda e^{r(x)}$ $(0 < x < 1)$ where

$$r(x) = 2M \begin{cases} x, & 0 \leq x \leq 1/2 \\ 1 - x, & 1/2 \leq x \leq 1. \end{cases}$$

Now we define v by $-v'' = e^r$ in $[0,1]$, $v(0) = v(1) = 0$, and by the maximum principle, we have

$$(9) \quad M = u(1/2) > v(1/2) = \lambda(4M^2)^{-1}((M-1)e^M + 1)$$

Hence an upper bound for u is given by the largest positive root M_0 of the equation $4M^3 = \lambda((M-1)e^M + 1)$. If λ is large enough the inequality (9) is false for all $M > 0$ and (5) has no solution. A rough estimate shows $M_0 \leq 24\lambda^{-1} + 1$. Now the problem (5) has no solutions (in case $\lambda > \lambda^*$) or two solutions (in case $0 < \lambda < \lambda^*$) which we assume to be isolated. All solutions belong to $\{u \in C^k[0,1] : u(x) < M_0 \text{ for } x \in [0,1]\}$ and $g(x,y) = \lambda e^y$ is sublinear on $[0,1] \times (-\infty, M_0)$. By a slight modification of theorem 3 we then obtain that every linear scheme (2) applied to (5) also has no solution u_h satisfying $D_h^0 u_h(x) < M_0 (x \in J_h)$ in case $\lambda > \lambda^*$ and two solutions satisfying $D_h^0 u_h(x) < M_0 (x \in J_h)$ in case $0 < \lambda < \lambda^*$. Both statements are true if $h \leq h_0$ where h_0, in general, depends on λ. Nothing can be said about the case $\lambda = \lambda^*$ since the unique solution of (5) in this case is not isolated in the sense of theorem 1.

References

[1] Atkinson, K.E.: The numerical evaluation of fixed points for completely continuous operators. SIAM J. Numer. Anal. (1973), 799-807.

[2] Beyn, W.-J.: Zur Stabilität von Differenzenverfahren für Systeme linearer gewöhnlicher Randwertaufgaben. Numer. Math. 29 (1978), 209-226.

[3] Bohl, E.: On the numerical treatment of a class of discrete bifurcation problems. To appear in IAC, Istituto per le Applicazioni del Calcolo, "Mauro Picone", Pubblicazioni Serie III.

[4] Bohl, E., Lorenz, J.: Inverse monotonicity and difference schemes of higher order. A summary for two-point boundary value problems. To appear in Aequ. Math.

[5] Collatz, L.: The numerical treatment of differential equations, 3rd ed. Berlin-Göttingen-Heidelberg, Springer 1966.

[6] Crandall, M.G., Rabinowitz, P.H.: Bifurcation, perturbation of simple eigenvalues and linearized stability. Arch. Rat. Mech. Anal. 52 (1973), 161-180.

[7] Grigorieff, R.D.: Die Konvergenz des Rand- und Eigenwertproblems linearer gewöhnlicher Differentialgleichungen. Numer. Math. 15 (1970), 15-48.

[8] Keller, H.B.: Approximation methods for nonlinear problems with application to two point boundary value problems. Math. Comput. 29 (1975), 464-474.

[9] Kreiss, H.-O.: Difference approximations for boundary and eigenvalue problems for ordinary differential equations. Math. Comput. 26 (1972), 605-624.

[10] Meyer-Spasche, R.: Numerische Behandlung von elliptischen Randwertproblemen mit mehreren Lösungen und von MHD Gleichgewichtsproblemen. Max Planck Institut für Plasmaphysik, Garching bei München, 1975.

[11] Protter, M.H., Weinberger, H.F.: Maximum principles in differential equations. Prentice Hall, Englewood Cliffs, N.J., 1967.

[12] Shampine, L.F.: Boundary value problems for ordinary differential equations I. SIAM J. Numer. Anal. 5 (1968), 219-242.

[13] Stetter, H.J.: Analysis of discretization methods for ordinary differential equations. Springer Tracts in Natural Philosophy, vol. 23. Berlin-Heidelberg-New York, Springer, 1973.

[14] Stummel, F.: Stability and discrete convergence of differentiable mappings. Rev. Roum. Math. Pures et Appl. Tome XXI, No 1 (1976), 63-96.

[15] Vainikko, G.: Funktionalanalysis der Diskretisierungs-methoden. Teubner Texte zur Mathematik, Leipzig, Teubner Verlag 1976.

[16] Vainikko, G.: Approximate methods for nonlinear equations. Nonlinear Analysis 2, (1978), 647-687.

Dr. Wolf-Jürgen Beyn
Institut für Numerische und
instrumentelle Mathematik der
Universität Münster
Roxeler Str. 64
D-4400 Münster

THE NUMERICAL SOLUTION OF AXISYMMETRIC FREE BOUNDARY POROUS FLOW WELL PROBLEMS USING VARIATIONAL INEQUALITIES

Colin W. Cryer and Hans Fetter

The free boundary problem for a fully penetrating well of radius r and filled with water to a depth h_w, in a layer of soil of depth H, radius R and permeability $k(x,y)$ can be formulated as follows: Find $\phi \in C^1[r,R]$ and $u \in C^2(\Omega) \cap C(\overline{\Omega})$ such that $(ku_x)_x + (ku_y)_y = 0$ in Ω, $u(R,y) = H$ for $0 < y < H$, $u_n(x,0) = 0$ for $r < x < R$, $u(r,y) = h_w$ for $0 < y < h_w$, $u(r,y) = y$ for $h_w < y < \phi(r)$, $u_n(x,\phi(x)) = 0$ and $u(x,\phi(x)) = \phi(x)$ for $r < x < R$, where $\Omega = \{(x,y$: $0 < y < \phi(x)\}$. The results of Benci [Annali di Mat. 100 (1974), 191-209] are used to derive a variational inequality and to prove existence and uniqueness. The problem is approximated using piecewise linear finite elements and $0(h)$ convergence of the approximate solutions is proved using recent results due to Brezzi, Hager, and Raviart.

1. Introduction

The steady state problem to be considered is shown in Figure 1.1. An axisymmetric well of radius r is sunk into a layer of soil of depth H and radius R. The bottom of the soil layer is impervious. The outer boundary of the soil adjoins a catchment area and the hydraulic head u is equal to the constant H along this boundary. The water seeps towards the well and a pump (not shown) maintains the water level in the well at a constant height h_w. The water-air interface is a free boundary which intersects the well wall at a height h_s.

The mathematical problem can now be formulated as follows (see Hantush [1964], Bear [1972], and Cryer [1976, p. 86]):

PROBLEM A (Classical)

Find functions $\phi(x)$ (the height of the free boundary) and $u(x,y)$ (the hydraulic head) such that (from the equation of continuity and Darcy's law):

$$\operatorname{div}(k \operatorname{grad} u) = \frac{\partial}{\partial x}\left(k \frac{\partial u}{\partial x}\right) + \frac{\partial}{\partial y}\left(k \frac{\partial u}{\partial y}\right) = 0, \quad \text{in } \Omega, \tag{1.1}$$

together with the boundary conditions,

$$u = H, \text{ on } AB(\Gamma_1), \quad \text{(constant hydraulic head)}, \tag{1.2}$$

$$\frac{\partial u}{\partial n} = 0, \text{ on } BC(\Gamma_4), \quad \text{(impervious boundary)}, \tag{1.3}$$

$$u = h_w, \text{ on } CD(\Gamma_2), \quad \text{(interface with water at rest)}, \tag{1.4}$$

$$u = y, \text{ on } DE(\Gamma_3'), \quad \text{(interface with air)}, \tag{1.5}$$

$$u = y, \text{ on } EA(\Gamma_0), \quad \text{(interface with air)}, \tag{1.6}$$

$$\frac{\partial u}{\partial n} = 0, \text{ on } EA(\Gamma_0), \quad \text{(streamline)}. \tag{1.7}$$

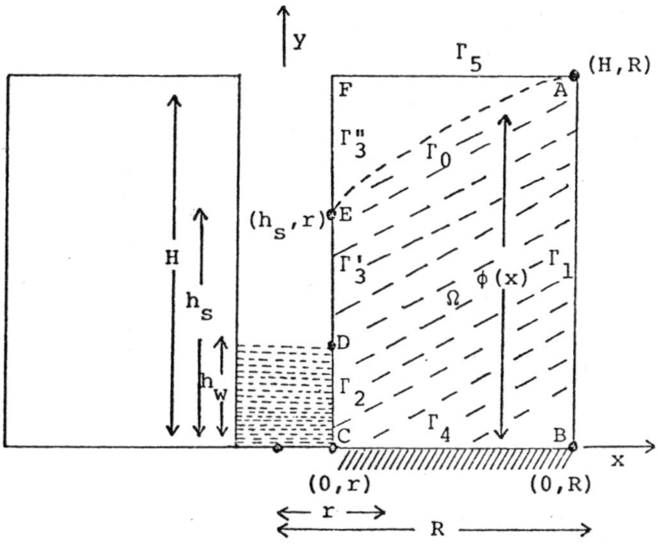

Figure 1.1: An axisymmetric fully penetrating well

Sponsored by the National Science Foundation under Grant No. MCS77-26732 with support facilities provided by the U. S. Army under Contract No. DAAG29-75-C-0024.

Here, Ω is the (unknown) domain,

$$\Omega = \{(x,y): 0 < y < \phi(x),\ r < x < R\} ,$$

and $\frac{\partial}{\partial n}$ denotes the outward normal derivative, Finally, $k = k(x,y) = x\kappa$ where the permeability of the soil is denoted by $\kappa = \kappa(x,y)$. It is assumed, that k is of the form

$$k(x,y) = \exp[f(x) + g(y)] \tag{1.8}$$

where $f(x)$ and $g(y)$ are continuously differentiable and

$$g'(y) \geq 0 . \qquad \square \tag{1.9}$$

In particular if the permeability κ is constant, $\kappa = 1$ say, then

$$k(x,y) = x = \exp[\ell n\ x]$$

so that

$$f(x) = \ell nx; \quad g(y) = 0 . \tag{1.10}$$

Since Baiocchi [1971] showed how certain free boundary problems related to fluid flow through porous media could be reformulated as variational inequalities, numerous studies have appeared in the literature which extend his results in many directions; Cryer [1976] and Baiocchi, Brezzi, and Comincioli [1976] give bibliographies. In this paper the results of Benci [1973, 1974] are applied to the well problem to obtain existence and uniqueness. A finite element method is then used to obtain numerical approximations, and error estimates are obtained.

Cryer and Fetter [1977] give a more detailed account of the present work. They also give references to earlier work and discuss some open questions.

After completing this work we heard that the case of constant κ had been formulated as a variational inequality and solved numerically by Elliott [1976, p. 62].

2. Formulation as a variational inequality

In this section we follow Benci [1973, 1974] and reformulate Problem A, as a variational inequality.

The first step is to introduce a "Baiocchi function" $w(x,y)$ defined on the rectangle

$$D = \{(x,y): r \le x \le R, \quad 0 \le y \le H\}, \tag{2.1}$$

as follows:

$$w(x,y) = \begin{cases} \int_y^{\phi(x)} \exp(g(t))\,[u(x,t) - t]dt, \\ \qquad \text{for } (x,y) \in \Omega, \\ 0, \quad \text{for } (x,y) \in D - \Omega. \end{cases} \tag{2.2}$$

The values of w on the boundary of D can be given explicitly; for a special case see (4.2).

We use the following function spaces (see Adams [1975]): $C(\bar{D})$, the space of functions which are continuous on $\bar{D}$, equipped with the supremum norm; $H^1(D)$, the Sobolev space of weakly differentiable functions on D, which is sometimes denoted by $H^{1,2}(D)$ or $W^{1,2}(D)$, and which is equipped with the norm $||\cdot||_{1,2}$; and $H_0^1(D)$, the subspace of $H^1(D)$ consisting of those elements of $H^1(D)$ which "vanish" on the boundary of D.

Let a be the bilinear operator defined on $H^1(D) \times H^1(D)$ by,

$$a(u,v) = \int_D \exp[f(x) - g(y)] \operatorname{grad} u \operatorname{grad} v \, dxdy ,$$
$$\equiv \int_D \exp[f(x) - g(y)] \, [u_x v_x + u_y v_y] dxdy . \tag{2.3}$$

Let j be the linear functional defined on $H^1(D)$ by,

$$j(v) = \int_D \exp[f(x)] v \, dx \, dy . \tag{2.4}$$

Let K be the closed convex set

$$K = \{v \in H^1(D) : v - w \in H_0^1(D) \text{ and } v \geq 0 \text{ a.e. in } D\} . \tag{2.5}$$

Then Benci [1973, 1974] proves

THEOREM 2.1

If u is a solution of Problem A and $g'(y) \geq 0$ then $w \in H^1(D) \cap C(\bar{D})$ and w satisfies the variational inequality: Find $w \in K$ such that

$$a(w,v-w) + j(v-w) \geq 0 , \tag{2.6}$$

for all $v \in K$. □

By assumption $f(x)$ and $g(y)$ are bounded. Thus, the bilinear functional a and the linear functional j are continuous on $H^1(D)$:

$$a(v,v) \leq \alpha_2 (\|v\|_{1,2})^2 , \tag{2.7}$$

$$|j(v)| \leq \beta_2 \|v\|_{1,2} , \tag{2.8}$$

for all $v \in H^1(D)$, where α_2 and β_2 are constants.

Also a is coercive on $H_0^1(D)$:

$$a(v,v) \geq \alpha_1 \; (\|v\|_{1,2})^2 \; , \tag{2.9}$$

for all $v \in H_0^1(D)$, where α_1 is a strictly positive constant.

It follows from the basic theory of variational inequalities (Stampacchia [1964]) that

THEOREM 2.2

There exists a unique solution $w \in H_0^1(D)$ *of the variational inequality formulation* (2.6) *of the axisymmetric well problem.* □

It also follows from the results of Benci [1974, p. 200] that

$$w \in H^{2,p}(D) \; , \tag{2.10}$$

for any p satisfying $1 < p < \infty$. Since D has the cone property it is a consequence of the Sobolev embedding theorem (Adams [1975, p. 97]) that

$$w \in C^1(\bar{D}) \; . \tag{2.11}$$

3. Numerical approximation

It has been shown in the previous section that the Baiocchi function w satisfies the variational inequality (2.6): Find $w \in K$ such that for all $v \in K$,

$$a(w,v-w) + j(v-w) \geq 0 \; . \tag{3.1}$$

There is a connection between the variational inequality (3.1) and the *unilateral minimization problem*

$$\min_{v \in K} J(v),$$

$$J(v) = a(v,v) + 2j(v).$$

This connection is given by the following theorem (Lions [1971, p. 9]):

THEOREM 3.1

Let $a(v,w)$ be a symmetric coercive bilinear form. Then w is a solution of the variational inequality (3.1) iff w is a solution of the unilateral minimization problem (3.2). □

We approximate w by choosing a finite-dimensional approximation K_h and solving the finite-dimensional problem: Find $w_h \in K_h$

$$J(w_h) = \underset{v_h \in K_h}{\mathrm{Min}} \; J(v_h). \tag{3.3}$$

The convex K_h is constructed as follows. The domain D is triangulated by first dividing D into small rectangles by lines parallel to the axes and then dividing each small rectangle by a straight line joining the bottom right and top left corners. The triangles are not necessarily uniform, but it is assumed that there is a constant $\beta > 0$ such that

$$\frac{1}{\beta} \text{ (maximum length of side) } \leq h \leq \beta \text{ (minimum length of side)}, \tag{3.4}$$

so that h is a measure of the fineness of the triangulation. The set of interior gridpoints will be denoted by D_h and the set of boundary gridpoints will be denoted by ∂D_h.

We denote by V_h the space of piecewise linear functions (linear finite elements) v_h corresponding to the triangulation. We set

$$K_h = \{v_h \in V_h : v_h \geq 0 \text{ in } D \text{ and } v_h = w \text{ on } \partial D_h\}, \quad (3.5)$$

or, equivalently,

$$K_h = \{v_h \in V_h : v_h \geq 0 \text{ in } D_h \text{ and } v_h = w \text{ on } \partial D_h\}. \quad (3.6)$$

The approximation w_h is readily computed as is shown in section 4. Here, we derive an error estimate for $\|w-w_h\|$ by combining the ideas of Brezzi and Sacchi [to appear] and Brezzi, Hager, and Raviart [to appear].

THEOREM 3.2

The piecewise linear approximate solution w_h exists and is unique. Furthermore,

$$\| w-w_h \|_{1,2} = O(h). \quad (3.7)$$

Proof: The existence and uniqueness of w_h is an immediate consequence of Theorem 3.1 together with the fact that a is a symmetric coercive bilinear form on $V_h \cap H_0^1(D)$.

We now introduce some notation. For any two functions $g_1, g_2 \in L^2(D)$ we set

$$(g_1, g_2) = \int_D g_1 g_2 dxdy. \quad (3.8)$$

From (2.10), $w \in H^2(D)$, so that w_x and $w_y \in H^1(D)$ and hence

$$Lw \equiv \operatorname{div} \exp[f(x) - g(y)] \operatorname{grad} w \in L^2(D). \quad (3.9)$$

For any $v_0 \in H_0^1(D)$ we thus have that

$$a(w,v_0) = \int_D \exp[f(x) - g(y)] \text{ grad } w \text{ grad } v_0 \, dxdy ,$$

$$= -\int_D v_0 \, Lw \, dxdy ,$$

$$= (-Lw, v_0) . \qquad (3.10)$$

Finally, we note that

$$j(v) = (e,v) , \qquad (3.11)$$

where

$$e(x,y) = \exp[f(x)] . \qquad (3.12)$$

If $v \in K$ then $v - w \in H_0^1(D)$ so that using (3.10) and (3.11) the variational inequality for w may be written in the equivalent form

$$(-Lw + e, v-w) \geq 0 , \qquad (3.13)$$

for all $v \in K$.

It can be shown that

$$-Lw + e \geq 0 \text{ a.e. in } D , \qquad (3.14)$$

and

$$(-Lw + e, w) = 0 . \qquad (3.15)$$

Finally, by assumption,

$$w \geq 0 \quad \text{a.e.} \quad \text{in} \quad D . \qquad (3.16)$$

Inequalities (3.14) and (3.16) together with equality (3.15) constitute a complementarity problem for w.

Since $-a(w_h, v_h - w_h) \leq (e, v_h - w_h)$ for all $v_h \in K_h$, we can prove that

$$a(w-w_h, w-w_h) \leq a(w-w_h, w-v_h) + (-Lw + e, v_h - w_h),$$

$$\leq \alpha_2 \| w-w_h \|_{1,2} \| w-v_h \|_{1,2} +$$

$$+ (-Lw + e, v_h - w_h), \qquad (3.17)$$

where α_2 is the constant introduced in (2.7). Using (3.14) and (3.15), we conclude that

$$(-Lw + e, v_h - w_h) = (-Lw + e, v_h - w) - (-Lw + e, w_h) +$$

$$+ (-Lw + e, w),$$

$$= (-Lw+e, v_h - w) - (-Lw + e, w_h),$$

$$\leq (-Lw + e, v_h - w), \qquad (3.18)$$

$$\leq \| -Lw + e \|_{0,2} \| v_h - w \|_{0,2} .$$

For any $v \in H^2(D)$ let v^I denote the piecewise linear interpolate to v. It follows from the work of Ciarlet and Raviart [1972] that there is a constant C independent of v and h such that

$$\| v-v^I \|_{m,2} \leq C \| v \|_{2,2} h^{2-m}, \text{ for } m = 0,1 . \qquad (3.19)$$

Next, we note that

$$\frac{1}{2}(\| w-w_h \|_{1,2})^2 \leq (\| w-w^I \|_{1,2})^2 + (\| w^I - w_h \|_{1,2})^2. \qquad (3.20)$$

Finally, we observe that $w^I - w_h \in H_0^1(D)$ so that, from the coercivity of a on $H_0^1(D)$ (see (2.9))

$$\alpha_1 (\| w^I - w_h \|_{1,2})^2 \leq a(w^I - w_h, w^I - w_h). \qquad (3.21)$$

We can now begin the final computations. We set $E = \| w-w_h \|_{1,2}$. Using (3.19), (3.20), and (3.21) we obtain

$$\frac{\alpha_1}{2} E^2 \leq \alpha_1 (C \|w\|_{2,2})^2 h^2 + a(w^I-w_h, w^I-w_h),$$

$$= a(w^I-w_h, w^I-w_h) + 0(h^2) ,$$

$$= a(w^I-w, w^I-w) + 2a(w^I-w, w-w_h) + a(w-w_h, w-w_h) +$$

$$+ 0(h^2)$$

$$\leq \alpha_2 (\| w^I-w \|_{1,2})^2 + 2\alpha_2 \| w^I-w \|_{1,2} \| w-w_h \|_{1,2} +$$

$$+ a(w-w_h, w-w_h) + 0(h^2) .$$

Using (3.19),

$$\frac{\alpha_1}{2} E^2 \leq \alpha_2 (C \| w \|_{2,2})^2 h^2 + 2\alpha_2 C \| w \|_{2,2} h E +$$

$$+ a(w-w_h, w-w_h) + 0(h^2) ,$$

$$= a(w-w_h, w-w_h) + 2C_1 h E + 0(h^2) ,$$

where $C_1 = \alpha_2 C \| w \|_{2,2}$

Using (3.17) and (3.18) with $v_h = w^I$,

$$\frac{\alpha_1}{2} E^2 \leq \alpha_2 (C \| w \|_{2,2}) h E + (-Lw + e, w^I - w_h) +$$

$$+ 2C_1 h E + 0(h^2) ,$$

$$\leq 3C_1 h E + \| -Lw + e \|_{0,2} \| w^I-w_h \|_{0,2} + 0(h^2) .$$

Using (3.19) with $m = 0$,

$$\frac{\alpha_1}{2} E^2 \leq 3C_1 \, h \, E + \| -Lw+e \|_{0,2} \, C \| w \|_{2,2} \, h^2 + 0(h^2) ,$$

$$= 3C_1 \, h \, E + 0(h^2) .$$

Thus, multiplying through by $\frac{2}{\alpha_1}$ we have that

$$E^2 \leq 2C_2 \, h \, E + 0(h^2)$$

with $C_2 = 6C_1/\alpha_1$. Hence,

$$(E - C_2 h)^2 \leq (C_2 h)^2 + 0(h^2) = 0(h^2) ,$$

so that

$$E - C_2 h = 0(h) ,$$

and finally,

$$E = \| w - w_h \|_{1,2} = 0(h) . \qquad \square$$

4. A Numerical Example

As an example we consider the specific case $r = 4.8$, $R = 76.8$, $h_w = 12$, $H = 48$, which was chosen because it had previously been considered by several authors.

Because the solution changes most rapidly near the well, the subdivisions were taken to be uniform in the y-direction and logarithmic in the x-direction. If n and m denote the number of subdivisions in the x- and y-directions, the coordinates of the gridpoints were given by

$$y_j = j\ H/m, \qquad 0 \le j \le m \ ,$$

$$x_i = r\ \exp[(i/n)\ \ln(R/r)], \qquad 0 \le i \le n \ .$$

The integer m was always chosen to be a multiple of 4 so that the corner D was a gridpoint; this was advisable since w is not smooth at the corner D.

The permeability κ was taken to be one so that $f(x) = \ln x$ and $g(y) = 0$. From (2.3), (2,4), and (3.2),

$$J(v) = \int_D x[v_x^2 + v_y^2 + 2v]dxdy \ . \tag{4.1}$$

The boundary values of w are found to be

$$w(x,H) = 0, \text{ on } AF\ ;\ w(R,y) = (H-y)^2/2, \text{ on } AB\ ;$$

$$w(r,y) = (h_w-y)^2/2, \text{ on } CD\ ;\ w(r,y) = 0 \text{ on } DF\ ;$$

$$w(x,0) = \frac{h_w^2 \ln(R/x) + H^2 \ln(x/r)}{2\ln(R/r)}, \text{ on } BC. \tag{4.2}$$

The problem (3.3) is of the form

$$\text{Minimize:} \quad V^T AV + 2b^T V \ ,$$

$$\text{Subject to:} \quad V_{ij} = W_{ij} \text{ on } \partial D_h, \tag{4.3}$$

$$V_{ij} \ge 0 \ ,$$

where A is a known $N \times N$ matrix, b is a known N-vector, and the solution V is an N-vector. V_{ij} and W_{ij} denote the values of V and w at the gridpoint (x_i, y_j).

The solution w_h of (4.3) was computed using S.O.R. with projection (Cryer [1971], Glowinski [1971], Glowinski, Lions, and Tremolieres [1976]). To choose the parameter ω we proceeded as follows. For the case $m = 16$, $n = 24$ computations were made with several values of ω and it was found that the optimum value of ω was approximately $1{\cdot}7$. For the general case we set

$$\omega = \frac{2}{1+\sin[\pi/\text{nfict}]}$$

where

$$\text{nfict} = {\cdot}8590\ [(n+1)(m+1)]^{1/2} .$$

The expression for ω is a modification of the theoretical optimum value for S.O.R. on a square (Varga [1962, p. 203]). The constant ${\cdot}8590$ was chosen so that $\omega = 1{\cdot}7$ when $m = 16$ and $n = 24$.

The computations presented no difficulties. The solution of the smallest problem is given in Table 4.1, where the position of the approximate free boundary is shown by the first zero term in each column. The approximate solution is identically zero on the vertical line $x = r$ so that it is not possible to determine the height h_s at which the free boundary intersects the well. As an approximation to h_s we take the height h_s' of the free boundary at the vertical gridline adjacent to the well. For example, from Table 4.1 we obtain $h_s' = 36$.

In Table 4.2 the values of h_s' for a sequence of decreasing grid lengths are given. The iterations were terminated when,

$$\| V^{10\ell} - V^{10(\ell-1)} \|_\infty < 10^{-6}$$

where V^k denotes the k-th iterate. In judging this

accuracy criterion, it should be remembered that $\| V \|_\infty = 1152$, so that the relative error is 10^{-9}

y \ x	4.80	7.61	12.09	19.20	30.47	48.38	76.80
48	0	0	0	0	0	0	0
36	0	0	0	0	3.03	31.59	72.00
24	0	17.55	43.61	81.33	133.09	204.06	288.00
12	0	88.58	182.02	283.14	394.37	517.10	648.00
0	72.00	252.00	432.00	612.00	792.00	972.00	1152.00

Table 4.1: Solution for m = 4, n = 6

m	n	h'_s	number of iterations
4	6	36.00	20
8	12	30.00	40
16	24	30.00	70
32	48	30.00	120
64	96	30.00	230

Table 4.2: Values of h'_s

The method of determining ω seemed satisfactory, although the ratios

$$\frac{\| V^{10\ell} - V^{10(\ell-1)} \|_2}{\| V^{10(\ell-1)} - V^{10(\ell-2)} \|_2}$$

oscillated so as to suggest that the dominant eigenvalue of the iteration was complex and hence that (from the theory of S.O.R.) reducing ω would improve the convergence.

For comparison, we compare in Table 4.3 the values of h_s obtained by different authors. With the exception

of the present computation, all the results are presented graphically so that we have had to estimate h_s from graphs.

Author	Method	h_s
Hall [1955, p. 29]	trial-free-boundary; finite differences	34.0
Taylor and Luthin [1969]	time-dependent; finite differences	34.0
Neuman and Witherspoon [1970]	trial free-boundary; finite elements	30.0
Neuman and Witherspoon [1971, p. 620]	time-dependent; finite differences	30.0
Present	Variational inequalities	30.0

Table 4.3: Computed values of h_s

The differences in Table 4.3 may be explained by the fact that the physical assumptions differed: Hall [1955] assumed capillarity and a lined well; Taylor and Luthin [1969] assumed partially saturated flow; and Neuman and Witherspoon [1970, 1971] made the same assumptions as in the present paper.

Finally, in Table 4.4 we give the computed values of w at a typical point $x = 19.2$ $y = 24$ for different values of m and n. We also give the differences between successive approximations and the ratios of successive differences. It can be seen that the results are consistent with the hypothesis that

$$\| w-w_h \|_\infty = 0(h^2) .$$

In Theorem 3.2 we, of course, only proved that

$$\| w-w_h \|_{1,2} = 0(h) .$$

m	n	w_h	Δw_h	ratio
4	6	81.333841		
8	12	83.478767	2.144926	
16	24	84.150541	.671774	3.193
32	48	84.298332	.147791	4.545
64	96	84.337269	.038930	3.796

Table 4.4: Values of w_h at $x = 19.2$, $y = 24.0$

Bibliography

[1] Adams, R. A.: Sobolev Spaces. New York, Academic Press, 1975.

[2] Baiocchi, C.: Sur un Problème à Frontière Libre Traduisant le Filtrage de Liquides à Travers des Milieux Poreux. Comptes. Rendus Acad. Sci. Paris A273 (1971), 1215-1217.

[3] Baiocchi, C., Brezzi, F. and Comincioli, V.: Free Boundary Problems in Fluid Flow Through Porous Media. In Proceedings Second International Symposium on Finite Element Methods in Flow Problems, Santa Margherita, Italy, 1976.

[4] Bear, J.: Dynamics of Fluids in Porous Media. New York, American Elsevier, 1972.

[5] Benci, V.: Su un Problema di Filtrazione in un Mezzo Poroso non Omogeneo. Rend. Acad. Naz. Lincei (8) 54 (1973), 10-15.

[6] Benci, V.: On a Filtration Problem Through a Porous Medium. Annali di Matem. (4) 100 (1974), 191-209.

[7] Brezzi, F., Hager, W. H., and Raviart, P. A.: Error Estimates for the Finite Element Solution of Variational Inequalities Part I: Primal theory. To appear.

[8] Brezzi, F. and Sacchi, G.: A Finite Element Approximation of a Variational Inequality Related to Hydraulics. Pubblicazioni No. 97, Laboratorio di Analisi Numerica del C.N.R., Università di Pavia, to appear.

[9] Ciarlet, P. G. and Raviart, P. A.: General Lagrange and Hermite Interpolation in R^n with applications to Finite Element Methods. Arch. Rational Mech. Anal. 46 (1972), 1977-199.

[10] Cryer, C. W.: The Solution of a Quadratic Programming Problem Using Systematic Over-relaxation. SIAM J. Control 9 (1971), 385-392.

[11] Cryer, C. W.: A Survey of Steady-state Porous Flow Free Boundary Problems. Technical Summary Report No. 1657, Mathematics Research Center, University of Wisconsin, Madison, Wisconsin, 1976.
[12] Cryer, C. W. and Fetter, H.: The Numerical Solution of Axisymmetric Free Boundary Porous Flow Well Problems Using Variational Inequalities. Technical Summary Report No. 1761, Mathematics Research Center, University of Wisconsin, 1977.
[13] Elliott, C. M.: Some Applications of the Finite Element Method in Numerical Analysis. D. Phil. Thesis, Oxford University, September 1976.
[14] Glowinski, R.: La Méthode de Relaxation. Rendiconti di Matematica 14, Universita Roma, (1971).
[15] Glowinski, R., Lions, J. L. and Tremolieres, R.: Analyse Numerique des Inéquations Variationnelles. Paris, Dunod, 1976.
[16] Hall, H. P.: An Investigation of Steady Flow Towards a Gravity Well. La Houille Blanche 10(1955), 8-35.
[17] Hantush, M. S.: Hydraulics of Wells. Advances of Hydroscience 1(1964), 281-432.
[18] Lions, J. L.: Optimal Control of Systems Governed by Partial Differential Equations. Berlin, Springer, 1971.
[19] Neuman, S. P. and Witherspoon, P. A.: Finite Element Method of Analyzing Steady Seepage with a Free Surface. Water Resources Res. 6(1970), 889-897.
[20] Neuman, S. P. and Witherspoon, P. A.: Analysis of Nonsteady Flow with a Free Surface Using the Finite Element Method. Water Resources Res. 7(1971), 611-623.
[21] Stampacchia, G.: Formes Bilinéaires Coercitives sur les Ensembles Convexes. Comptes Rendus Acad. Sci. Paris 258(1964), 4413-4416.
[22] Taylor, G. S. and Luthin, J. N.: Computer Methods for Transient Analysis of Water-table Aquifers. Water Resources Res. 5(1969), 144-152.
[23] Varga, R. S.: Matrix Iterative Analysis. Englewood Cliffs, Prentice-Hall (1962).

Computer Sciences Department
University of Wisconsin
Madison, Wisconsin 53706

AN ITERATION METHOD FOR SOLVING NONLINEAR EIGENVALUE PROBLEMS

Kurt Georg

In a recent paper [7] the convergence of an inverse iteration type algorithm for a certain class of nonlinear elliptic eigenvalue problems was discussed. Such algorithms have been used successfully in plasma physics [11] , but no satisfactory theoretical justification of convergence was known. While in [7] only the nondiscretized case was discussed, here an analogous algorithm for nonlinear eigenvalue problems in $\mathbb{R}^N$ will be treated. This algorithm is interesting in itself, but can also be interpreted as a suitably discretized version of the algorithm discussed in [7] .

Subject Classifications. AMS(MOS): 65H10, 65N25, 90C30.

1. INTRODUCTION.

Let us illustrate the situation by the following simple but already significant example. Consider the eigenvalue problem

$$(1.1)\qquad \lambda u''(t) + \varphi(u(t)) = 0, \quad u(0) = u(1) = 0,$$

where $\varphi : \mathbb{R} \longrightarrow (0,+\infty)$ is twice continuously differentiable, increasing and $\lim_{t\to+\infty} t^{-1}\varphi(t) = +\infty$. We approximate the eigenvalue problem (1.1) by uniform central differences and hence define a symmetric positive definite linear map $L : \mathbb{R}^N \longrightarrow \mathbb{R}^N$

by

(1.2) $$L = (N+1)^2 \begin{pmatrix} 2 & -1 & & 0 \\ -1 & \ddots & \ddots & \\ & \ddots & \ddots & -1 \\ 0 & & -1 & 2 \end{pmatrix}$$

and a smooth potential operator $f : \mathbb{R}^N \longrightarrow \mathbb{R}^N$ by

(1.3) $$f\begin{pmatrix} \xi_1 \\ \vdots \\ \xi_N \end{pmatrix} = \begin{pmatrix} \varphi(\xi_1) \\ \vdots \\ \varphi(\xi_N) \end{pmatrix} .$$

Now the approximating eigenvalue problem in $\mathbb{R}^N$ is

(1.4) $$\lambda Lx = f(x) .$$

As is known, see for example [2-5,12], the above hypothesis on φ implies the existence of a critical eigenvalue $\lambda^* > 0$ such that the eigenvalue problem (1.1) has no solution for $\lambda \in (0,\lambda^*)$ and at least two solutions for $\lambda \in (\lambda^*,+\infty)$, and it is readily seen that the same is true for the approximating eigenvalue problem (1.4). The situation can be illustrated by the following picture:

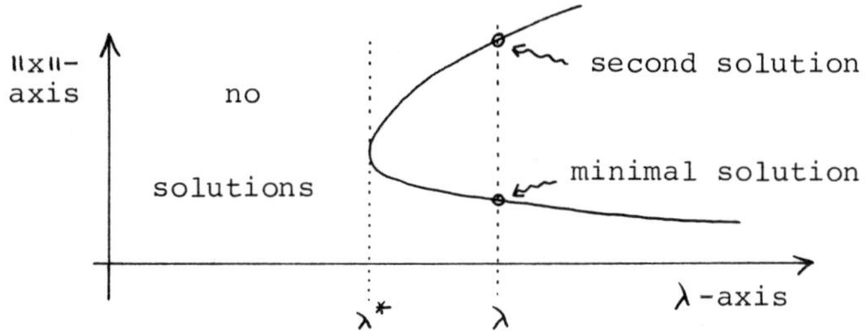

For $\lambda > \lambda^*$, the Picard iteration

(1.5) $$\lambda Lx_{n+1} = f(x_n) ,$$

starting with $x_1=0$, converges monotonically to the minimal solution of (1.4), see for example [3]. The second solution however is unstable under this iteration. If we assume that 0 is a regular value of the map $x \longrightarrow f(x) - Lx$, then clearly Newton's iteration

(1.6) $$(f'(x_n)-\lambda L)(x_{n+1}-x_n) + f(x_n) - \lambda Lx_n = 0$$

converges locally quadratically to any solution of (1.4). But the domain of convergence to the minimal solution is dominating, hence Newton's iteration (1.6) has starting difficulties for approximating the second solution. If we assume that 0 is a regular value of the map $(\lambda, x) \rightarrow f(x) - \lambda Lx$, one can use a so-called embedding method to run from the easily computable minimal solution to the second solution along the branch of solutions, see for example [1,8,10,11,13] . One also may use a procedure given in [1] to start in the minimal solution and stop in the second solution. This procedure works for a fixed λ-level and can be considered an improvement of Jeppson's device [9]. The algorithm which will be discussed here is motivated by a different point of view. Instead of fixing the λ-level and looking for a solution of (1.4), we consider a norm of x to have a fixed value and look for a solution of (1.4) where the eigenvalue $\lambda > 0$ now is an unknown parameter.

2. FORMULATION OF THE PROBLEM.

We now define the problem which will be considered. Let $L : \mathbb{R}^N \rightarrow \mathbb{R}^N$ be a linear symmetric positive definite map and $f : \mathbb{R}^N \rightarrow \mathbb{R}^N$ a smooth potential operator, more precisely: f is twice continuously differentiable, and the Frechet derivative $f'(x)$ is symmetric for all $x \in \mathbb{R}^N$. We consider the nonlinear eigenvalue problem

$$(2.1) \qquad \lambda Lx = f(x) \ .$$

As already mentioned above, this formulation contains suitable discretizations of nonlinear elliptic eigenvalue problems as treated in [7]. We consider in $\mathbb{R}^N$ the scalar product

$$(2.2) \qquad \langle x,y \rangle := x^T Ly$$

and the norm

$$(2.3) \qquad \|x\| = \langle x,x \rangle^{1/2} .$$

We fix a real number $R > 0$ and look for a solution of the eigenvalue problem (2.1) with $\|x\| = R$ where $\lambda > 0$ now is an unknown parameter. The following algorithm corresponds to the Picard iteration (1.5) :

(2.4) $$x_{n+1} = R\|L^{-1}f(x_n)\|^{-1}L^{-1}f(x_n) .$$

We call this the inverse iteration method, since in the linear case it coincides with the known inverse iteration method to approximate the eigenvector belonging to the largest characteristic number of L . Hence we have the following well-known facts:

(2.5) LEMMA. Let $f : \mathbb{R}^N \longrightarrow \mathbb{R}^N$ be the identity map, and let the largest characteristic number λ of L be simple. Suppose that x is a normalized eigenvector of L belonging to λ , i.e. $\|x\|=R$ and $\lambda Lx=x$. If we start algorithm (2.4) with a point $x_1 \in \mathbb{R}^N$ such that $x^T x_1 > 0$, then the sequence $x_1, x_2, \ldots$, generated by (2.4) , converges linearly to x . If μ denotes the second largest characteristic number of L , then the contraction factor is $\lambda^{-1}\mu$, i.e. for all $\varepsilon > 0$ there exists an $n_0 > 0$ such that $\|x-x_{n+1}\| \leq (\lambda^{-1}\mu+\varepsilon)\|x-x_n\|$ for all $n \geq n_0$.

Our aim now is to prove a similar result for the case that f is any nonlinear map which satisfies the given conditions. Befor doing so, let us point out that also Newton'n method is available in this context. Consider the map $G : \mathbb{R}^N \times \mathbb{R} \longrightarrow \mathbb{R}^N \times \mathbb{R}$, defined by

(2.6) $$G\begin{pmatrix} x \\ \lambda \end{pmatrix} = \begin{pmatrix} f(x) - \lambda Lx \\ x^T Lx - R^2 \end{pmatrix} .$$

Clearly, a solution of (2.1) with prescribed norm $\|x\|=R$ corresponds to a zero point of G , and we can write Newton's method for finding a zero point of G in the following way:

(2.7) $$\begin{pmatrix} f'(x_n)-\lambda_n L & , -Lx_n \\ 2x_n^T L & , 0 \end{pmatrix} \cdot \begin{pmatrix} x_{n+1}-x_n \\ \lambda_{n+1}-\lambda_n \end{pmatrix} + \begin{pmatrix} x_n^T Lx_n - R^2 \\ f(x_n)-\lambda_n Lx_n \end{pmatrix} = 0.$$

Hence, if $\binom{x}{\lambda}$ is a regular zero point of G , then the iteration (2.7) converges locally quadratically to $\binom{x}{\lambda}$.

3. AN AUXILIARY NONLINEAR PROGRAMMING PROBLEM.

Since f was supposed to be a potential operator, we can define the potential $p : \mathbb{R}^N \to \mathbb{R}$ by

$$(3.1) \qquad p(x) = \int_0^1 x^T f(tx)\, dt ,$$

and the gradient of p equals f. On the other hand, the gradient of the norm (2.3) equals $\|x\|^{-1} Lx$. We consider the nonlinear programming problem:

(3.2) PROBLEM. Maximize $p(x)$ subject to $\|x\|=R$.

Then, by using the Lagrange multiplier rule, we immediately get the following result:

(3.3) LEMMA. A point $x \in \mathbb{R}^N$ with norm $\|x\|=R$ is a critical point of the problem (3.2) if and only if there exists a $\lambda \in \mathbb{R}$ such that $\binom{x}{\lambda}$ solves the eigenvalue problem (2.1), i.e. if and only if $\binom{x}{\lambda}$ is a zero point of the map G in (2.6).

Let x be such a critical point of (3.2), and denote the manifold given by the constraint with

$$(3.4) \qquad S = \{ y \in \mathbb{R}^N : \|y\|=R \} .$$

Let $\chi : \mathbb{R}^{N-1} \to S$ be a local chart such that $\chi(0)=x$. Then the gradient of $p \circ \chi$ vanishes at 0, and we call as usual x a nondegenerate critical point if the Hessian of $p \circ \chi$ has full rank at 0. We identify in an obvious way the tangent space of S at x with the orthogonal complement of x:

$$(3.5) \qquad T_x = \{ y \in \mathbb{R}^N : \langle y, x \rangle = 0 \} ,$$

and we define a linear operator $H_x : T_x \to T_x$, the "restricted Hessian of p at x", by

$$(3.6) \qquad \langle H_x y, z \rangle = y^T f'(x) z \quad \text{for all } y, z \in T_x .$$

A routine calculation shows the following facts, see [6,7] for similar calculations.

(3.7) LEMMA. Let x be a critical point of (3.2), i.e. $x \in \mathbb{R}^N$, $\|x\|=R$, and $\lambda Lx=f(x)$ for some $\lambda \in \mathbb{R}$. Then the following three conditions are equivalent:

(a) x is a nondegenerate critical point.

(b) $\binom{x}{\lambda}$ is a regular zero point of the map G, cf. (2.6), and hence Newton's method (2.7) works.

(c) λ does not belong to the spectrum $\sigma(H_x)$.

Furthermore, if x is nondegenerate, then the following two conditions are equivalent :

(d) x is a local optimal point of (3.2).

(e) $\lambda > \sigma(H_x)$.

4. THE CONVERGENCE OF THE INVERSE ITERATION.

Motivated by the inverse iteration (2.4), let us define a "fixed point operator" $C : \{x \in S : f(x) \neq 0\} \longrightarrow S$ by

$$Cx = R\|L^{-1}f(x)\|^{-1}L^{-1}f(x) . \tag{4.1}$$

Clearly, the inverse iteration (2.4) can be written in the equivalent form

$$x_{n+1} = Cx_n , \tag{4.2}$$

and $x \in S$ is a fixed point of C if and only if $\lambda Lx=f(x)$ for some $\lambda > 0$. The Frechet derivative $C'(x)$ of C at x is a linear map of the tangent spaces involved and can be easily calculated in the following way, see [7] for a similar result :

(4.3) LEMMA. Let $x \in S$ be a fixed point of C, i.e. $\lambda Lx=f(x)$ for some $\lambda > 0$. Then $C'(x) = \lambda^{-1}H_x$.

In a fixed point x of C, the local behavior of the inverse iteration (2.4) is controlled by the spectral radius of $C'(x) = \bar{\lambda}^{-1} H_x$. Note that H_x is selfadjoint with respect to the scalar product (2.2) , and hence the spectral radius of $C'(x)$ equals the norm $\|C'(x)\|$. Hence, if x is a fixed point of C , then $\|C'(x)\| < 1$ means that the inverse iteration (2.4) converges linearly to x in some neighborhood of x . The contraction constant is $\|C'(x)\|$. Combining the results (3.7) and (4.3) , one immediately gets the following behavior of the inverse iteration method:

(4.4) THEOREM. Let $x \in S$ be a fixed point of C such that $\|C'(x)\| < 1$. Then x is a nondegenerate local optimal point of the nonlinear programming problem (3.2) .

(4.5) THEOREM. Let $x \in S$ be a fixed point of C , and suppose that the spectral radius of the restricted Hessian H_x is an eigenvalue of H_x . If x is a nondegenerate local optimal point of (3.2) , then $\|C'(x)\| < 1$.

5. FINAL REMARKS.

(5.1) The condition in (4.5) , that the spectral radius of the restricted Hessian H_x is an eigenvalue of H_x , can be equivalently formulated in the following way:

$$\sup \{ y^T f'(x) y \; : \; y \in T_x \} + \inf \{ z^T f'(x) z \; : \; z \in T_x \} \geq 0 \, ,$$

and hence is fullfilled e.g. if $f'(x)$ is positive semi-definite.

(5.2) In the linear case, i.e. if $f : \mathbb{R}^N \rightarrow \mathbb{R}^N$ is the identity map, theorem(4.5) specializes to lemma (2.5) , and also the contraction constant $\|C'(x)\|$ coincides with the one given there. The only difference is that (4.5) is a local result, which is not astonishing, since there is much freedom in the choice of the nonlinearity f .

(5.3) As we have seen, the inverse iteration method (2.4) works for nondegenerate local optima of the nonlinear programming problem (3.2), whereas Newton's method (2.7) works for all nondegenerate critical points, cf. lemma (3.7). But let us point out that one inverse iteration step (2.4) involves essentially one evaluation of $f(x)$ and one solving of a linear equation $Ly=z$, where L can be e.g. decomposed once by Cholesky's method which respects also band structure. On the other hand, one Newton step (2.7) involves essentially one evaluation of Lx, $f(x)$ and $f'(x)$ and one solving of a full nonsymmetric linear system. Essentially the same amount of work is involved by a step of the embedding method mentioned in section 1.

(5.4) Though (4.5) is a local result, numerical experience suggests that for a large class of problems the type of convergence is "nearly global". In fact, the inverse iteration method can be interpreted as a kind of gradient method, cf. [7] for details.

(5.5) If one wants to calculate a solution of the eigenvalue problem (2.1) for a given eigenvalue λ, e.g. if one wishes to calculate the second solution for a given λ, cf. section 1, one may use the norm level R as a shooting parameter and apply the inverse iteration method several times. In a similar way one may also calculate the critical eigenvalue λ^* mentioned in section 1. In many cases a few applications of the inverse iteration method will be sufficient, and hence the method is reasonable because an inverse iteration step does not cost much. Several numerical calculations for simple problems were done, and in particular the algorithm was found very useful to calculate the critical eigenvalue λ^*. For numerical applications to nonlinear elliptic eigenvalue problems we refer the reader to [14] and the various papers mentioned in [11].

6. REFERENCES

1 Allgower,E. and Georg,K.: Simplicial and continuation methods for approximating fixed points and solutions to systems of equations. To appear in SIAM Review (1979).

2 Amann,H.: On the number of solutions of asymptotically superlinear two point boundary value problems. Arch.Rational Mech. Anal. 55 (1974), 207-213.

3 Amann,H.: Fixed point equations and nonlinear eigenvalue problems in ordered Banach spaces. SIAM Review 18(1976), 620-709.

4 Crandall,M.G. and Rabinowitz,P.H.: Some continuation and variational methods for positive solutions of nonlinear elliptic eigenvalue problems. Arch. Rational Mech. Anal. 58 (1975), 207-218.

5 Dancer,E.N.: Global solution branches for positive maps. Arch.Rational Mech. Anal. 52 (1973), 181-192.

6 Fiacco,A.V. and MacCormick,G.P.: Nonlinear programming: sequential unconstraint minimization techniques. New York, John Wiley 1968.

7 Georg,K.: On the convergence of an inverse iteration method for nonlinear elliptic eigenvalue problems. To appear in Numer. Math. (1979).

8 Haselgrove,C.: Solution of nonlinear equations and of differential equations with two-point boundary conditions. Comput. J. 4 (1961), 255-259.

9 Jeppson,M.M.: A search for the fixed points of a continuous mapping. In: Mathematical topics in economics theory and computation, R.H.Day and S.M.Robinson (eds.),1972, 122-129.

10 Keller,H.B.: Numerical solution of bifurcation and nonlinear eigenvalue problems. In: Applications of bifurcation theory, P.H.Rabinowitz (ed.), New York, Academic Press 1977, 359-384.

11 Lackner,K.: Computation of ideal MHD equilibria. Computer Physics Communications 12 (1976), 33-44.

12 Laetsch,T.: The number of solutions of a nonlinear two point boundary value problem. Indiana Univ. J. Math. 20 (1970), 1-13.

13 Menzel,R. and Schwetlick,H.: Zur Lösung parameterabhängiger nichtlinearer Gleichungen mit singulären Jacobi-Matrizen. Numer. Math. 30 (1978), 65-79.

14 Meyer-Spasche,R.: Numerical treatment of Dirichlet problems with several solutions. ISNM 31, Basel and Stuttgart, Birkhäuser 1976.

Institut für Angewandte Mathematik
der Universität Bonn
Wegelerstr. 6
D - 5300 Bonn

AUFWANDSOPTIMALE SCHRITTWEITENSTEUERUNG BEI EINBETTUNGSMETHODEN

H.Hackl,Hj.Wacker,W.Zulehner

Zusammenfassung:Bei der Lösung nichtlinearer Probleme mit Einbettungsmethoden hat die Schrittweitensteuerung wesentlichen Einfluß auf den Aufwand.Für ein Prädiktor-Korrektor Verfahren (hier:trivialer Prädiktor,allgemeiner Korrektor) wird ein Modell aufgestellt,welches den Rechenaufwand (=Gesamtzahl der Prädiktor-Korrektorschritte) minimiert.Das auf globalen Größen basierende Modell kann explizit gelöst werden.Für das Newtonverfahren als Korrektor läßt sich eine implementierbare Version formulieren.Die Wirksamkeit der Schrittweitensteuerung wird mit einer bekannten Methode von W.C.Rheinboldt an Hand einiger Beispiele verglichen.

1.Problemstellung

Zu lösen sei die nichtlineare Gleichung $T_1(x)=o$.Die Lösung erfolge mit Hilfe von Einbettung:

$$T(x,s)=o,\ s\in[o,1] \wedge T(x,1)=T_1(x) \wedge T(x_o,o)=o$$

Nach Festlegung der Homotopie soll ein Stufenverfahren verwendet werden,d.h.:man diskretisiert das Homotopieintervall $o=s_o\leq s_1\leq\ldots\leq s_N=1$ und löst sukzessive die Probleme $T(x,s_i)=o$ mit einem lokalen Iterationsverfahren.Eine Startlösung $x_i^{(o)}$ für das lokale Iterationsverfahren verschafft man sich mit Hilfe von x_{i-1}

(allgemeiner: $x_{i-1},\ldots,x_{i-p}$).

Im Zusammenhang mit Einbettungsverfahren arbeitet man heute an vier Problemkreisen:

a) Wahl einer problemangepaßten Homotopie

b) Anwendung von Einbettungsmethoden in anderen Gebieten (etwa bei Optimierungsaufgaben)

c) Bewältigung der "singulären Situation"

d) Wahl von geeigneten Schrittweiten $\Delta s_i := s_i - s_{i-1}$.

Im folgenden wollen wir uns ausschließlich mit der letztgenannten Aufgabe befassen.

Die bisherigen Versuche in Richtung Schrittweitensteuerung lassen sich grob in vier Gruppen einteilen:

(I) Heuristische Vorgehensweisen: Eine naheliegende Möglichkeit besteht etwa in der Vorschrift: $\Delta s_i := 2\Delta s_{i-1}$. Bei Mißerfolg wird solange halbiert, bis man entweder fortsetzen kann oder eine singuläre Situation "erkennt". Vorschläge dieser Art-wenn auch wesentlich ausgeklügelter-finden sich auch in neueren Arbeiten, z.B. bei W.F.Schmidt [10] : $\Delta s_i := \lambda_i \Delta s_{i-1}$, wobei λ_i aus lokalen Daten berechnet wird.

(II) Die theoretischen Ansätze zielten bereits sehr früh dahin, mit Hilfe globaler Konstanten eine gleichmäßige maximal zulässige Schrittweite zu berechnen. Wird Δs_i kleiner als eine gewisse Schranke S_o gewählt, so ist das Stufenverfahren durchführbar, d.h. der Übergang von Stufe $i-1 \to i$ ist mit dem betrachteten lokalen Verfahren erfolgreich. Als Näherung für $x(s_i)$ wird oft $x(s_{i-1})$ gewählt (trivialer Prädiktorschritt). S_o hängt von globalen Größen ab. Es gibt implementierbare Varianten, die berücksichtigen, daß $x(s_i)$ i.a. nicht exakt erreichbar ist. (z.B. Meyer [6] , Avila [1] , Wacker [12]).

(III) Selbststeuernde Verfahren arbeiten zum Teil mit lokalen Schätungen globaler Größen. Rheinboldt [8] verschafft sich obere und untere Schranken für den lokalen Konvergenzradius, Deuflhard [2] berechnet mit Hilfe lokaler Größen eine Schrittweite,die zulässig und gleichzeitig maximal ist.Leder [5] minimiert das Funktional $\|H(z)\|_2^2$ mit $H(z):=(T(x,s),m(1-s))^T$ $(m>o)$ mit dem Abstiegsverfahren von Goldstine-Armijo.Schwetlick [11] verwendet die Idee des hinreichend kleinen Anstiegs, wobei ebenfalls lokal gesteuert wird.

(IV)Aufwandsminimale Schrittweitensteuerungen:Den meisten bisherigen Arbeiten liegt die Philosophie der maximalen Stufenbreite zu Grunde,d.h.man erwartet sich bei Verwendung maximal möglicher Stufenbreiten gleichzeitig einen minimalen Gesamtaufwand.Diese Einstellung ist insofern verständlich,als sie bei Vernachlässigung des Aufwandes in den einzelnen Stufen durchaus zutrifft.In der Praxis-gerade etwa beim Newtonverfahren-kann diese Vernachlässigung kaum verantwortet werden.

Betrachten wir die Stufen $s_o,s_1,...,s_N$.Der Übergang von Stufe $i-1 \to i$ erfordere k_i Iterationen.Dann ist der Aufwand für den gesamten Lösungsprozess ungefähr proportional zu $k_1+...+k_N$.Die Größe k_i hängt von der Güte der Approximation $x_i^{(o)}$ $(:= x_{i-1}^{(k_{i-1})}$ beim trivialen Prädiktorschritt) ab.D.h. große Stufenbreiten erfordern große k_i,kleine Stufenbreiten kleine k_i.Es ist keineswegs trivial einsichtig,das Minimum des Gesamtaufwandes bei "Δs möglichst groß" anzunehmen.Dieser Gedanke taucht erstmals bei Ribarič/Seliškar [9] auf.Allerdings werden dort keine expliziten Steuerungen erhalten. Kung [4] konstruiert eine Problemkette und minimiert die Gesamtzahl der Newtonschritte mit Hilfe eines Parameters.Dabei handelt es sich nicht im strengen Sinn um Einbettung.Die Arbeiten hier in Linz [13],[14] sind im folgenden näher beschrieben,da sie Vorstufen der vorgeschlagenen implementierbaren Schrittweitensteuerung darstellen.

2.Optimale Schrittweitensteuerung

2.1.Vorstufen der Lösung

a)In [13] wurde eine Aufwandsanalyse für das globalisierte Verfahren des Minimalen Residuums durchgeführt.
Unter der Annahme einer gleichmäßigen Stufenbreite Δs sowie gleich vielen Iterationen k auf jeder Stufe konnte eine obere Schranke $\Phi(k,\Delta s)$ für den Gesamtaufwand (=Gesamtzahl der Iterationen) angegeben werden.Die Forderung Endfehler$\leq\bar{\varepsilon},\bar{\varepsilon}$ vorgegeben, lieferte mit Hilfe der Fehlerfortpflanzung des speziellen Verfahrens $[\alpha(\beta\Delta s+\bar{\varepsilon})+\gamma]^k(\beta\Delta s+\bar{\varepsilon})\leq\bar{\varepsilon}$.Hieraus gewinnt man eine obere Schranke $k(\Delta s)$ für k.Man nimmt an,daß während der Rechnug am Ende der einzelnen Stufen stets die Fehlergrenze $\bar{\varepsilon}$ eingehalten wird.
Für das Optimierungs problem $\Phi(k(\Delta s),\Delta s)=\min!,\Delta s\varepsilon(o,S_1)$ konnte die Existenz eines Optimums im Innern nachgewiesen werden.
Die Lösung Δs_{opt}-sowie die damit erhältiche Iterationszahl k_{opt}- sind in Abhängigkeit der globalen Konstanten α,β,γ berechenbar.

b)In [14] wurde ein Modell für die Aufwandsminimierung des globalisierten Newtonverfahrens erstellt und gelöst.
Wie oben wird angenommen:gleichmäßige Stufeneinteilung und gleichviele Iterationen pro Stufe.Die Minimierung der oberen Schranke $\Phi(k,\Delta s)$ wird wieder auf eine Minimierung bezüglich Δs zurückgeführt,indem man die Rekursionsformel

$C^{-1}[C(A\Delta s+\varepsilon)]^{2^k}\leq\varepsilon,\varepsilon$ Genauigkeit in den Zwischenstufen,

ausnützt.$\Phi(k(\Delta s,\varepsilon),\Delta s)$ läßt sich bezüglich Δs <u>und</u> ε minimieren.
Die Minimierung kann weitgehend problemunabhängig durchgeführt werden und zeigt klar,daß Δs_{opt} <u>nicht</u> nahe bei S_o liegt;es gilt:

$$\Delta s_{opt}\approx o.62\ S_o!$$

Der Nachteil des Modells liegt in der Verwendung globaler Konstanten.Man könnte sich jedoch-ähnlich wie bei [2],[8]-mit lokalen Schätzungen behelfen.Das folgende Modell erlaubt jedoch einen wesentlich leichteren Übergang vom Modell zu einer implementierbaren Version.

2.2. Die Problemstellung für das allgemeine Modell

Wir fassen die Berechnung der Stufe s_i als Prädiktor-Korrektor Verfahren auf:

(P) Trivialer Prädiktorschritt: $\tilde{x}_i := x_{i-1}$ (letzte Näherung der Stufe i-1)

(K) Korrektorschritt: $x_i := \Phi(\tilde{x}_i, s_i)$ (z.B. $\Phi(x.s)$ ist das Ergebnis einer Newtoniteration mit Startwert x in der Stufe s).

Wir treffen folgende Annahmen für Prädiktor-und Korrektorschritt

(V1) $\bigvee_{A>o} \bigwedge_{x\varepsilon X} \bigwedge_{s,t\varepsilon[o,1]} \|T(x,t)\| \leq \|T(x,s)\| + A|t-s|$

(V2) $\bigwedge_{(x,s)\varepsilon X\times[o,1]} \|T(\Phi(x,s),s)\| \leq \phi(\|T(x,s)\|)$

wobei: $\phi : [o,\infty) \to [o,\infty)$, monoton, konvex, stetig differenzierbar, $\phi(\eta) < \eta$ für ein $\eta > o$.

Bezeichnungen: ε_{min}: der kleinere Fixpunkt

$$\varepsilon_{max}: \begin{cases} \text{der größere Fixpunkt} \\ +\infty, \text{falls nur ein Fixpunkt existiert} \end{cases}$$

$$\varepsilon^*: \begin{cases} \min_{t>\varepsilon_{min}} \{\phi'(t)=1\} & \text{falls } \{\phi'^{-1}(1)\} \neq \emptyset \\ +\infty & \text{sonst} \end{cases}$$

Es gilt: $\bigwedge_{u\epsilon(\varepsilon_{min},\varepsilon_{max})} \phi(u) < u \wedge \varepsilon\epsilon(\varepsilon_{min},\varepsilon_{max}) \vee \varepsilon_{max} = \varepsilon^* = \infty$.

Wir setzen: $\varepsilon_i := \|T(x_i,s_i)\| \wedge \Delta s_i := s_i - s_{i-1}$

$$\varepsilon_i = \|T(x_i,s_i)\| = \|T(\Phi(\tilde{x}_i,s_i),s_i)\| \leq \phi(\|T(\tilde{x}_i,s_i)\|) \leq$$

$$\leq \phi(\|T(x_{i-1},s_{i-1})\| + A\Delta s_i) = \phi(\varepsilon_{i-1} + A\Delta s_i)$$

Damit läßt sich der Fehler jeder Stufe (genauer: eine obere Schranke, die der Einfachheit wieder mit ε_i bezeichnet wird) rekursiv auf den Eingangsfehler zurückführen, sobald die Stufeneinteilung bekannt ist:

$$\varepsilon_i(\Delta s_1, \ldots \Delta s_i) := \phi(\varepsilon_{i-1}(\Delta s_1, \ldots \Delta s_{i-1}) + A\Delta s_i); \varepsilon_o := \|T(x_o,o)\|$$

Wir betrachten nun Zerlegungen $o \le s_o \le \ldots \le s_N = 1$, wobei wir auch gleiche Stufen zulassen. Da wir nur den trivialen Prädiktor - schritt verwenden, ist der Gesamtaufwand im Wesentlichen proportional der Gesamtzahl N der Korrektorschritte. Damit können wir formulieren:

Problem: Man wähle $N \in \mathbb{N}$, N minimal, und Schrittweiten $\Delta s_i \ge o$, $i=1,\ldots,N$, $\sum_{i=1}^{N} \Delta s_i = 1$ mit $\varepsilon_N(\Delta s_1,\ldots,\Delta s_N) \le \bar{\varepsilon}$.

2.3. Das Hilfsproblem und seine Lösung

Hilfsproblem: Für festes $N \in \mathbb{N}$ wähle man Schrittweiten $\Delta t_i \ge o$, $i=1,\ldots,N$, $\sum_{i=1}^{N} \Delta t_i = 1$, sodaß ε_N minimal wird.

Auf die Bedeutung des Hilfsproblems für das obige Problem haben schon Ribarič und Seliškar [9] hingewiesen.

<u>Satz 1</u> (Drei Phasensatz):

Für den Prädiktor-Korrektorschritt gelte (V1) und (V2). Dann liefert die folgende "3 Phasensteuerung" $\Delta t := (\Delta t_1,\ldots,\Delta t_N)$ die Lösung des Hilfsproblems: $(t_o := o, t_k := \sum_{j=1}^{N} \Delta t_j)$

Phase I :	$\Delta t_i := o$	für $i<N \wedge \varepsilon_{i-1} \ge \varepsilon^*$
Phase II :	$\Delta t_i := (\varepsilon^* - \varepsilon_{i-1})/A$	für $1-t_{i-1} > (\varepsilon^* - \varepsilon_{i-1})/A \wedge i<N$
Phase III:	$\Delta t_i := 1-\Delta t_{i-1}$	für $(1-t_{i-1} \le (\varepsilon^* - \varepsilon_{i-1})/A) \vee (t_{i-1}=1) \vee (1-t_{i-1} > (\varepsilon^* - \varepsilon_{i-1})/A \wedge i=N)$

(D.h.: In Phase I wird solange gerechnet bis der Fehler ε^* unterschritten ist oder i=N.
In Phase II wird der Homotopiepfad bis auf den letzten Schritt durchlaufen.
In Phase III wird nach s=1 gesprungen und dann-falls i<N-weiteriteriert.

Beweis:

(1) Eigenschaften der Steuerung:

Phase I: Es gilt $\Delta t_i=o \wedge t_i=o$ nach Definition von Phase I ($t_o=o$). Damit und wegen $\varepsilon_{i-1} \geq \varepsilon^*$ folgt: $\bigwedge_{t_i \text{ Phase I}} \phi'(\varepsilon_{i-1}+A\Delta t_i) \leq 1$

Phase II: Sei t_{i-1} die letzte Stufe von Phase I. Dann gilt wegen Definition von Phase II: $\Delta t_i=(\varepsilon^*-\varepsilon_{i-1})/A>o$ (sonst Phase I) $\varepsilon_{i-1}+A\Delta t_i=\varepsilon^* \rightarrow \varepsilon_i=\phi(\varepsilon_{i-1}+A\Delta t_i)=\phi(\varepsilon^*)$. Wegen $\phi(\varepsilon^*)<\varepsilon^*$ folgt: $\Delta t_{i+1}=(\varepsilon^*-\phi(\varepsilon^*))/A>o$ usw.. Allgemein: $\Delta t_i>o \wedge o<t_i<1$ (letzteres wegen Definition von Phase II). Ist t_i aus Phase II $\rightarrow$ $\varepsilon_{i-1}+A\Delta t_i=\varepsilon^* \rightarrow \phi'(\varepsilon_{i-1}+A\Delta t_i)=1$.

Phase III: Es gilt $t_i=1$ (Def.) Ist t_i aus Phase III $\wedge i \neq N \rightarrow$ $\phi'(\varepsilon_{i-1}+A\Delta t_i) \leq 1$. Denn: Schritt 1 in Phase III: $t_{i-1}<1 \rightarrow \varepsilon_{i-1}+A\Delta t_i \leq \varepsilon^*$ $(\Delta t_i=1-t_{i-1}) \rightarrow \phi'(\varepsilon_{i-1}+A\Delta t_i) \leq 1$. Weitere Schritte: $t_i=1 \rightarrow$ $\varepsilon_i=\phi(\varepsilon_{i-1}+A\Delta t_i) \leq \phi(\varepsilon^*) \leq \varepsilon^*$ usw..

(2) Existenz einer Lösung des Hilfsproblems:

$\varepsilon_N(\Delta t_1,\ldots,\Delta t_N)$ ist stetig (ϕ ist stetig).

$K:=\{(\Delta t_1,\ldots,\Delta t_N) \mid \sum_{i=1}^{N} \Delta t_i=1 \wedge \Delta t_i \geq o, i=1,2,\ldots,N\}$ ist kompakt.

$\rightarrow \varepsilon_N$ nimmt sein Minimum auf K an.

Damit ist die Existenz einer Lösung des folgenden Optimierungsproblems nachgewiesen (Hilfsproblem!):

$$\begin{aligned} &\varepsilon_N(\Delta t_1,\ldots,\Delta t_N)=\min! \\ &h(\Delta t)=\sum_{i=1}^{N} \Delta t_i-1=o \qquad (*) \\ &g_k(\Delta t)=-\Delta t_k \leq o \;, k=1,\ldots,N \end{aligned}$$

(3) Das Zielfunktional ist konvex und stetig differenzierbar (ϕ konvex, monoton, stetig differenzierbar), die Nebenbedingungen sind linear:

$\Delta t=(\Delta t_1,\ldots,\Delta t_N)$ ist optimal für $(*) \overset{!}{\Longleftrightarrow}$ Es gelten für $(*)$ im Punkt Δt die Kuhn-Tucker Bedingungen

$$\bigvee_{\lambda \in \mathbb{R}} \; \bigvee_{\mu_1,\ldots,\mu_N \geq o} \; \bigwedge_{i=1,\ldots,N} \frac{\partial \varepsilon_N(\Delta t)}{\partial t_i} = \lambda+\mu_i \wedge \mu_i \Delta t_i=o$$

Wir geben für (*) eine Lösung der Kuhn-Tucker Bedingungen (λ, μ_i) an:

a) Wegen $\sum_{i=1}^{N} \Delta t_i = 1$ existiert ein Index i_o mit $t_{i_o} > o$.

$$\lambda := \frac{\partial \varepsilon_N(\Delta t)}{\partial \Delta t_{i_o}} \; ; \; \mu_i := \frac{\partial \varepsilon_N}{\partial \Delta t_i} - \frac{\partial \varepsilon_N}{\partial \Delta t_{i_o}} \, , \; i=1,\dots,N$$

Damit sind bereits die Gleichungen erfüllt.

b) Wir zeigen: $\mu_i \geq o \wedge \mu_i \Delta t_i = o$

Es gilt: $\frac{\partial \varepsilon_{N(\Delta t)}}{\partial \Delta t_i} = A \prod_{j=i}^{N} \phi'(\varepsilon_{j-1} + A\Delta t_j)$

$$\mu_i = \begin{cases} A \prod_{j=i_o}^{N} \phi'(\varepsilon_{j-1} + A\Phi t_j) \left[\prod_{j=i}^{i_o-1} \phi'(\varepsilon_{j-1} + A\Delta t_j) - 1 \right] & i < i_o \\ A \prod_{j=i}^{N} \phi'(\varepsilon_{j-1} + A\Delta t_j) \left[1 - \prod_{j=i_o}^{i-1} \phi'(\varepsilon_{j-1} + A\Delta t_j) \right] & i \geq i_o \end{cases} \qquad (**)$$

Fall 1: $t_i = o, \Delta t_i = o \rightarrow \mu_i \Delta t_i = o$. Die Zeiger $\{i,\dots,i_o - 1\}$ sind sämtlich aus Phase I $\rightarrow$ (wegen (1)) $\phi'(\varepsilon_{i-1} + A\Delta t_i) \leq 1 \rightarrow \mu_i \geq o$.

Fall 2: $o < t_i < 1 \wedge \Delta t_i > o$. Ist $i < i_o$, so sind sämtliche Zeiger $\{i,\dots,i_o - 1\}$ aus Phase II (höchstens i_o selbst kannaus Phase III sein; Phase I entfällt wegen $t_i > o$) $\longrightarrow$ (wegen (1)) $\phi'(\varepsilon_{i-1} + A\Delta t_i) = 1 \rightarrow \mu_i = o$. Ist $i \geq i_o$, so sind alle Zeiger $\{i_o,\dots,i-1\}$ aus Phase II (höchstens i selbst kann aus Phase III sein; wegen $t_{i_o} > o$ ist i_o aus Phase II). $\longrightarrow$ (wegen (1)) $\phi'(\varepsilon_{i-1} + A\Delta t_i) \overset{\circ}{=} 1 \rightarrow \mu_i = o$.

Fall 3: $t_i = 1, \Delta t_i = o \rightarrow \mu_i \Delta t_i = o$. $\mu_i \geq o$ folgt aus (**) analog zu Fall 2 wegen $\phi'(\varepsilon_{i-1} + A\Delta t_i) \leq 1, i \neq N$.

□

2.4. Die optimale Schrittweitensteuerung

<u>Satz 2</u> :

(1) Die Voraussetzungen (V1) und (V2) seien erfüllt.

(2) $\varepsilon_o < \varepsilon_{max} \wedge \varepsilon_{min} < \bar{\varepsilon}$ ($\bar{\varepsilon}$: vorgeschriebene Endgenauigkeit).

(3) Die Steuerung des Prozesses sei folgendermaßen definiert:

$$s_i := \begin{cases} 1-s_{i-1} & \text{f. } \phi(\varepsilon_{i-1}+A(1-s_{i-1})) \le \bar{\varepsilon} \\ o & \phi(\varepsilon_{i-1}+A(1-s_{i-1})) > \bar{\varepsilon} \wedge \varepsilon_{i-1} > \varepsilon^* \\ (\varepsilon^* - \varepsilon_{i-1})/A & \phi(\varepsilon_{i-1}+A(1-s_{i-1})) > \bar{\varepsilon} \wedge \varepsilon_{i-1} \le \varepsilon^* \\ & \quad \wedge (\varepsilon^* - \varepsilon_{i-1})/A \le 1-s_{i-1} \\ 1-s_{i-1} & \phi(\varepsilon_{i-1}+A(1-s_{i-1})) > \bar{\varepsilon} \wedge \varepsilon_{i-1} \le \varepsilon^* \wedge \\ & \quad \wedge (\varepsilon^* - \varepsilon_{i-1})/A > 1-s_{i-1} \end{cases}$$

Dann gilt:

(1) Es gibt ein $N \in \mathbb{N}$ mit $\sum_{i=1}^{N} \Delta s_i = 1 \wedge \varepsilon_N \le \bar{\varepsilon}$.

(2) Sei $\bar{N} \in \mathbb{N}$ die kleinste Zahl mit $\sum_{i=1}^{\bar{N}} \Delta s_i = 1 \wedge \varepsilon_{\bar{N}} \le \bar{\varepsilon}$

Dann ist $\Delta s := (\Delta s_1, \ldots, \Delta s_{\bar{N}})$ die gesuchte Schrittweitensteuerung.

Beweis:

Zu (1): Die Steuerung zerfällt in dieselben drei Phasen wie die optimale Steuerung von Satz 1. Zu zeigen ist: alle drei Phasen sind nach endlich vielen Schritten beendet.

Phase I ist beendet, wenn $\Delta s_i > o$.

Annahme: $\bigwedge_{i \in N} \Delta s_i = o \rightarrow \varepsilon_i = \phi(\varepsilon_{i-1})$. Wegen $\varepsilon_o < \varepsilon_{max}$ gilt: $\lim_{i\to\infty} \varepsilon_i = \varepsilon_{min} < \varepsilon^*$

(Wegen ε_i monoton und beschränkt durch ε_{min}).

$\rightarrow \bigvee_{i \in \mathbb{N}} \varepsilon_{i-1} < \varepsilon \rightarrow \Delta s_i > o$ Widerspruch.

Phase II ist beendet, wenn $s_i = 1$. Sei i_o Ende von Phase I: $s_{i_o} = o \wedge$

$\Delta s_{i_o+1} = (\varepsilon^* - \varepsilon_{i_o})/A > o \wedge \varepsilon_{i_o+1} = \phi(\varepsilon^*)$.

Annahme: $\bigwedge_{i \geq i_o+2} \Delta s_i = (\varepsilon^* - \phi(\varepsilon^*))/A \rightarrow \lim_{i\to\infty} s_i = \infty \rightarrow$ Widerspruch.

Phase III ist beendet, wenn $\varepsilon_i \leq \bar{\varepsilon} \wedge s_i = 1$. Sei i_1 Ende von Phase II

$\varepsilon_{i_1} < \varepsilon_{max}$ $(\varepsilon < \infty \rightarrow \varepsilon_{i_1} \leq \varepsilon_{max}; \varepsilon^* = \infty \rightarrow \varepsilon_{i_1} < \infty$, trivial).

Annahme: $\bigwedge_{i \geq i_1+1} \varepsilon_i > \bar{\varepsilon} \wedge s_i = 1 \rightarrow \varepsilon_i = \phi(\varepsilon_{i-1})$. Wegen $\lim_{i\to\infty} \varepsilon_i = \varepsilon_{min} \wedge \bar{\varepsilon} > \varepsilon_{min}$

gilt: $\bigvee_{i_2 \in \mathbb{N}} \varepsilon_{i_2} \leq \bar{\varepsilon}$ Widerspruch.

Zu (2) Annahme: Es gibt eine Steuerung $\Delta t := (\Delta t_1, \ldots, \Delta t_M)$ mit

$\sum_{i=1}^{M} \Delta t_i = 1 \wedge \Delta t_i \geq o, i=1,\ldots,M \wedge \varepsilon_M < \bar{\varepsilon} \wedge M < \bar{N}$.

$\bar{\varepsilon} \underset{\text{Vor.}}{\geq} \varepsilon_M(\Delta t) \underset{\text{Satz 1}}{\geq} \varepsilon_M(\overline{\Delta s})$ mit $\overline{\Delta s} := (\Delta s_1, \ldots, \Delta s_{M-1}, 1 - s_{M-1})$

$\phi(\varepsilon_{M-1} + A(1 - s_{m-1})) \leq \bar{\varepsilon} \rightarrow \Delta s_M = 1 - s_{M-1}$. Für die verkürtzte Steuerung

gilt dann: $\sum_{i=1}^{M} \Delta s_i = 1 \wedge \Delta s_i \geq o, i=1,\ldots,M \wedge \bar{\varepsilon}_M \leq \bar{\varepsilon}. \rightarrow M \leq \bar{N}$ im Widerspruch

zur Definition von $\bar{N}$.

□

Bem 1: Phase I und/oder Phase II können entfallen, Phase III nie!

Bem 2: Im "Normalfall" (mehr als 1 Schritt in Phase II) wird dort im Wesentlichen mit gleichmäßiger Stufenbreite $\Delta s_c := (\varepsilon^* - \phi(\varepsilon^*))/A$ und gleicher Zwischengenauigkeit $\varepsilon_e := \phi(\varepsilon^*)$ gerechnet.
(1.Schritt von Phase II: $\Delta s_i = (\varepsilon^* - \varepsilon_{i-1})/A \rightarrow \varepsilon_i = \phi(\varepsilon_{i-1} + A\Delta s_i) =$

$$= \phi(\varepsilon_{i-1} + A(\varepsilon^* - \varepsilon_{i-1})/A) = \phi(\varepsilon^*)$$

2.Schritt von Phase II: $\Delta s_{i+1} = (\varepsilon^* - \phi(\varepsilon^*))/A \rightarrow \varepsilon_{i+1} = \phi(\varepsilon^*)$ usw.)

Bem 3: Ist ϕ strikt konvex, so ist die Lösung eindeutig.

3. Anwendungen auf einige Iterationsverfahren

3.1. Iterationsverfahren der Konvergenzordnung $p>1$: $\phi(x) = Cx^p$

Es gilt: $\varepsilon_{min} = 0$, $\varepsilon_{max} = C^{-1/(p-1)}$, $\varepsilon^* = (pC)^{-1/(p-1)}$

Aus $A\Delta s < \varepsilon_{max}$ erhält man die Grenzschrittweite $S_o := C^{-1/(p-1)}/A$
Bei Durchlaufen des Homotopieintervalles (PhaseII) wird mit der Schrittweite $\Delta s_e = \frac{(pC)^{-1/(p-1)}}{A} \cdot (1 - \frac{1}{p}) = (p-1)p^{-p/(p-1)} \cdot S_o$ gerechnet

Zugehörige Genauigkeit: $\varepsilon_e = C \cdot (pC)^{-p/(p-1)}$

Mit Hilfe von Δs_e erhält man eine obere Schranke N_e für die Anzahl der Iterationen bei Durchlaufen des Homotopieintervalls (Phase II):

$$N_e = \frac{1}{\Delta s_e} = \frac{1}{p-1} \cdot p^{-p/(p-1)} \cdot \frac{1}{S_o}$$

Bemerkung : Betrachtet man Δs_e und S_o in Abhängigkeit von $p>1$, so erhält man:

$$\lim_{p\to\infty} \Delta s_e(p)/S_o(p)=\lim_{p\to\infty}((p-1)p^{-p/(p-1)})=1$$

D.h. bei wachsender Konvergenzordnung wächst die optimale Schrittweite $\Delta s_e(p)$ bezogen auf die Grenzschrittweite $S_o(p)$.

Spezialfall:Newtonverfahren (p=2)

$\Phi(x,s):=x-T_x(x,s)^{-1}T(x,s)\wedge\phi(x)=Cx^2$

Wir erhalten:

$S_o=1/CA, \Delta s_e=1/4CA=S_o/4, \varepsilon_e=1/4C, N_e=4CA=4/S_o$

Wir verglichen das hier vorgestellte 3-Phasen-Modell (3PM) während Phase II mit dem in [14] behandelten Modell (N.V) für das Newtonverfahren:

	(N.V)	(3PM)
optimale Schrittweite	o.62 S_o	o.25 S_o
Genauigkeit in Phase II	o.1o AS_o	o.25 AS_o
Iterationen Pro Stufe	2.63	1
Gesamtzahl der Iterationen	$4.26/S_o$	$4/S_o$

Zusammenfassung:Das Modell (3PM) arbeitet mit kleineren Schritt weiten,geringerer Genauigkeit in den Zwischenstufen und mit etwas geringerem Aufwand als das Modell (N.V).

3.2.Das Verfahren des minimalen Residuums

$$\Phi(x,s):=x-\frac{(T(x,s),T_x(x,s))}{\|T_x(x,s)T(x,s)\|^2}T(x,s)$$

ϕ hat folgende Form (siehe [13]):$\phi(x)=(Cx+B)x, B>1$

Damit gilt:

$\varepsilon_{min}=o, \varepsilon_{max}=(1-B)/C, \varepsilon^*=(1-B)/2C$

Für die Grenzschrittweite ergibt sich:$S_o=(1-B)/2C$

Schrittweite in Phase II:$\Delta s_e=(1-B)^2/4CA=S_o.(1-B)/4$

Zwischengenauigkeit in Phase II:$\varepsilon_e=(1-B^2)/4C$

Obere Schranke für die Anzahl der Iterationen in Phase II:

$$N_e = \frac{1}{\Delta s_e} = \frac{4}{1-B} \cdot \frac{1}{S_o}$$

In [13] wurde ein Modell zur Aufwandsminimierung für das Verfahren des minimalen Residuums diskutiert. Bei Anwendung analoger Techniken wie in [14] erhält man ein Modell (M.R) für das globalisierte Verfahren.

Vergleich der Modelle (3PM) und (M.R) für einige Werte von B (Phase II):

	B=o	B=o.3	B=o.6
Anzahl der Iterationen in (M.R)	$7.69/S_o$	$1o.3o/S_o$	$16.42/S_o$
Anzahl der Iterationen in (3PM)	$4/S_o$	$5.71/S_o$	$1o/S_o$

Zusammenfassung: Der Aufwand in (3PM) ist wesentlich kleiner als in (M.R).

3.3. Lineare Iterationsverfahren: $\phi(x)=Cx, C<1$

Aus Satz 2 folgt wegen $\overset{*}{\varepsilon}=\infty$ sofort $s_1=1$ und damit $\Delta s=(1,o,\ldots o)$ bis $\varepsilon_N \leq \bar{\varepsilon}$. Der Algorithmus arbeitet optimal ohne Einbettung!

4. Der Algorithmus (I3PM)

Auf Grund von Satz 2 wurde für das Newtonverfahren der folgende implementierbare Algorithmus (I3PM) konstruiert:

0. Festlegung von Anfangswerten für A, C, C_o; $\Delta\varepsilon^* := 0.1, \varepsilon^* := \frac{1}{2C}$
1. $i:=0$, $x_i := x_o$, $\varepsilon_i := \|T(x_o,0)\|$, $s_i := 0$
2. $i := i+1$
3. Wenn $\varepsilon_{i-1} \geq \varepsilon^*$ oder $s_{i-1}=1$, dann $s_i := s_{i-1}$, go to 7
4. $\Delta s_i := \min(1-s_{i-1}, (\varepsilon^* - \varepsilon_{i-1})/A)$, $s_i := s_{i-1} + \Delta s_i$,
   $\tilde{\varepsilon}_i := \|T(x_{i-1}, s_i)\|$
5. Wenn $\tilde{\varepsilon}_i < \varepsilon^*(1-\Delta\varepsilon^*)$, dann $x_i := x_{i-1}$, $A := |\tilde{\varepsilon}_i - \varepsilon_{i-1}|/\Delta s_i$,
   go to 2
6. Wenn $\tilde{\varepsilon}_i > \varepsilon^*(1+\Delta\varepsilon^*)$, dann $A := |\tilde{\varepsilon}_i - \varepsilon_{i-1}|/\Delta s_i$, go to 4
7. $x_i := \Phi(x_{i-1}, s_i)$, $\varepsilon_i := \|T(x_i, s_i)\|$
8. Wenn $s_i = 1$ und $\varepsilon_i \leq \bar{\varepsilon}$: stop (Lösung)
9. $C := \max(C_o, \varepsilon_i/\tilde{\varepsilon}_i^2)$, $\varepsilon^* := 1/(2C)$
10. Wenn $\varepsilon_i \geq \tilde{\varepsilon}_i$, go to 3
11. Go to 2

Erklärung:
Die Punkte 1, 2, 3, 4, 7, 8, 11 werden unmittelbar durch Satz 2 nahegelegt, die übrigen Teile berücksichtigen die tatsächliche Situation:
Die Punkte 5, 6:
Nach dem Prädiktorschritt müßte gelten: $\tilde{\varepsilon}_i = \varepsilon^*$. In (I3PM) wird diese Bedingung ersetzt durch $\tilde{\varepsilon}_i \in [\varepsilon^*(1-\Delta\varepsilon^*), \varepsilon^*(1+\Delta\varepsilon^*)]$
Ist $\tilde{\varepsilon}_i$ zu klein, wird ohne Korrektorschritt weitergegangen und A neu gesetzt.
Ist $\tilde{\varepsilon}_i$ zu groß, wird Δs_i neuerlich mit einem modifizierten A berechnet.
(Überschreitet A eine vorgegebene obere Schranke $\bar{A}$(hier $\bar{A} := 10^6$), ist zu befürchten, daß (V1) nicht erfüllt ist.- Abbruch)
Die Punkte 9, 10:
Nach dem Korrektorschritt müßte gelten: $\varepsilon_i < \tilde{\varepsilon}_i$
Bei Verletzung dieser Bedingung wird die Schrittweite Δs_i mit

einem modifizierten C neu berechnet.
Ist die Bedingung bei zwei aufeinanderfolgenden Durchläufen in der selben Stufe s_i verletzt, wird der gesamte Prozeß mit einer größeren unteren Schranke C_o für C neu gestartet. (d. h. man verlangt eine größere Genauigkeit der Zwischenlösungen (x_i, s_i))
In allen Fällen wird nach jeder Iteration C neu gesetzt.
(Überschreitet C eine vorgegebene obere Schranke $\bar{C}$(hier $\bar{C}:=10^6$), ist zu befürchten, daß (V2) mit $\phi(x) = Cx^2$ nicht erfüllt ist.- Abbruch).

5. Numerische Experimente

Einige numerische Resultate bei Verwendung von (I3PM) (alle Rechnungen wurden auf einer Anlage IBM 360/44 mit doppelter Genauigkeit durchgeführt):

Beispiel 1:

Rheinboldt[7] (S. 173-174) löst mit einem 1-stufigen SOR-Newton-Verfahren folgendes nichtlineare Zweipunkt-Randwertproblem:

$$- \frac{d}{dt}\left[c\left(\frac{du}{dt}\right) \frac{du}{dt}\right] = f(t), \quad t \in (0,1)$$

$$u(0) = u(1) = 0$$

$$\text{mit} \quad c(z) := 1+z^2 \quad \text{und} \quad f(t) := 6000(1-2t)^2 + 20$$

Exakte Lösung: $u(t) = 10t(1-t)$

Diskretisierung: (1) gleichmäßige Maschenbreite $h=1/(n+1)$
(2) Approximation der linken Seite durch Hintereinanderschaltung von Vorwärts- und Rückwärtsdiffenzenoperator.

Ergebnis: $A(x)x = b, \quad x \in \mathbb{R}^n, \quad A = (a_{ij}), \; b = (b_i)$

$$a_{ij} := \begin{cases} -(\alpha_i + \alpha_{i-1})/h & \text{für } i=j \\ \alpha_l/h & \text{für } |i-j| = 1, \; l = \min(i,j) \\ 0 & \text{sonst} \end{cases}$$

$$\alpha_i := c\left[(x_{i+1}-x_i)/h\right] \qquad (x_0 := x_{n+1} := 0)$$

$$b_i := 10.i.h(1-i.h)$$

Einbettung: $T(x,s) := A(x)x - sb$

Ergebnisse mit (I3PM) für $C=0.5$, $A=1$, $C_0=0$:

	n=4	n=9	n=19	n=39
Iterationen bis s≥0.1	14	16	19	20
Iterationen bis s=1	16	19	21	23

Bemerkung: (1) Die Iterationszahl hängt nur schwach von der Dimension n ab, im Gegensatz zu dem von Rheinboldt verwendeten SOR-Newton-Verfahren.

(2) Auf Grund der Größe der rechten Seite b benötigt das Verfahren sehr lange, um auf s≥0.1 zu kommen.

(3) Das Newtonverfahren ohne Einbettung versagt in allen Fällen mit Startwert $x_0=0$.

Beispiel 2:

Rheinboldt[8] untersucht das elliptische Randwertproblem:

$$-\frac{\partial}{\partial x}\left[q\left(\frac{\partial u}{\partial x}^2 + \frac{\partial u}{\partial y}^2\right)\frac{\partial u}{\partial x}\right] - \frac{\partial}{\partial y}\left[q\left(\frac{\partial u}{\partial x}^2 + \frac{\partial u}{\partial y}^2\right)\frac{\partial u}{\partial y}\right] = w \quad \text{in } \Omega := [0,1]^2$$

$$u = 0 \quad \text{auf } \partial\Omega$$

Die Methode der finiten Elemente mit stückweise linearen Funktionen auf einer gleichmäßigen Einteilung von Ω mit Maschenbreite h=1/(m+1) liefert bei konstanter rechter Seite w:

$$(Q_N+Q_W+Q_S+Q_O)x_{ij} - Q_N x_{i,j+1} - Q_W x_{i-1,j} - Q_S x_{i,j-1} - Q_O x_{i+1,j} =$$
$$= h^2 w \quad \text{für } i,j = 1,2,\dots,m$$

$$x_{kl} = 0 \quad \text{für } (kh,lh) \in \partial\Omega$$

wobei: $2Q_N = q(\Delta_x(i,j+1)^2+\Delta_y(i,j)^2) + q(\Delta_x(i-1,j)^2+\Delta_y(i,j)^2)$

$2Q_W = q(\Delta_x(i-1,j)^2+\Delta_y(i,j)^2) + q(\Delta_x(i-1,j)^2+\Delta_y(i-1,j-1)^2)$

$2Q_S = q(\Delta_x(i-1,j-1)^2+\Delta_y(i,j-1)^2) + q(\Delta_x(i,j)^2+\Delta_y(i,j-1)^2)$

$2Q_O = q(\Delta_x(i,j)^2+\Delta_y(i,j-1)^2) + q(\Delta_x(i,j)^2+\Delta_y(i+1,j)^2)$

und $\Delta_x(k,l) = \frac{1}{h}(x_{k+1,l}-x_{k,l})$, $\Delta_y(k,l) = \frac{1}{h}(x_{k,l+1}-x_{k,l})$

Dieses Gleichungssystem hat die Gestalt $A(x)x = b$.

Als Einbettung wird verwendet: $T(x,s) := A(x)x - sb$

Folgende konkrete Funktionen q(t) und Werte w wurden analog zu Rheinboldt[8] bei unterschiedlicher Maschenbreite untersucht:

a) $q(t) := e^{5t}$, w=5, m=7

Die Parameterwahl $C = C_o = 5$, $A = 1$ in (I3PM) liefert:

s_i	$s_{i+1}-s_i$	Newton-Iterationen
0.18286	0.20858	1
0.39144	0.15547	2
0.54691	0.20928	1
0.75617	0.10554	1
0.86171	0.13829	1
1.00000	-	-

Gesamtzahl der Newton-Iterationen 6

(für kleinere Werte C_o schreitet die Schrittweitensteuerung zu optimistisch vor, sodaß man den Konvergenzbereich des Newtonverfahren verläßt.) Für $C_o=5$ konnte also nach 6 Newton-iterationen der Konvergenzbereich des Newtonverfahren für s=1 erreicht werden.

Rheinboldt[8] benötigt 20 Iterationen um s=1 zu erreichen.

Das Newtonverfahren ohne Einbettung divergiert mit dem Startwert $x_o=0$.

b) $q_o = 1,\ q_1 = 10,\ w = 15$

$$q(t) := \begin{cases} q_o & \text{für } t \le 0.15 \\ (q_o+q_1)/2+(q_1-q_o)(3\bar{t}-\bar{t}^3)/4, & \bar{t}=(40t-13)/7,\ 0.15 \le t \le 0.5 \\ q_1 & \text{für } t \ge 0.5 \end{cases}$$

(q ist eine "geglättete" Stufenfunktion)

Parameterwahl: $A = 1,\ C = \max(C_o, 0.5)$
Für verschiedene Setzungen von C_o ergibt sich:

	$C_o=0$	$C_o=0.5$	$C_o=1$	$C_o=2.5$	$C_o=5$	Rhb 8
m=2	∞	28	23	∞	31	30
m=3	∞	26	35	34	32	36
m=5	∞	∞	∞	32	36	41

(∞ ... Konvergenzbereich wird verlassen.)

In jedem der Fälle m=2,3,5 versagt das Newtonverfahren ohne Einbettung mit Startwert $x_o=0$.

An den vorgelegten Ergebnissen erkennt man einen Nachteil von (I3PM): Die Festlegung von A, C(d.h. die Fixierung der ersten Schrittweite) und C_o (d.h. die Fixierung einer oberen Schranke für die Zwischengenauigkeiten) beeinflußt stark die Iterationszahl. Dieser Effekt wirkt sich vor allem bei Beispielen unangenehm aus, deren Konvergenzbereich bei Iteration an der Stelle s von s stark abhängt, wo also die Annahme von globalen Fehlerabschätzungen wie (V2) eine zu grobe Vereinfachung darstell.

Weitere numerische Beispiele zu (I3PM) finden sich in [3].

6. Literaturverzeichnis

[1] J. H. Avila. The feasibility of continuation methods for nonlinear equations. SIAM J. Numer. Anal., 11(1974), pp. 102-120.

[2] P. Deuflhard. A stepsize control for continuation methods with special application to multiple shooting techniques. Preprint no. 7627, TU München, 1976, pp. 1-76.

[3] J. Hackl, Hj. Wacker, W. Zulehner. On optimal stepsize control for continuation methods. Preprint no. 101, Univ. Linz, 1978, pp. 1-20.

[4] H. T. Kung. The complexity of obtaining starting points for solving operator equations by Newton's method. Analytic Computational Complexity, J. F. Traub, ed., Academic Press, New York, 1976, pp. 35-55.

[5] D. Leder. Automatische Schrittweitensteuerung bei global konvergenten Einbettungsmethoden. Z. Angew. Math. Mech., 54(1970), pp. 319-324.

[6] G. Meyer. On solving nonlinear equations with a one-parameter operator imbedding. SIAM J. Numer. Anal., 5(1968), pp. 739-752.

[7] W. C. Rheinboldt. On the solution of large, sparse sets of nonlinear equations. Computational Mechanics, A. Dold, B. Eckmann, ed., Springer Verlag, New York, 1975, pp. 169-194.

[8] W. C. Rheinboldt. On the solution of some nonlinear equations arising in the application of finite element methods. Math. of Finite Elements, J. Whiteman, ed., Academic Press, London, 1976, pp. 465-482.

[9] M. Ribaric, M. Seliskar. On optimization of stepsize in the continuation method. Math. Balkanica, 4(1974), pp. 517-521.

[10] W. F. Schmidt. Adaptive stepsize selection for use with the continuation method. Internat. J. Numer. Methods Engrg., 12(1978), pp. 677-694.

[11] H. Schwetlick. Ein neues Prinzip zur Konstruktion implementierbarer, global konvergenter Einbettungsalgorithmen. Beiträge Numer. Math., 4(1975), pp. 215-228, 5(1976), pp. 201-206.

[12] Hj. Wacker. Ein Iterationsverfahren zur Lösung spezieller Randwertprobleme. Computing, 8(1972), pp. 275-291.

[13] Hj. Wacker. Minimierung des Rechenaufwandes für spezielle Iterationsverfahren vom Typ minimales Residuum. Computing, 18(1977), pp. 209-224.

[14] Hj. Wacker, E. Zarzer, W. Zulehner. Optimal stepsize control for the globalized Newton method. Continuation Mehtods, Hj. Wacker, ed., Academic Press, New York, 1978, pp. 249-277.

Johann Hackl
Wiener Allianz L.vers.-A.G.
Postfach 1500
A-1131 Wien

Hansjörg Wacker, Walter Zulehner
Institut für Mathematik
Universität Linz
A-4045 Linz-Auhof

EXPLICIT HERMITIAN METHODS FOR THE NUMERICAL SOLUTION OF PARABOLIC PARTIAL DIFFERENTIAL EQUATIONS

Gerhard Joubert

Explicit hermitian methods, which have smaller truncation errors and better stability properties than presently available explicit methods, are derived for the one-dimensional nonhomogeneous parabolic differential equation. As these hermitian methods are not defined for all internal points of the difference grid used, smoothing methods which enable their practical application are formulated. Numerical results for a linear and a nonlinear example are given.

1. INTRODUCTION.

A number of methods which can be used to improve the accuracy of difference methods for the numerical treatment of partial differential equations are available. One possibility is to use hermitian formulas as originally proposed by Collatz [5] and subsequently investigated by a number of authors. In [4] a survey of these methods as applied to the solution of parabolic equations is given.

As is well-known explicit difference methods offer computational advantages, especially in the case of nonlinear problems, over implicit methods. On the other hand their use is often limited by rather restrictive stability requirements. The aim with this paper is to investigate explicit hermitian formulas with weaker stability requirements than those presently available and to formulate a smoothing method which enables the practical application of these formulas. Numerical results obtained with these explicit procedures for a linear and a nonlinear example are compared with results obtained with standard difference methods.

In order to describe the construction of hermitian formulas consider the one-dimensional parabolic differential equation

$$Lu = u_t - u_{xx} = f(x,t) \tag{1}$$

with $u = u(x,t)$ and prescribed initial and boundary values

$$\begin{aligned} u(x,0) &= g(x), && 0\leq x\leq 1 \\ u(0,t) &= u(1,t) = 0, && 0<t\leq T. \end{aligned} \tag{2}$$

2. HERMITIAN FORMULAS

In order to describe the construction of hermitian formulas in the case of (1) consider a rectangular grid, with mesh-widths Δx and Δt in the x- and t- directions respectively, defined over the domain of definition of the differential equation. Indicate the grid points by $P_{p,q}$ and choose a linear combination:

$$\phi = \sum_{q=-1}^{n} \sum_{p=-m}^{m} [b_{p,-q}\, u(P_{p,-q}) + c_{p,-q}(\Delta x)^2\, Lu(P_{p,-q})], \tag{3}$$

$$n \geq 0,\ m \geq 1 .$$

In the remainder of this paper only symmetric explicit two-level formulas, defined over at most five points in the x-direction, i.e. with $n = 0$, $m \leq 2$, will be considered.

The aim is to choose the coefficients $b_{p,-q}$ and $c_{p,-q}$ in such a way that the truncation error is minimized if a Taylor series expansion of the terms in ϕ is made. Substituting 0 for the remainder terms and using (1) the equation

$$\phi_\Delta = \sum_{q=-1}^{n} \sum_{p=-m}^{m} [b_{p,-q} U_{j+p,k-q} + c_{p,-q} (\Delta x)^2 f_{j+p,k-q}] = 0 \tag{4}$$

is obtained, with $U_{j,k} = U(j\Delta x, k\Delta t) \approx u(x,t)$ and $f_{j,k} = f(j\Delta x, k\Delta t)$. In the case of explicit formulas, (4) can be used directly to compute the values $U_{j,k+1}$ from known values on the time-levels $t = k\Delta t$, $t = (k-1)\Delta t$, ..., $t = (k-n)\Delta t$ for $j = 0,1,\ldots,M$ with $M\Delta x = 1$.

The symmetry requirement implies that

$$b_{-p,-q} = b_{p,-q},\ c_{-p,-q} = c_{p,-q},\ p = 1,2,\ldots,m; \quad q = 0,1,\ldots,n. \tag{5}$$

Furthermore let

$$r = \frac{\Delta t}{(\Delta x)^2}. \tag{6}$$

Various methods can be used to construct formulas ϕ. A very simple method to do this without using Taylor expansions was used by Collatz [4,5] to investigate formulas with $n = 0$, $m \leq 1$.

In order to obtain formulas with a first order truncation error it must be required that

(7) $\phi = 0$ for $u = 1, t, x^2$

and then, because of symmetry,

(8) $\phi = 0$ for $u = x, x^3, tx$.

To obtain formulas with a smaller truncation error it must furthermore be required that

(9) $\phi = 0$ for $u = t^2,\ tx^2,\ x^4$.

Then ϕ is also zero for $u = x^5,\ tx^3,\ t^2x$.

Conditions (7) and (9) give the following system of 6 equations in 12 unknowns:

(10)

	$b_{0,0}$	$b_{1,0}$	$b_{2,0}$	$b_{0,1}$	$b_{1,1}$	$b_{2,1}$	$c_{0,0}$	$c_{1,0}$	$c_{2,0}$	$c_{0,1}$	$c_{1,1}$	$c_{2,1}$
1	1	2	2	1	2	2	0	0	0	0	0	0
t	0	0	0	r	2r	2r	1	2	2	1	2	2
x^2	0	2	8	0	2	8	-2	-4	-4	-2	-4	-4
t^2	0	0	0	r	2r	2r	0	0	0	2	4	4
tx^2	0	0	0	0	2r	8r	0	2	8	-2r	2(1-2r)	4(2-r)
x^4	0	2	32	0	2	32	0	-24	-96	0	-24	-96

Here, for example, the first row should be read as

$$b_{0,0} + 2b_{1,0} + 2b_{2,0} + b_{0,1} + 2b_{1,1} + 2b_{2,1} = 0.$$

As only explicit equations are to be considered let

(11) $b_{1,1} = b_{2,1} = c_{1,1} = c_{2,1} = 0.$

In addition to these, let also

(12) $c_{2,0} = 0,\quad b_{0,1} = -1.$

If only the first three equations in (10) are considered, two more values, say $c_{1,0}$ and $c_{0,1}$, can be chosen zero, giving

$$(13)\qquad \begin{aligned} b_{0,0} &= 1 - 2r + 6b_{2,0} \\ b_{1,0} &= r - 4b_{2,0} \\ c_{0,0} &= r. \end{aligned}$$

If $m = 1$, then $b_{2,0} = 0$, giving the formula

$$(14)\quad \phi_\Delta = (1-2r)U_{j,k} + r(U_{j-1,k} + U_{j+1,k}) - U_{j,k+1} + \\ + \Delta t f_{j,k} = 0,$$

or

$$(15)\quad U_{j,k+1} = (1-2r)U_{j,k} + r(U_{j-1,k} + U_{j+1,k}) + \Delta t f_{j,k}.$$

With $m = 2$, i.e. $b_{2,0} \neq 0$, the formula

$$(16)\quad U_{j,k+1} = b_{0,0}U_{j,k} + b_{1,0}(U_{j-1,k} + U_{j+1,k}) + \\ + b_{2,0}(U_{j-2,k} + U_{j+2,k}) + \Delta t f_{j,k}$$

is obtained.

Written in the usual way the discretization errors of these formulas are given by

$$(17)\qquad E = O(\Delta t + (\Delta x)^2).$$

Other formulas, with the same discretization error, can be obtained if e.g. $c_{0,0}$ is chosen 0 instead of $c_{1,0}$ or $c_{0,1}$.

In order to obtain formulas with improved accuracy, consider all the equations in (10). These have the solution

$$(18)\quad \begin{aligned} b_{0,0} &= \tfrac{1}{2}(6r^2 - 5r+2) \\ b_{1,0} &= \tfrac{2r}{3}(2 - 3r) \\ b_{2,0} &= \tfrac{r}{12}(6r-1) \\ c_{0,0} &= \tfrac{r}{2}(1-2r) \\ c_{1,0} &= \tfrac{r^2}{2} \\ c_{0,1} &= \tfrac{r}{2}. \end{aligned}$$

If $m' = 1$ then $b_{2,0} = 0$ or $r = \frac{1}{6}$, giving the formula [4]:

$$(19)\quad \phi_\Delta = \tfrac{2}{3} U_{j,k} + \tfrac{1}{6}(U_{j-1,k} + U_{j+1,k}) - U_{j,k+1} + \\ + 6\Delta t\,[\tfrac{1}{18} f_{j,k} + \tfrac{1}{72}(f_{j-1,k} + f_{j+1,k}) + \tfrac{1}{12} f_{j,k+1}]$$

or

$$(20)\quad U_{j,k+1} = \tfrac{2}{3} U_{j,k} + \tfrac{1}{6}(U_{j-1,k} + U_{j+1,k}) + \\ + \Delta t\,[\tfrac{1}{3} f_{j,k} + \tfrac{1}{12}(f_{j-1,k} + f_{j+1,k}) + \tfrac{1}{2} f_{j,k+1}].$$

For $m = 2$, i.e. $b_{2,0} \neq 0$, the formula becomes:

$$(21)\quad U_{j,k+1} = b_{0,0}\, U_{j,k} + b_{1,0}\,(U_{j-1,k} + U_{j+1,k}) + \\ + b_{2,0}(U_{j-2,k} + U_{j+2,k}) + \Delta t\,[(\tfrac{1-2r}{2}) f_{j,k} + \tfrac{r}{2}(f_{j-1,k} + f_{j+1,k}) + \\ + \tfrac{1}{2} f_{j,k+1}].$$

The discretization errors of the formulas (20) and (21) are given by

$$(22)\quad E = O(\,(\Delta t)^2 + (\Delta x)^4).$$

Note that the formulas (15) and (16) can be obtained from a straightforward extension of the equivalent finite difference approximations for the homogeneous diffusion equation $Lu = 0$. The accuracy of these equations cannot, however, be improved by choosing $r = \frac{1}{6}$ in the case of (15) or $b_{2,0} = \frac{r(6r-1)}{12}$ in the case of (16). For (1) improved accuracy can, however, be obtained by using hermitian formulas such as (20) and (21).

The stability of (15), (16), (20) and (21) can be shown by using the Lax-Richtmyer stability definition [7]. The following results can easily be shown to hold [6]:

Theorem 1

The difference equation (15) is stable for $0 < r \leq \frac{1}{2}$.

Theorem 2

If the coefficients of (16) are chosen such that the conditions

$$
\begin{aligned}
0 < r \leq 1 &: \quad \frac{2r-1}{8} \leq b_{2,0} \leq \frac{r}{4} \\
1 \leq r \leq 2 &: \quad \frac{r^2}{8} \leq b_{2,0} \leq \frac{r}{4},
\end{aligned}
\tag{23}
$$

then (16) is a consistent and stable approximation of (1).

The consistency and stability conditions (16) and (23) can be satisfied simultaneously for all $0 < r \leq 2$. A similar result to theorem 2 holds for (21), but with the conditions (13) replaced by (18). In this case all conditions can be simultaneously satisfied for all $0 < r \leq \frac{2}{3}$. The stability of (20) follows as a special case of this result.

3. SMOOTHING FORMULAS

The hermitian formula (3) with $m \geq 2$ is not defined for all internal points of the difference grid used. As in the case of difference equations with $m \geq 2$ for $Lu = 0$, such a formula can be written as a combination of a so-called basic difference formula with $m = 1$ and a suitable smoothing formula [6]. If the smoothing formula is defined for all internal grid points, then the new algorithm is also defined for all internal grid points.

In the case of (3) with $n = 0$, $m = 2$ the following smoothing algorithm can be used:

<u>Algorithm</u>

<u>Step 1</u>: Set $k = 0$.

<u>Step 2</u>: Compute values $U_{j,k+1}$, $U_{j,k+2}$, $j = 1,2,\ldots,M-1$, successively from the known values $U_{j,k}$, $j = 0,1,\ldots,M$, and the boundary values $U_{0,k+1}$, $U_{M,k+1}$ by means of (15) in the usual way.

<u>Step 3</u>: Compute values $U'_{j,k+1}$, $j = 1,2,\ldots,M-1$, from the known and computed values $U_{j,k}$, $U_{j,k+1}$, $U_{j,k+2}$, $j=0,1,\ldots,M$, by means of a suitable smoothing formula.

<u>Step 4</u>: Replace the values $U_{j,k+1}$, $j = 1,2,\ldots,M-1$, computed in step 2 by the smoothed values $U'_{j,k+1}$, set $k = k+1$ and if $k\Delta t < T$ then go to step 2 else stop.

A suitable smoothing formula which can be used in the case of the hermitian formulas (21) (and (20)) is given by the following result:

Theorem 3

Given an approximate solution of (1), (2) for $t = k\Delta t$, and values for $t = (k+1)\Delta t$, $t = (k+2)\Delta t$ computed according to step 2 of the algorithm, then the smoothing formula

$$(24)\quad U'_{j,k+1} = \sum_{\ell=0}^{2} a_{0,\ell}\, U_{j,k+\ell} + \Delta t \sum_{\ell=0}^{1} \sum_{i=-1}^{1} \hat{a}_{i,\ell}\, f_{j+i,k+\ell},$$

$j = 1,2,\ldots,M-1$, with the $a_{0,\ell}$ and $\hat{a}_{i,\ell}$ chosen such that

$$(25)\quad \begin{aligned} a_{0,2} &= \frac{1}{r^2}\, b_{2,0} \\ a_{0,1} &= 1 - 2a_{0,2} \\ a_{0,0} &= a_{0,2} \\ \hat{a}_{0,1} &= a_{0,2} - \frac{1}{2} \\ \hat{a}_{-1,1} &= \hat{a}_{1,1} = 0 \\ \hat{a}_{0,0} &= \frac{2}{3} - a_{0,2} \\ \hat{a}_{-1,0} &= \hat{a}_{1,0} = -\frac{1}{12} \end{aligned}$$

with $b_{2,0}$ the coefficient from (21), hold, applied to these values on the time-levels $t = k\Delta t$, $t = (k+1)\Delta t$, $t = (k+2)\Delta t$ according to step 3 of the algorithm, results in a computational procedure which is equivalent to (21).

Proof

The proof of the theorem follows easily if (15) is substituted into the right-hand side of (24).

A similar algorithm and smoothing formula can be derived for the equation (16), the only change to the algorithm being that only one cycle need be computed with the formula (15) in step 1. A similar result to that in theorem 3 can then be shown to hold for the smoothing formula:

$$(26)\quad U'_{j,k+1} = \sum_{\ell=0}^{1} \sum_{i=-1}^{1} a_{i,\ell} U_{j+i,k+\ell} + \Delta t \hat{a}_{1,0} (f_{j-1,k} + f_{j+1,k})$$

with

$$(27)\quad \begin{aligned} a_{0,1} &= 1 \\ a_{-1,1} &= a_{1,1} = \frac{1}{r} b_{2,0} \\ a_{0,0} &= 4b_{2,0} \\ a_{-1,0} &= a_{1,0} = -\left(\frac{1+2r}{r}\right) b_{2,0} \\ \hat{a}_{1,0} &= \frac{1}{r} b_{2,0} \end{aligned}$$

4. NUMERICAL RESULTS

4.1 A linear problem

In table 1 numerical results computed with the methods given above are compared with the well-known Crank-Nicolson implicit method, which is unconditionally stable, but requires the solution of a system of equations with each time-step [1,7]:

$$(28)\quad (1+r)\, U_{j,k+1} - \frac{r}{2} (U_{j-1,k+1} + U_{j+1,k+1})$$
$$= (1-r) U_{j,k} + \frac{r}{2} (U_{j-1,k} + U_{j+1,k}) - \Delta t f_{j,k+\frac{1}{2}}.$$

The problem considered is (1) with

$$(29)\quad f(x,t) = x(x-1)e^{-t} [\cos(t^2) + 2t \sin(t^2)] - 2\cos(t^2)e^{-t},$$

and the initial and boundary conditions:

$$(30) \quad \begin{aligned} u(x,0) &= x(1-x), \quad 0 \leq x \leq 1 \\ u(0,t) &= u(1,t) = 0, \quad 0 < t \leq T. \end{aligned}$$

The solution is given by

$$(31) \qquad u(x,t) = \cos(t^2)e^{-t}x(1-x).$$

For each t-value only the biggest absolute error is given, which in the given results occurred at x = 0,5 in each case.

Method	r	Discretization error	t=0,1	t=0,2	t=0,5	t=1,0
(15)	0,5	$E=O(\Delta t+(\Delta x)^2)$	$3,83.10^{-5}$	$4,48.10^{-5}$	$1,29.10^{-5}$	$7,41.10^{-6}$
(15)	$\frac{1}{6}$	$E=O(\Delta t+(\Delta x)^2)$	$1,26.10^{-5}$	$1,48.10^{-5}$	$4,33.10^{-6}$	$2,47.10^{-6}$
(20)	$\frac{1}{6}$	$E=O((\Delta t)^2+(\Delta x)^4)$	$9,30.10^{-8}$	$1,08.10^{-7}$	$2,30.10^{-8}$	$1,21.10^{-8}$
(21)+(24)	0,5	$E=O((\Delta t)^2+(\Delta x)^4)$	$8,47.10^{-7}$	$9,84.10^{-7}$	$2,12.10^{-7}$	$1,12.10^{-7}$
(28)	0,5	$E=O((\Delta t)^2+(\Delta x)^2)$	$4,25.10^{-5}$	$4,89.10^{-5}$	$1,04.10^{-5}$	$5,62.10^{-6}$

TABLE 1

The computational work required per time-step by the various methods is given in table 2.

Method	Arithmetic Operations per Time-Step			Function Evaluations per Time-Step
	Multiplications	Divisions	Additions/ Subtractions	
(15)	3(M-1)	-	3(M-1)	M-1
(20)*	15(M-1)	-	18(M-1)	3(M+1)
(21)+(24)	6(M+2)	-	2(4M+3)	M+1
(28)	4(M-1)	2(M-1)	4(M-1)	M-1

TABLE 2

Except in the case of (20) the number of function evaluations is virtually the same for each method with M large. It should be noted that on most serial computers the time required to execute a division is considerably longer than for a multiplication.

4.2 A nonlinear problem

In order to study the behaviour of the abovementioned formulas when used to solve nonlinear problems, the one-dimensional Burgers equation

$$(32) \qquad Lu = u_t - u_{xx} = -uu_x, \quad -\pi \le x \le 0, \quad 0 < t \le T$$

---

* In order to compare the computational work required by (20) with that required by the other methods, the work required for three time steps is given.

with initial and boundary values

$$u(x,0) = R \sin x \quad , \quad -\pi \leq x \leq 0$$

$$u(-\pi,t) = u(0,t) = 0, \qquad 0 < t \leq T,$$

with R the Reynold's number, was considered. The analytic solution of this equation is given e.g. by Benton and Platzmann [2].

The stability conditions given for the explicit hermitian formulas also hold in this case.

Numerical results were computed with (15),(16) and (21) for R = 1, 10 and 20. For the results given in table 3 the mesh widths $\Delta x = \frac{\pi}{20}$, $\Delta t = 0{,}01$ and for those given in table 4 the mesh widths $\Delta x = \frac{\pi}{40}$, $\Delta t = 0{,}0025$ were used respectively. In table 3 numerical results obtained with the Crank-Nicolson method for R = 20 are also given. In both the tables 3 and 4 only the biggest absolute errors obtained in each case for the indicated time levels are given. The best results were obtained by replacing $U_{j,k}$ by $\frac{1}{3}(U_{j-1,k} + U_{j,k} + U_{j+1,k})$ as in [3].

5. CONCLUSIONS

In the linear case better results can be obtained with explicit hermitian methods than with the Crank-Nicolson method. The smoothing procedure (21) + (24) gives improved results at no additional expense in computational work compared to (28).

In the nonlinear case the results obtained with methods (15) and (16) are comparable with those obtained with the Crank-Nicolson method. The comparatively poor results obtained with method (21) + (24) in this case result from the fact that the right hand side of (32) cannot be approximated with a second

R	Method	t=0,1	t=0,2	t=0,3	t=0,5	t=1,0
1,0	(15)	$8{,}00.10^{-4}$	$1{,}06.10^{-3}$	$1{,}13.10^{-3}$	$1{,}10.10^{-3}$	$1{,}06.10^{-3}$
$b_{0,2}$ = -0,001	(16)	$4{,}7.10^{-4}$	$5{,}7.10^{-4}$	$5{,}8.10^{-4}$	$7{,}3.10^{-4}$	$1{,}07.10^{-3}$
	(21)	$5{,}9.10^{-4}$	$8{,}9.10^{-4}$	$1{,}03.10^{-3}$	$9{,}7.10^{-4}$	$4{,}3.10^{-4}$
10,0	(15)	$3{,}80.10^{-1}$	$3{,}63.10^{-1}$	$1{,}05.10^{-1}$	$7{,}06.10^{-2}$	$3{,}57.10^{-2}$
$b_{0,2}$ = -0,001	(16)	$3{,}50.10^{-1}$	$3{,}60.10^{-1}$	$7{,}64.10^{-2}$	$4{,}55.10^{-2}$	$2{,}45.10^{-2}$
	(21)	$3{,}81.10^{-1}$	$5{,}70.10^{-1}$	$1{,}89.10^{-1}$	$8{,}00.10^{-2}$	$3{,}42.10^{-2}$
20,0	(15)	3,65	$5{,}04.10^{-1}$	$3{,}27.10^{-1}$	$1{,}81.10^{-1}$	$6{,}55.10^{-2}$
$b_{0,2}$ = -0,001	(16)	3,90	$4{,}29.10^{-1}$	$2{,}71.10^{-1}$	$1{,}53.10^{-1}$	$5{,}15.10^{-2}$
	(21)	7,47	$5{,}52.10^{-1}$	$3{,}71.10^{-1}$	$1{,}90.10^{-1}$	$6{,}26.10^{-2}$
	Crank-Nicolson	8,703	3,356	1,048	$2{,}25.10^{-1}$	$3{,}7.10^{-2}$

TABLE 3

R	Method	t=0,1	t=0,2	t=0,3	t=0,5	t=1,0
1,0	(15)	$2,0.10^{-4}$	$2,6.10^{-4}$	$2,8.10^{-4}$	$2,7.10^{-4}$	$2,7.10^{-4}$
$b_{0,2}$ = -0,001	(16)	$2,9.10^{-4}$	$4,6.10^{-4}$	$5,5.10^{-4}$	$5,7.10^{-4}$	$3,8.10^{-4}$
	(21)	$5,7.10^{-4}$	$8,9.10^{-4}$	$1,04.10^{-3}$	$9,9.10^{-4}$	$4,2.10^{-4}$
10,0	(15)	$8,86.10^{-2}$	$8,64.10^{-2}$	$2,51.10^{-2}$	$1,70.10^{-2}$	$8,73.10^{-3}$
$b_{0,2}$ = -0,001	(16)	$7,00.10^{-2}$	$7,90.10^{-2}$	$3,44.10^{-2}$	$1,06.10^{-2}$	$5,44.10^{-3}$
	(21)	$8,68.10^{-2}$	$1,22.10^{-1}$	$4,50.10^{-2}$	$1,92.10^{-2}$	$8,36.10^{-3}$
20,0	(15)	$6,90.10^{-1}$	$1,14.10^{-1}$	$7,79.10^{-2}$	$4,32.10^{-2}$	$1,59.10^{-2}$
$b_{0,2}$ = -0,001	(16)	$6,99.10^{-1}$	$4,75.10^{-2}$	$2,57.10^{-2}$	$1,63.10^{-2}$	$3,11.10^{3}$
	(21)	1,06	$1,19.10^{-1}$	$8,64.10^{-2}$	$4,57.10^{-2}$	$1,53.10^{-2}$

TABLE 4

order discretization error within the limitation $m \leq 2$, $n = 0$. This reduces the overall error of this method to first order. Better results can be obtained for (32) by using implicit hermitian methods [1].

From the results obtained it appears that the smoothing method can be successfully applied to explicit hermitian formulas, resulting in explicit computational procedures which compare favourably with existing methods.

ACKNOWLEDGEMENTS

Part of the research was done at the Institut für Angewandte Mathematik, University of Hamburg with a grant of the Alexander von Humboldt-Foundation, Bonn-Bad Godesberg, West-Germany. The investigation of the applications to nonlinear problems was sponsored by the Atomic Energy Board, South Africa.

REFERENCES

[1] Adam, Y.: A hermitian finite difference method for the solution of parabolic equations. Comp. and Maths. with Applications. 1 (1975), 393-406.

[2] Benton, E.R. and Platzmann, G.W.: A table of solutions of the one-dimensional Burgers equation. Quarterly of Applied Maths. 30 (1972), 195-212.

[3] Bivins, R.L. and Metropolis, N.C.: Significance arithmetic: Application to a partial differential equation. IEEE Trans. on Computers. C-26 (1977), 639-642.

[4] Collatz, L.: Hermitian methods for initial value problems in partial differential equations. Topics in Numerical Analysis, Proceedings of the Royal Irish Academy Conference on Numerical Analysis, 1972. Edited by J.J.H. Miller. London, Academic 1973.

[5] Collatz, L.: The Numerical Treatment of Differential Equations. Berlin, Springer 1960.

[6] Joubert, G.R.: Explicit difference approximations of the one-dimensional diffusion equation, using a smoothing technique. Numerische Mathematik 17 (1971), 409-430.

[7] Richtmyer, R.D. and Morton, K.W.: Difference Methods for Initial Value Problems. New York, Interscience 1967.

Computer Science Department
University of Natal
DURBAN
South Africa

ZUR EINSCHLIESSUNG DES BETRAGSKLEINSTEN EIGENWERTES BEI EIGENWERTAUFGABEN MIT GEWÖHNLICHEN DIFFERENTIAL-GLEICHUNGEN VIERTER ORDNUNG

Peter P. Klein

Sufficient conditions are stated for the general eigenvalue problem $My = \lambda Ny$ with linear, ordinary, selfadjoint differential expressions M and N of order 4 and 2 respectively to be equivalent with an eigenvalue problem involving a linear, compact, positive integral operator. By means of the theory for such operators the existence of a nonnegative eigenfunction belonging to the smallest positive eigenvalue of the original problem is concluded. The bounds for this eigenvalue, stemming from the quotient theorem for positive operators, are in accordance with those given in [1].

Bezeichnungen: RWA, EWA, EW, EV, EF seien die Abkürzungen für Randwertaufgabe, Eigenwertaufgabe, Eigenwert, Eigenvektor, Eigenfunktion; IGL, DGL, RB seien die Abkürzungen für Integralgleichung, Differentialgleichung, Randbedingung. θ bezeichne das Nullelement eines linearen Raumes. $C^k[x_1, x_2]$ sei die Menge der im Intervall $[x_1, x_2]$ k-mal stetig differenzierbaren Funktionen.

Einleitung

Gegeben sei die EWA

$$\text{DGL: } My(x) = \lambda Ny(x) \text{ in } x_1 \leqslant x \leqslant x_2$$

$$\text{RB: } \begin{cases} y(x_i) = 0 \text{ oder } M_0 y(x_i) = \lambda N_0 y(x_i) & (i = 1, 2) \\ y'(x_i) = 0 \text{ oder } M_1 y(x_i) = \lambda N_1 y(x_i) & (i = 1, 2) \end{cases} \tag{1}$$

wobei gesetzt ist:

$My(x) = (p_2(x)y''(x))'' - (p_1(x)y'(x))'$, $Ny(x) = -(q_1(x)y'(x))' + q_0(x)y(x)$

mit reellen Funktionen $p_\mu \in C^\mu[x_1, x_2]$ $(\mu = 1, 2)$, $p_2(x) > 0$ in $x_1 \leqslant x \leqslant x_2$, sowie $q_\nu \in C^\nu[x_1, x_2]$ $(\nu = 0, 1)$, $q_\nu \not\equiv 0$ für $\nu = 0$ oder $\nu = 1$,

und für $i = 1, 2$ gesetzt ist:

$M_o y(x_i) = g_{oi} y(x_i) + (-1)^i (-(p_2 y'')' + p_1 y')(x_i)$, $M_1 y(x_i) = g_{1i} y'(x_i) + (-1)^i (p_2 y'')(x_i)$
$N_o y(x_i) = h_{oi} y(x_i) + (-1)^i ((q_1 y')(x_i) + k_{1i} y'(x_i))$, $N_1 y(x_i) = h_{1i} y'(x_i) + (-1)^i k_{oi} y(x_i)$
mit reellen Konstanten $g_{\nu i}$, $h_{\nu i}$, $k_{\nu i}$ ($\nu = 0, 1$; $i = 1, 2$).
Liegt die wesentliche RB $y^{(\nu)}(x_i) = 0$ vor, so sei $k_{\nu i} = 0$ gesetzt. Je nach Art der ersten beiden RB bei der EWA (1) sind folgende Fälle zu unterscheiden:

RB	$y(x_1)=0$ $y(x_2)=0$	$y(x_1)=0$ $M_o y(x_2) = \lambda N_o y(x_2)$	$M_o y(x_1) = \lambda N_o y(x_1)$ $y(x_2)=0$	$M_o y(x_1) = \lambda N_o y(x_1)$ $M_o y(x_2) = \lambda N_o y(x_2)$
EWA	1.1	1.2.1	1.2.2	1.3

In [1] ist ein Quotientensatz für allgemeine EWA der Form $My = \lambda Ny$ angegeben worden, wobei M und N Differentialausdrücke der Ordnung 2m und 2n sind. Im Fall $m = 2$, $n = 1$ ist die hier behandelte EWA spezieller wegen $p_o \equiv 0$; die Randausdrücke N_o, N_1 sind aber durch die zusätzlichen Terme $k_{1i} y'(x_i)$, $k_{oi} y(x_i)$ etwas allgemeiner. Gilt $k_{oi} = k_{1i}$ ($i = 1, 2$), so läßt sich die EWA (1) als natürliche EWA im Sinne von [9] auffassen.

§ 1 Hilfsmittel

Vorgelegt sei zunächst die RWA

DGL: $My(x) = r(x)$ in $x_1 \leqslant x \leqslant x_2$

$$\text{RB:} \begin{cases} y(x_i) = 0 \text{ oder } M_o y(x_i) = r_i & (i = 1, 2) \\ y'(x_i) = 0 \text{ oder } M_1 y(x_i) = s_i & (i = 1, 2) \end{cases} \tag{2}$$

mit $r \in C[x_1, x_2]$ und Konstanten r_i, s_i.
Für diese RWA wird eine entsprechende Fallunterscheidung getroffen wie für die EWA. Bei der Angabe hinreichender Bedingungen für die Existenz einer zur RWA (2) gehörigen Greenschen Funktion G bildet die folgende RWA den Ausgangspunkt:

$$\begin{aligned} &\text{DGL: } Lz(x) = -(p_2(x)z'(x))' + p_1(x)z(x) = s(x) \text{ in } x_1 \leqslant x \leqslant x_2 \\ &\text{RB: } z(x_i) = 0 \text{ oder } g_{1i} z(x_i) + (-1)^i (p_2 z')(x_i) = s_i \quad (i = 1, 2) \end{aligned} \tag{3}$$

mit $s \in C[x_1, x_2]$.

Unter der Voraussetzung

(V 1) Die homogene RWA (3) hat nur die triviale Lösung

gibt es zur RWA (3) eine Greensche Funktion H, die sich in folgender Weise darstellen läßt (vgl. z. B. [7], S. 328)

$$H(x,\xi) = \begin{cases} a^{-1}\, u(x)\, v(\xi) & x_1 \leqslant \xi \leqslant x \leqslant x_2 \\ a^{-1}\, v(x)\, u(\xi) & x_1 \leqslant x \leqslant \xi \leqslant x_2 \end{cases} \tag{4}$$

mit nicht identisch verschwindenden Funktionen u, v und einer Konstanten a, die den Bedingungen genügen:

$Lv(x) = 0$ in $x_1 \leqslant x \leqslant x_2$, $v(x_1) = 0$ oder $g_{11}v(x_1) - (p_2v')(x_1) = 0$

$Lu(x) = 0$ in $x_1 \leqslant x \leqslant x_2$, $u(x_2) = 0$ oder $g_{12}u(x_2) + (p_2u')(x_2) = 0$

$p_2(x)\,[u(x)\,v'(x) - u'(x)\,v(x)] = a.$

Im Fall $s \equiv 0$ ist die Lösung der RWA (3) gegeben durch

$$h(x) = s_1 a^{-1}\, u(x)v(x_1) + s_2 a^{-1}\, v(x)\,u(x_2) = \sum_{i=1}^{2} s_i H(x, x_i). \tag{5}$$

Liegt für ein $i \in \{1, 2\}$ die RB $z(x_i) = 0$ vor, so kann s_i eine beliebige Zahl sein wegen $H(x, x_i) \equiv 0$.

Satz 1. 1: Gegeben sei die RWA (2). Unter den Voraussetzungen (V 1), (V 2) existiert die zugehörige Greensche Funktion G gemäß Tabelle 1.

Die Lösung der RWA (2) lautet dann

$$y(x) = \sum_{i=1}^{2} r_i\, G(x, x_i) + \sum_{i=1}^{2} s_i\, G_\xi(x, x_i) + \int_{x_1}^{x_2} G(x,\xi)\, r(\xi)\, d\xi .$$

Liegt für ein $i \in \{1, 2\}$ die RB $y(x_i) = 0$ oder $y'(x_i) = 0$ vor, so können r_i oder s_i beliebige Zahlen sein wegen $G(x, x_i) \equiv 0$ oder $G_\xi(x, x_i) \equiv 0$.

Beweis: Sei y Lösung der RWA (2). Wird gesetzt $z = y'$, so ergibt sich nach einer Integration, daß z Lösung der RWA (3) mit geeigneten rechten Seiten $s(x)$, $s_i (i = 1, 2)$ ist. Mit der Greenschen Funktion H der RWA (3) und der Funktion h aus (5) folgt eine Darstellung für z und nach einer weiteren Integration eine Darstellung für y. Die Integrationskonstanten sind durch die ersten beiden RB festgelegt.

Bemerkung 1. 3: Die beiden Darstellungen von G bei der RWA (2. 1) sind gleich, da für H_γ mit $\gamma = \frac{1}{\eta}$ gilt: $\int_{x_1}^{x_2} H_\gamma(s,t)dt \equiv 0$, $\int_{x_1}^{x_2} H_\gamma(s,t)ds \equiv 0$.

Bei der RWA (2. 3) folgt die Übereinstimmung der beiden Darstellungen von G mit Hilfe der für die RWA (2. 1) geltenden Gleichung.

Definition 1.2: Es gelte (V 1). H sei die Greensche Funktion der RWA (3). Es sei gesetzt:

$$\eta = \int_{x_1}^{x_2} \left(\int_{x_1}^{x_2} H(s,t)\,dt \right) ds, \quad \Delta = g_{o1} + g_{o2} + g_{o1}\, g_{o2}\, \eta \;, \quad H_\gamma(x,\xi) = H(x,\xi) - \gamma \int_{x_1}^{x_2} H(x,t)\,dt \int_{x_1}^{x_2} H(s,\xi)\,ds.$$

RWA	RB	Vor. (V 2)	γ	Greensche Funktion $G(x,\xi)$ =
2.1	$y(x_1) = 0$ $y(x_2) = 0$	$\eta \neq 0$	$\frac{1}{\eta}$	$\int_{x_1}^{x} \left(\int_{x_1}^{\xi} H_\gamma(s,t)\,dt \right) ds = \int_{x}^{x_2} \left(\int_{\xi}^{x_2} H_\gamma(s,t)\,dt \right) ds$
2.2.1	$y(x_1) = 0$ $M_o y(x_2) = r_2$	$1 + g_{o2}\eta \neq 0$	$\frac{g_{o2}}{1+g_{o2}\eta}$	$\int_{x_1}^{x} \left(\int_{x_1}^{\xi} H_\gamma(s,t)\,dt \right) ds$
2.2.2	$M_o y(x_1) = r_1$ $y(x_2) = 0$	$1 + g_{o1}\eta \neq 0$	$\frac{g_{o1}}{1+g_{o1}\eta}$	$\int_{x}^{x_2} \left(\int_{\xi}^{x_2} H_\gamma(s,t)\,dt \right) ds$
2.3	$M_o y(x_1) = r_1$ $M_o y(x_2) = r_2$	$\eta \neq 0$ und $\Delta \neq 0$	$\frac{g_{o1}\, g_{o2}}{\Delta}$	$\int_{x_1}^{x} \left(\int_{x_1}^{\xi} H_\gamma(s,t)\,dt \right) ds + \frac{1}{\Delta} \left\{ 1 + g_{o2} \left[\int_{x}^{x_2} \left(\int_{\xi}^{x_2} H(s,t)\,dt \right) ds - \int_{x_1}^{x} \left(\int_{x_1}^{\xi} H(s,t)\,dt \right) ds \right] \right\} =$ $= \int_{x}^{x_2} \left(\int_{\xi}^{x_2} H_\gamma(s,t)\,dt \right) ds + \frac{1}{\Delta} \left\{ 1 + g_{o1} \left[\int_{x_1}^{x} \left(\int_{x_1}^{\xi} H(s,t)\,dt \right) ds - \int_{x}^{x_2} \left(\int_{\xi}^{x_2} H(s,t)\,dt \right) ds \right] \right\}$

Tabelle 1

Bemerkung 1.4: Formal ergibt sich die Greensche Funktion G der RWA (2.2.i) aus der Greenschen Funktion der RWA (2.3) durch den Grenzübergang $g_{oi} \longrightarrow \infty$, der auch bewirkt, daß die natürliche RB $\frac{1}{g_{oi}} M_o y(x_i) = \frac{r_i}{g_{oi}}$ in die wesentliche RB $y(x_i) = 0$ übergeht. Werden die Grenzübergänge $g_{o1} \longrightarrow \infty$, $g_{o2} \longrightarrow \infty$ nacheinander ausgeführt, so ergibt sich die Greensche Funktion der RWA (2.1).

Folgerung 1.5: 1. Für die RWA (2.1), (2.2), (2.3) gilt: $G_{x\xi} = H_\gamma$.

2. Liegt die RWA (2.1) vor, so haben die Funktionen $G_{x\xi}$, G_x, G_ξ Vorzeichenwechsel in $[x_1, x_2] \times [x_1, x_2]$,
3. Für die RWA (2.2) und (2.3) zeigt Tabelle 2 unter der Zusatzvoraussetzung (V 3) das Vorzeichenverhalten der Funktionen G, G_ξ, G_x, $G_{x\xi}$ in $[x_1, x_2] \times [x_1, x_2]$.

RWA	RB	Vor. (V 3)		Folgerung	
2.2.1	$y(x_1)=0$ $M_o y(x_2)=r_2$	$H_\gamma \geq 0$ (für 2.2.1 und 2.2.2)		$G \geq 0$, $G_x \geq 0$	$G_\xi \geq 0$, $G_{x\xi} \geq 0$
2.2.2	$M_o y(x_1)=r_1$ $y(x_2)=0$			$G \geq 0$, $G_x \leq 0$	$G_\xi \leq 0$, $G_{x\xi} \geq 0$
2.3	$M_o y(x_1)=r_1$ $M_o y(x_2)=r_2$	$H_\gamma \geq 0$		$G_{x\xi} \geq 0$	
		$g_{o1} > 0$ $g_{o2} = 0$	$H \geq 0$	$G \geq 0$, $G_x \geq 0$	$G_\xi \geq 0$, $G_{x\xi} \geq 0$
		$g_{o1} = 0$ $g_{o2} > 0$	$H \geq 0$	$G \geq 0$, $G_x \leq 0$	$G_\xi \leq 0$, $G_{x\xi} \geq 0$

Tabelle 2 (bei Funktionen gilt das Vorzeichen in $[x_1, x_2] \times [x_1, x_2]$.)

Beweis: 1. Die Gleichung $G_{x\xi} = H_\gamma$ ergibt sich aus den in Tabelle 1 gegebenen Darstellungen für G. 2. Im Fall der RWA (2.1) gilt mit $\gamma = \frac{1}{\eta}$:

$$\int_{x_1}^{x_2} G_{x\xi}(s,t)dt = \int_{x_1}^{x_2} H_\gamma(s,t)dt \equiv 0$$

$$\int_{x_1}^{x_2} G_x(s,\xi)ds = \int_{x_1}^{x_2}\left(\int_{x_1}^{\xi} H_\gamma(s,t)dt\right)ds = \int_{x_1}^{\xi}\left(\int_{x_1}^{x_2} H_\gamma(s,t)ds\right)dt \equiv 0$$

$$\int_{x_1}^{x_2} G_\xi(x,t)dt = \int_{x_1}^{x_2}\left(\int_{x_1}^{x} H_\gamma(s,t)ds\right)dt = \int_{x_1}^{x}\left(\int_{x_1}^{x_2} H_\gamma(s,t)dt\right)ds \equiv 0.$$

Da keine der Funktionen $G_{x\xi}$, G_x, G_ξ gleich der Nullfunktion sein kann - sonst wäre G die Nullfunktion - muß jede das Vorzeichen wechseln.

3. Für die RWA (2. 2) und die RWA (2. 3) ergibt sich unter der Zusatzvoraussetzung (V 3) das Vorzeichen von G, G_ξ, G_x, $G_{x\xi}$ aus der Darstellung von G in Tabelle 1.

§ 2 Eine Eigenwertaufgabe mit positivem Operator

Mit der zur RWA (2) gehörigen Greenschen Funktion G geht die EWA (1) über in die Integrodifferentialgleichung:

$$y(x) = g(x) + \int_{x_1}^{x_2} G(x,\xi)\,\lambda\,[-(q_1y')' + q_0y](\xi)d\xi \quad \text{mit}$$

$$g(x) = \sum_{i=1}^{2}\lambda[h_{oi}y(x_i) + (-1)^i((q_1y')(x_i) + k_{1i}y'(x_i))]\,G(x,x_i) +$$
$$+ \sum_{i=1}^{2}\lambda[h_{1i}y'(x_i) + (-1)^i k_{oi}y(x_i)]\,G_\xi(x,x_i).$$

Durch partielle Integration und geeignetes Zusammenfassen ergibt sich die gemischte Integralgleichung (vgl. [10], S. 120)

$$y(x) = \lambda\Big\{\sum_{i=1}^{2}(h_{oi}G(x,x_i) + (-1)^i k_{oi}G_\xi(x,x_i))y(x_i) + \int_{x_1}^{x_2} G(x,\xi)(q_oy)(\xi)d\xi \; + \tag{6}$$
$$+ \sum_{i=1}^{2}((-1)^i k_{1i}G(x,x_i) + h_{1i}G_\xi(x,x_i))y'(x_i) + \int_{x_1}^{x_2} G_\xi(x,\xi)(q_1y')(\xi)d\xi\Big\}.$$

Mit den Bezeichnungen

$$G_i(x,\xi) = \frac{1}{x_2-x_1}(h_{oi}G(x,x_i) + (-1)^i k_{oi}G_\xi(x,x_i)) \quad (i = 1,2)$$

$$G_3(x,\xi) = G(x,\xi)q_o(\xi)$$

$$G_{3+i}(x,\xi) = \frac{1}{x_2-x_1}((-1)^i k_{1i}G(x,x_i) + h_{1i}G_\xi(x,x_i)) \quad (i = 1, 2)$$

$$G_6(x,\xi) = G_\xi(x,\xi)\,q_1(\xi)$$

- wobei G_i, G_{i+3} $(i = 1,2)$ nicht von ξ abhängen - erhält man aus (6) die IGL

$$y(x) = \lambda \int_{x_1}^{x_2} \Big(\sum_{i=1}^{2} G_i(x,\xi) y(x_i) + G_3(x,\xi) y(\xi) + \sum_{i=1}^{2} G_{3+i}(x,\xi) y'(x_i) + G_6(x,\xi) y'(\xi)\Big) d\xi . \quad (7)$$

Diese IGL vereinfacht sich, wenn eine der Funktionen G_i identisch Null ist. Das tritt in folgenden Fällen ein: Bei Vorliegen der wesentlichen RB $y(x_i) = 0$ für $i = 1$ oder $i = 2$ gilt $G_i(x,\xi) \equiv 0$ wegen $G(x, x_i) \equiv 0$ und $k_{oi} = 0$; bei Vorliegen der anderen wesentlichen RB $y'(x_i) = 0$ für $i = 1$ oder $i = 2$ gilt $G_{3+i}(x,\xi) \equiv 0$ wegen $k_{1i} = 0$ und $G_\xi(x, x_i) \equiv 0$. Liegt wenigstens eine natürliche RB vor und gilt für ein $i \in \{1,2\}$ $h_{oi} = k_{oi} = 0$ bzw. $k_{1i} = h_{1i} = 0$, so ist die Funktion G_i bzw. G_{3+i} ebenfalls identisch Null. Schließlich ist G_3 bzw. G_6 gleich der Nullfunktion, wenn gilt $q_o \equiv 0$ bzw. $q_1 \equiv 0$. Andererseits ergibt sich wegen der Voraussetzung $q_\nu \not\equiv 0$ für $\nu = 0$ oder $\nu = 1$ auch $G_3 \not\equiv 0$ oder $G_6 \not\equiv 0$.

Definition 2.1: Gegeben sei die EWA (1); es gelte (V 1), (V 2). $I = \{ j \in \mathbb{N} \mid j \leqslant 6,\ G_j \not\equiv 0 \}$ sei eine Indexmenge; $|I|$ sei die Anzahl ihrer Elemente. Für $v \in C^1[x_1, x_2]$ sei gesetzt in $x_1 \leqslant x \leqslant x_2$: $v_i(x) = v(x_i)$ $(i = 1,2)$, $v_3(x) = v(x)$, $v_{3+i}(x) = v'(x_i)$ $(i = 1,2)$, $v_6(x) = v'(x)$. $\mathfrak{v} = (v_j)_{j\in I}$ bezeichne den zur Funktion v gehörigen $|I|$-Vektor.

Sei R bzw. $\widetilde{R}$ die Menge der $|I|$-Vektoren, deren Komponenten im Intervall $[x_1, x_2]$ definierte reell- bzw. komplexwertige, stetige Funktionen sind. Es sei gesetzt:

$$\mathcal{G} = (G_{ij})_{(i,j)\in I\times I} \quad \begin{cases} G_{ij}(x,\xi) = G_j(x_i,\xi) & (i = 1,2;\ 1 \leqslant j \leqslant 6) \\ G_{3j}(x,\xi) = G_j(x,\xi) & (1 \leqslant j \leqslant 6) \\ G_{3+i,j}(x,\xi) = \frac{\partial}{\partial x} G_j(x_i,\xi) & (i = 1,2;\ 1 \leqslant j \leqslant 6) \\ G_{6j}(x,\xi) = \frac{\partial}{\partial x} G_j(x,\xi) & (1 \leqslant j \leqslant 6) \end{cases} \quad (8)$$

Da die Funktionen G_{ij} $(1 \leqslant i,\ j \leqslant 6)$ auf $[x_1, x_2] \times [x_1, x_2]$ stetig sind, existiert zu jedem $\varepsilon > 0$ ein $\delta > 0$, so daß für alle $x', x'' \in [x_1, x_2]$

$$\text{mit } |x' - x''| < \delta \text{ gilt: } \int_{x_1}^{x_2} |G_{ij}(x',\xi) - G_{ij}(x'',\xi)| d\xi < \varepsilon . \quad (9)$$

Der Operator $\mathcal{P}\mathfrak{v}(x) = \int_{x_1}^{x_2} \mathcal{G}(x,\xi)\, \mathfrak{v}(\xi) d\xi$, $\mathfrak{v} \in \widetilde{R}$

ist dann auf $\widetilde{R}$ definiert und bildet $\widetilde{R}$ in sich ab. Da die Elemente von $\mathcal{G}$

reellwertige Funktionen sind, gilt auch: $\mathfrak{R} R \subset R$.

Satz 2.2: Unter den Voraussetzungen (V 1), (V 2) ist die EWA (1) äquivalent zu der EWA: $\mathfrak{R}\mathfrak{y} = \varkappa \mathfrak{y}$ mit $\varkappa \neq 0$. (10)
Die EW stehen in der Beziehung $\varkappa = \frac{1}{\lambda}$.

Beweis: Offenbar sind die EWA (1) und (7) äquivalent. Es sei y eine EF zum EW λ. $\mathfrak{y}$ bezeichne den zur Funktion y gehörigen $|I|$-Vektor. Es gilt $\lambda \neq 0$ und $\mathfrak{y} \neq \theta$; wäre $\lambda = 0$ oder $\mathfrak{y} = \theta$, so müßte y wegen (7) identisch Null sein. Unter Verwendung von (8) geht die IGL (7) in das IGL-System $\mathfrak{y} = \lambda \mathfrak{R}\mathfrak{y}$ und mit $\varkappa = \frac{1}{\lambda}$ in (10) über. Umgekehrt sei $\mathfrak{y} = (y_j)_{j \in I}$ ein EV der EWA (10) zum EW $\varkappa \neq 0$. Es sei gesetzt: $\lambda = \frac{1}{\varkappa}$ und $z(x) = \lambda \int_{x_1}^{x_2} \sum_{j \in I} G_j(x, \xi) y_j(\xi) d\xi$. Für den zur Funktion z gehörigen $|I|$-Vektor $\mathfrak{z}$ gilt: $\mathfrak{z} = \lambda \mathfrak{R}\mathfrak{y} = \mathfrak{y}$. Es kann z nicht die Nullfunktion sein, da sonst $\mathfrak{z}$ und somit $\mathfrak{y}$ der Nullvektor wäre. Werden in der Definitionsgleichung von z die Komponenten von $\mathfrak{y}$ durch solche von $\mathfrak{z}$ ersetzt, so ergibt sich (7) mit z an Stelle von y.

Da die Elemente der Matrix $\mathfrak{G}$ die Eigenschaft (9) haben, ist $\mathfrak{R}$ ein vollstetiger Operator auf $\widetilde{R}$ bzw. R, wenn dort die Maximumnorm zugrundegelegt wird (vgl. [4], S. 276 f). Werden zu (V 1), (V 2) als Voraussetzungen (V 3), (V 4) gemäß Tabelle 3 hinzugenommen, so bildet $\mathfrak{R}$ den Kegel $K \subset R$ in sich ab und ist somit ein positiver Operator im Sinne von [8]. Entsprechend gilt für den komplexen Kegel $\widetilde{K} = K + iK$ im Raum $\widetilde{R}$: $\mathfrak{R}\widetilde{K} \subset \widetilde{K}$. Im Falle der EWA (1.1) werden durch Voraussetzung (V 4) nur spezielle EWA zugelassen. Diese Einschränkung ist erforderlich, da die Funktionen $G_{x\xi}$, G_x, G_ξ nach Folgerung 1.5.2 das Vorzeichen wechseln. Bei der EWA (1.3) werden, wenn nicht eine der Konstanten g_{oi} $(i = 1, 2)$ Null ist, nur Aussagen für die Eingliedklasse (vgl. [5]) gemacht.

Zur Anwendung des Quotientensatzes für positive Operatoren wird folgendes Hilfsmittel benötigt:

Lemma 2.4: Gegeben sei die EWA (1); es gelte (V 1) - (V 4). Ferner sei $v_o \in C^2[x_1, x_2]$ und für den zugehörigen $|I|$-Vektor $\mathfrak{v}_o = (v_{oj})_{j \in I}$ gelte:

<u>Definition 2. 3:</u> $K_1 = \{ \mathfrak{v} \in R \mid \mathfrak{v} = (v_j)_{j \in I};\quad v_j(x) \geqslant 0 \text{ in } x_1 \leqslant x \leqslant x_2 \text{ für } j \in I \}$

$K_2 = \{ \mathfrak{v} \in R \mid \mathfrak{v} = (v_j)_{j \in I};\quad v_j(x) \gtreqless 0 \text{ in } x_1 \leqslant x \leqslant x_2 \text{ für } j \in \begin{matrix} I_o \\ I_1 \end{matrix} \} \text{ mit } \begin{matrix} I_o = I \cap \{1,2,3\} \\ I_1 = I \cap \{4,5,6\} \end{matrix}$

EWA	RB	Vor. (V 3)		Vor. (V 4)		Vorzeichen von G_{ij}	Kegel K
1. 1	$y(x_1) = 0$ $y(x_2) = 0$	$G \geqslant 0$		$k_{o1} = 0$ $k_{o2} = 0$	$h_{1i} = 0\ (i=1,2)$ $q_o \geqslant 0,\ q_1 \equiv 0$	$G_{33} \geqslant 0$	K_1
1. 2. 1	$y(x_1) = 0$ $M_o y(x_2) = \lambda N_o y(x_2)$	$H_\gamma \geqslant 0$		$k_{o1} = 0$	$h_{\nu i} \geqslant 0,\ k_{\nu i} \geqslant 0$ $(\nu = 0,1;\ i = 1,2)$ $q_\nu \geqslant 0\ (\nu = 0,1)$	$G_{ij} \geqslant 0,\ (i,j) \in I \times I$	K_1
1. 2. 2	$M_o y(x_1) = \lambda N_o y(x_1)$ $y(x_2) = 0$	$H_\gamma \geqslant 0$		$k_{o2} = 0$	$h_{\nu i} \geqslant 0,\ k_{\nu i} \geqslant 0$ $(\nu = 0,1;\ i = 1,2)$ $q_\nu \geqslant 0\ (\nu = 0,1)$	$G_{ij} \geqslant 0,\ (i,j) \in I_o \times I_o \cup I_1 \times I_1$ $G_{ij} \leqslant 0,\ (i,j) \in I_o \times I_1 \cup I_1 \times I_o$	K_2
1. 3	$M_o y(x_1) = \lambda N_o y(x_1)$ $M_o y(x_2) = \lambda N_o y(x_2)$	$G \geqslant 0$		$h_{\nu i} = k_{\nu i} = 0$ $(\nu = 0,1;\ i=1,2)$	$q_o \geqslant 0,\ q_1 \equiv 0$	$G_{33} \geqslant 0$	K_1
		$H_\gamma \geqslant 0$			$q_o \equiv 0,\ q_1 \geqslant 0$	$G_{66} \geqslant 0$	
		$g_{o1} > 0$ $g_{o2} = 0$	$H \geqslant 0$	$(-1)^i k_{\nu i} \geqslant 0$ $(\nu = 0,1;\ i=1,2)$	$h_{\nu i} \geqslant 0$ $(\nu = 0,1;\ i=1,2)$ $q_\nu \geqslant 0\ (\nu = 0,1)$	$G_{ij} \geqslant 0,\ (i,j) \in I \times I$	K_1
		$g_{o1} = 0$ $g_{o2} > 0$	$H \geqslant 0$	$(-1)^i k_{\nu i} \leqslant 0$ $(\nu = 0,1;\ i=1,2)$		$G_{ij} \geqslant 0,\ (i,j) \in I_o \times I_o \cup I_1 \times I_1$ $G_{ij} \leqslant 0,\ (i,j) \in I_o \times I_1 \cup I_1 \times I_o$	K_2

Tabelle 3 (bei Funktionen gilt das Vorzeichen in $[x_1, x_2]$ bzw. $[x_1, x_2] \times [x_1, x_2]$)

(i) $\mathfrak{v}_o \in K$ (Definition von K gemäß Tabelle 3)

(ii) Die Komponenten von $\mathfrak{v}_o$ haben keine Nullstellen im Intervall (x_1, x_2).

(iii) Im Fall $q_\nu \not\equiv 0$ für $\nu = 0$ oder $\nu = 1$ ist die Vielfachheit der Nullstellen von $v_o^{(\nu)}$ in den Randpunkten x_i $(i = 1, 2)$ nicht größer als durch die wesentlichen RB der EWA (1) angegeben wird.

Dann wird durch $l(\mathfrak{v}) = \underset{j \in I}{\mathrm{Max}} \; \sup_{x_1 < x < x_2} \dfrac{(\mathfrak{R}\mathfrak{v})_j(x)}{v_{oj}(x)}$, $\mathfrak{v} \in R$

ein reellwertiges Funktional auf R definiert mit den Eigenschaften: l ist nichtnegativ, subadditiv und positiv homogen auf K. Ferner gilt:
$\mathfrak{R}\mathfrak{v} \leqslant l(\mathfrak{v})\,\mathfrak{v}_o$ für alle $\mathfrak{v} \in K$.

Beweis: Es sei $\mathfrak{v} = (v_j)_{j \in I}$ aus R. Wird gesetzt $w(x) = \int_{x_1}^{x_2} \sum_{j \in I} G_j(x, \xi) v_j(\xi) d\xi$ so gilt für den zur Funktion w gehörigen $|I|$-Vektor $\mathfrak{w}$: $\mathfrak{w} = \mathfrak{R}\mathfrak{v}$. Da w Lösung der RWA (2) ist bei geeigneten rechten Seiten $r(x)$, r_i, $s_i (i = 1, 2)$, so erfüllt w insbesondere die wesentlichen RB. Im Fall $q_\nu \not\equiv 0$ für $\nu = 0$ oder $\nu = 1$ sind die Quotienten $\Psi_\nu(x) = \dfrac{w^{(\nu)}(x)}{v_o^{(\nu)}(x)}$ in $x_1 < x < x_2$ wegen (ii) definiert und stetig. In den Randpunkten $x_i (i = 1, 2)$ sind die Quotienten stetig ergänzbar, da dort die Vielfachheit der Nennernullstellen nicht größer ist als die der Zählernullstellen. Damit sind die Quotienten Ψ_ν in (x_1, x_2) beschränkt und das Funktional l nimmt für jedes $\mathfrak{v} \in R$ einen endlichen Wert an. Wegen $\mathfrak{R} K \subset K$ ist l auf K nichtnegativ; die restlichen Eigenschaften folgen aus der Definition von l.

Iteration: Es sei $v_o \in C^2 [x_1 , x_2]$,und $v_1 \in C^4 [x_1, x_2]$ sei Lösung der RWA

DGL: $Mv_1(x) = Nv_o(x)$ in $x_1 \leqslant x \leqslant x_2$

$$\text{RB:} \quad \begin{cases} v_1(x_i) = 0 \text{ oder } M_o v_1(x_i) = N_o v_o(x_i) \quad (i = 1, 2) \\ v_1'(x_i) = 0 \text{ oder } M_1 v_1(x_i) = N_1 v_o(x_i) \quad (i = 1, 2). \end{cases} \tag{11}$$

Die zu den Funktionen v_k $(k = 0, 1)$ gehörigen $|I|$-Vektoren seien mit $\mathfrak{v}_k = (v_{kj})_{j \in I}$ bezeichnet. Haben die Komponenten von $\mathfrak{v}_1$ keine Nullstellen im Intervall (x_1, x_2), so sei gesetzt: $\phi_j(x) = \dfrac{v_{oj}(x)}{v_{1j}(x)}$ $(x_1 < x < x_2,\ j \in I)$

sowie: $\phi_{min} = \underset{j \in I}{\mathrm{Min}} \; \inf_{x_1 < x < x_2} \phi_j(x)$, $\phi_{max} = \underset{j \in I}{\mathrm{Max}} \; \sup_{x_1 < x < x_2} \phi_j(x)$.

Dabei kann ϕ_{max} den Wert ∞ annehmen.

Satz 2.5: Gegeben sei die EWA (1); es gelte (V 1) - (V 4). Es sei $v_o \in C^2 [x_1, x_2]$ und erfülle die Bedingungen (i), (ii), (iii) aus Lemma 2.4; $v_1 \in C^4 [x_1, x_2]$ sei Lösung der RWA (11). Die Komponenten von $\mathfrak{w}_1$ seien nullstellenfrei im Intervall (x_1, x_2) und es gelte $\phi_{max} < \infty$. Dann besitzt die EWA (1) einen reellen, positiven EW λ_o mit einer nichtnegativen EF; λ_o ist betragskleinster EW der EWA (1) und es gilt die Einschließung: $\phi_{min} \leqslant \lambda_o \leqslant \phi_{max}$.

Beweis: Für die Lösung v_1 der RWA (11) gilt die Darstellung

$v_1(x) = \int_{x_1}^{x_2} \sum_{j \in I} G_j(x, \xi) v_{oj}(\xi) d\xi$. Für den zur Funktion v_1 gehörigen $|I|$-Vektor $\mathfrak{w}_1$ folgt dann: $\mathfrak{w}_1 = \mathcal{R} \mathfrak{w}_o$. Aus $\mathfrak{w}_o \in K$ ergibt sich $\mathfrak{w}_1 \in K$, da $\mathcal{R}$ positiver Operator ist. Die Quotienten $\phi_j(x)$ $(x_1 < x < x_2,\ j \in I)$ sind definiert und positiv. Damit gilt $\phi_{min} \geqslant 0$; $\phi_{min} = 0$ ist jedoch ausgeschlossen, da dies wegen des Zusammenhanges $\phi_{min} = \frac{1}{l(\mathfrak{w}_o)}$ zu $l(\mathfrak{w}_o) = \infty$ führt, was der Aussage von Lemma 2.4 widerspricht. Nach Definition von ϕ_{max} gilt: $\mathfrak{w}_o \leqslant \phi_{max} \mathfrak{w}_1$. Es folgt $\mu \mathfrak{w}_o \leqslant \mathfrak{w}_1$ mit $\mu = \frac{1}{\phi_{max}}$, wobei $\mu > 0$ ist. Nach dem Quotientensatz für lineare, vollstetige, positive Integraloperatoren (vgl. [4], S. 277) besitzt $\mathcal{R}$ einen reellen, positiven EW $\varkappa_o$, der alle anderen EW $\varkappa$ von $\mathcal{R}$ betragsmäßig übertrifft. Zum EW $\varkappa_o$ gibt es einen EV $\mathfrak{w} \in K$. Es gilt die Einschließung: $\mu \leqslant \lambda_o \leqslant l\,(\mathfrak{w}_o)$. Damit ist $\lambda_o = \frac{1}{\varkappa_o}$ betragskleinster EW derEWA (1); zu λ_o gibt es eine nicht-negative EF v und es gilt die Einschließung: $\phi_{min} \leqslant \lambda_o \leqslant \phi_{max}$.

Bemerkung 2.6: Sind die Funktionen q_o und q_1 beide von der Nullfunktion verschieden, so gilt:

$$\phi_{min} = \operatorname*{Min}_{\nu = o,1} \left\{ \operatorname*{Min}_{x_1 \leqslant x \leqslant x_2} \frac{v_o^{(\nu)}(x)}{v_1^{(\nu)}(x)} \right\}, \quad \phi_{max} = \operatorname*{Max}_{\nu = o,1} \left\{ \operatorname*{Max}_{x_1 \leqslant x \leqslant x_2} \frac{v_o^{(\nu)}(x)}{v_1^{(\nu)}(x)} \right\};$$

dabei sind die Quotienten $\frac{v_o^{(\nu)}(x)}{v_1^{(\nu)}(x)}$ $(\nu = 0, 1)$ in den Randpunkten stetig zu ergänzen. Die Einschließung für λ_o hat dann dieselbe Form wie in [1].

§ 3 Spezialfälle und Beispiele

Der folgende Satz gibt bei den EWA (1.2), (1.3) hinreichende Bedingungen für (V 1), (V 2), (V 3) an.

Satz 3.1: Es gelte (V 1'), (V 2') gemäß der folgenden Übersicht:

EWA	Vor. (V 1')	Vor. (V 2')
1.2.1	$p_2(x) > 0$, $p_1(x) \geqslant 0$ in $x_1 \leqslant x \leqslant x_2$	$g_{o2} \geqslant 0$
1.2.2	$g_{1i} \geqslant 0$ $(i = 1, 2)$	$g_{o1} \geqslant 0$
1.3	Der Fall $p_1 \equiv 0$ und $g_{11} = g_{12} = 0$ sei ausgeschlossen.	$g_{oi} \geqslant 0$ $(i = 1, 2)$, $g_{o1} + g_{o2} > 0$

Dann sind die Bedingungen (V 1), (V 2) erfüllt, und es gilt $H_\gamma(x, \xi) > 0$ in $(x_1, x_2) \times (x_1, x_2)$, falls g_{oi} für $i = 1$ oder $i = 2$ genügend klein ist.

Beweis: Aus (V 1') folgt (V 1): Die RWA (3) ist von monotoner Art (vgl. z.B. [6]), d.h. die zugehörige Greensche Funktion H existiert und ist nichtnegativ. Aus (V 2') ergibt sich (V 2) (siehe Tabelle 1) wegen $\eta > 0$. Unter Voraussetzung (V 1') gilt nach [3], S. 526, für die Greensche Funktion H in der Gestalt (4):

1. $u(x) \neq 0$ in $[x_1, x_2)$; entweder u ist konstant oder streng monoton fallend, wenn u als positiv angenommen wird.
2. $v(x) \neq 0$ in $(x_1, x_2]$; entweder v ist konstant oder streng monoton wachsend, wenn v als positiv angenommen wird.

Hiermit ergibt sich für $x \in (x_1, x_2)$:

$$\int_{x_1}^{x_2} H(x,t)dt = \int_{x_1}^{x} a^{-1} u(x)\, v(t)dt + \int_{x}^{x_2} a^{-1} v(x)\, u(t)dt =$$

$$= a^{-1} u(x)\, v(x) \left\{ \int_{x_1}^{x} \frac{v(t)}{v(x)} dt + \int_{x}^{x_2} \frac{u(t)}{u(x)} dt \right\} \leqslant a^{-1} u(x) v(x)\, (x_2 - x_1).$$

Entsprechend gilt für $\xi \in (x_1, x_2)$: $\int_{x_1}^{x_2} H(s, \xi)ds \leqslant a^{-1} u(\xi)\, v(\xi)\, (x_2 - x_1)$.

Damit folgt für H_γ (siehe Definition 1.2) in $(x_1, x_2) \times (x_1, x_2)$:

$$H_\gamma(x,\xi) \geqslant H(x,\xi) - \gamma a^{-2} u(x)v(\xi)v(x)u(\xi)(x_2 - x_1)^2 =$$

$$= \begin{cases} a^{-1} u(x)v(\xi)\,[1 - \gamma a^{-1} v(x)u(\xi)(x_2 - x_1)^2] & \text{falls } \xi \leqslant x \\ a^{-1} v(x)u(\xi)\,[1 - \gamma a^{-1} u(x)v(\xi)(x_2 - x_1)^2] & \text{falls } x \leqslant \xi \end{cases}$$

$$\geqslant H(x,\xi)\,[1 - \gamma a^{-1} u(x_1)v(x_2)(x_2 - x_1)^2].$$

Da bei den EWA (1.2), (1.3) nach Definition von γ (siehe Tabelle 1) gilt $\lim\limits_{g_{oi}\to o} \gamma = 0$ mit i = 1 oder i = 2, ist für genügend kleines g_{oi} der Ausdruck $[1 - \gamma a^{-1} u(x_1)v(x_2)(x_2 - x_1)^2]$ noch positiv.

Bemerkung 3.2: Liegt die EWA (1.2) vor und gilt (V 1'), so ist (V 3) auch für $g_{oi} < 0$ erfüllt, wenn nur $1 + g_{oi}\eta > 0$ bleibt.

Bemerkung 3.3: Im Fall $p_1 \equiv 0$ können die unter (V 1') an g_{1i} (i = 1, 2) gestellten Forderungen, um $H(x,\xi) > 0$ in $(x_1, x_2) \times (x_1, x_2)$ zu garantieren, gemäß Tabelle 4 weiter abgeschwächt werden (vgl. [2], S. 269).

Es sei gesetzt: $x_1 = 0$, $x_2 = 1$; $\varphi(x) = \int_0^x \frac{1}{p_2(t)}\,dt$.

RB	Bedingung für g_{1i}	$H(x,\xi)$ für $\xi \leqslant x$
$z(0)=0$ $z(1)=0$	–	$\frac{[\varphi(1) - \varphi(x)]\,\varphi(\xi)}{\varphi(1)}$
$z(0)=0$ $g_{12}z(1)+(p_2z')(1) = s_2$	$1+g_{12}\varphi(1)>0$	$\frac{[1+g_{12}(\varphi(1)-\varphi(x))]\,\varphi(\xi)}{1+g_{12}\varphi(1)}$
$g_{11}z(0)-(p_2z')(0)=s_1$ $z(1)=0$	$1+g_{11}\varphi(1)>0$	$\frac{[\varphi(1) - \varphi(x)](1+g_{11}\varphi(\xi))}{1+g_{11}\varphi(1)}$
$g_{11}z(0)-(p_2z')(0)=s_1$ $g_{12}z(1)+(p_2z')(1) = s_2$	$g_{11}+g_{12}+g_{11}g_{12}\varphi(1)>0$ $1+g_{11}\varphi(1)>0,\ 1+g_{12}\varphi(1)>0$	$\frac{[1+g_{12}(\varphi(1)-\varphi(x))](1+g_{11}\varphi(\xi))}{g_{11}+g_{12}+g_{11}g_{12}\varphi(1)}$

Tabelle 4

Dabei ergibt sich die Greensche Funktion H nach (4) aus dem Fundamentalsystem $\{1, \varphi\}$ der DGL $Lz = -(p_2z')' = 0$.

Beispiele für EWA (1.2): Die Bedingungen (V 1'), (V 2'), (V 4) lassen sich an den folgenden Beispielen, die aus [5] entnommen sind, unmittelbar nachprüfen. Es wird gesetzt $x_1 = 0$, $x_2 = 1$, und es werden die Bezeichnungen verwendet:

c Federkonstante	F Querschnittsfläche
$c_1, c_2, \ldots$ Konstanten	D Flanschkonstante
α Biegesteifigkeit	C Torsionssteifigkeit
ϱ Dichte	J_p polares Flächenträgheitsmoment
	G Gewicht

1. Biegeschwingungen eines Stabes, ein Ende frei
   $(\alpha y'')'' = \lambda \varrho F y;\quad y(0) = y'(0) = 0,\quad y''(1) = y'''(1) = 0.$
2. Torsionsschwingungen von I-Profilen mit Berücksichtigung von Flanschbiegung
   $Dy^{IV} - Cy'' = \lambda \varrho J_p y;\quad y''(0) = 0,\ Dy'''(0) - Cy'(0) = 0,\quad y(1) = y'(1) = 0.$
3. Kippen von I-Trägern mit Berücksichtigung von Flanschbiegung
   $Dy^{IV} - Cy'' = \lambda x^2 y;\quad y''(0) = 0,\ Dy'''(0) - Cy'(0) = 0,\quad y(1) = y'(1) = 0.$
4. Stabknickung mit Berücksichtigung von Eigengewicht
   $(\alpha y'')'' - (Gy')' = -\lambda y'';\quad y'(0) = (\alpha y'')'(0) = 0,\quad y(1) = y''(1) = 0.$
5. Kippen eines Stabes infolge Torsion
   $y^{IV} = \lambda[-(x^2 y')' + 2y];\quad y'(0) = y'''(0) = 0,\quad y(1) = y'(1) = 0.$
6. Biegeschwingungen eines Stabes mit Endmasse
   $(\alpha y'')'' = \lambda \varrho F y;\quad y(0) = y'(0) = 0,\quad y''(1) = \lambda(c_1 y'(1) + c_2 y(1)),$
   $-y'''(1) = \lambda(c_3 y(1) + c_2 y'(1)).$
7. Knickstab mit elastischer Zwischenstütze
   $(\alpha y'')'' = -\lambda y'';\quad y(0) = y''(0) = 0,\quad y'(1) = 0,\ cy(1) - (\alpha y'')'(1) = 0.$
8. Knicken eines Stabes, linkes Ende elastisch gestützt, rechtes Ende eingespannt
   $(\alpha y'')'' = -\lambda y'';\quad y''(0) = 0,\ cy(0) + (\alpha y'')'(0) = \lambda(-y'(0)),\ y(1) = y'(1) = 0.$

Bemerkung 3.4: Bei den Beispielen 7, 8 läßt sich über das Ergebnis von Satz 3.1 hinaus zeigen, daß mit den Bezeichnungen $\Psi(x) = \int_0^x \frac{t}{\alpha(t)}\,dt$, $\Phi(x) = \int_0^x \Psi(t)\,dt$ für positive Konstanten c gilt:

$$c \leqslant \frac{1}{\Psi(1)} \iff H_\gamma(x,\xi) > 0 \quad \text{in } (0,1) \times (0,1)$$

Beweis: In beiden Beispielen hat die RWA (3) die Gestalt

$-(\alpha z')' = s;\ z'(0) = 0,\ z(1) = 0.$ Mit $\varphi(x) = \int_0^x \frac{1}{\alpha(t)}\,dt$ lautet die zugehörige Greensche Funktion $H(x,\xi) = \begin{cases} \varphi(1) - \varphi(x) & \text{für } \xi \leqslant x \\ \varphi(1) - \varphi(\xi) & \text{für } x \leqslant \xi . \end{cases}$

Es folgt $\int_0^1 H(x,t)dt = \Psi(1) - \Psi(x)$, sowie $\eta = \int_0^1 \int_0^1 H(s,t)dt\,ds = \Psi(1) \cdot 1 - \Psi(1)$.

Für $c > 0$ gilt $1 + c\eta > 0$, da H nichtnegativ ist. Mit $\gamma = \frac{c}{1+c\eta}$ lautet

$$H_\gamma(x,\xi) = \begin{cases} \varphi(1) - \varphi(x) - \gamma[\Psi(1) - \Psi(x)][\Psi(1) - \Psi(\xi)] & \text{für } \xi \leqslant x \\ \varphi(1) - \varphi(\xi) - \gamma[\Psi(1) - \Psi(x)][\Psi(1) - \Psi(\xi)] & \text{für } x \leqslant \xi . \end{cases}$$

Für $0 < \xi \leqslant x < 1$ gilt:

$$H_\gamma(x,\xi) > H_\gamma(x,0) = \int_x^1 \frac{1}{\alpha(t)}dt - \gamma \int_x^1 \frac{t}{\alpha(t)}\,dt \cdot \Psi(1) \geqslant (1 - \gamma\Psi(1)1) \int_x^1 \frac{1}{\alpha(t)}\,dt.$$

Entsprechendes ergibt sich für $0 < x \leqslant \xi < 1$. Die Bedingungen $c \leqslant \frac{1}{\Psi(1)}$ und $1 - \gamma\Psi(1)1 \geqslant 0$ sind gleichwertig. Umgekehrt nimmt auch $H_\gamma(x,0) = (\varphi(1) - \varphi(x))\left\{1 - \gamma\frac{\Psi(1) - \Psi(x)}{\varphi(1) - \varphi(x)}\Psi(1)\right\}$ wegen

$\lim_{x\to 1} \frac{\Psi(1) - \Psi(x)}{\varphi(1) - \varphi(x)} = 1$ im Fall $c > \frac{1}{\Psi(1)}$ negative Werte an.

Numerisches Beispiel: Es wird folgende EWA behandelt

$$(xy'')'' - (\tfrac{1}{x}y')' = \lambda[-(xy')' + xy]; \quad \begin{cases} \lim_{x\to o} [(xy'')' - \frac{1}{x}y'] = 0, & y(1) = 0 \\ y'(0) = 0 & , \ y'(1) = 0. \end{cases} \qquad (12)$$

Diese EWA ergibt sich durch Spezialisierung aus einer EWA, die die Eigenschwingungen gedrückter Kreisplatten beschreibt (vgl. [5]):

$$(xy'')'' - (\tfrac{1}{x}y')' + \frac{P}{N}(xy')' = \frac{m\,\omega^2}{N}xy; \quad \begin{cases} \lim_{x\to o} [(xy'')' - \frac{1}{x}y' + cy] = 0, & y(1) = 0 \\ y'(0) = 0 & , \ y'(1) = 0 \end{cases}$$

(P Druckkraft, N Plattenfaktor, m Masse, ω Kreisfrequenz).

Wird zunächst das Verhältnis P/ω^2 konstant gehalten, indem gesetzt wird $P = \lambda P_o$, $\omega^2 = \lambda\omega_o^2$ (vgl. [9], S. 115), so geht die DGL über in: $(xy'')'' - (\frac{1}{x}y')' = \lambda[-\frac{P_o}{N}(xy')' + \frac{m\,\omega_o^2}{N}xy]$. Die willkürliche Wahl

$\frac{P_o}{N} = \frac{m\,\omega_o^2}{N} = 1$ und $1 = 1$ führt im Falle $c = 0$ auf die EWA (12). Die Voraussetzungen an die Koeffizientenfunktionen der EWA (1) sind hier verletzt, da $p_2(x) = x$ eine Nullstelle und $p_1(x) = \frac{1}{x}$ eine Unendlichkeitsstelle in $x = 0$ hat. Dennoch läßt sich zeigen, daß die EWA (12) äquivalent zu einer EWA mit einem linearen, vollstetigen, positiven Integraloperator ist. Die zur RWA (3) gehörige Greensche Funktion $H(x,\xi) = \begin{cases} \frac{1}{2}(\frac{1}{x} - x)\xi & \text{für } \xi \leqslant x \\ \frac{1}{2}x(\frac{1}{\xi} - \xi) & \text{für } x \leqslant \xi \end{cases}$

ist im Punkt (0, 0) unstetig, aber noch beschränkt. Wegen $c = 0$ ergibt sich als Greensche Funktion der RWA (2): $G(x,\xi) = \int_x^1 \int_\xi^1 H(s,t)\,dt\,ds$.

Die EWA (10) lautet:

$$\mathfrak{P}\mathfrak{y} = \varkappa\mathfrak{y} \quad \text{mit} \quad \varkappa = \frac{1}{\lambda}, \quad \mathfrak{P}\mathfrak{y}(x) = \int_{x_1}^{x_2} \mathfrak{G}(x,\xi)\,\mathfrak{y}(\xi)d\xi,$$

$$\mathfrak{y}(x) = \begin{pmatrix} y_3(x) \\ y_6(x) \end{pmatrix}, \quad \mathfrak{G}(x,\xi) = \begin{pmatrix} G(x,\xi)\xi & G_\xi(x,\xi)\xi \\ G_x(x,\xi)\xi & G_{x\xi}(x,\xi)\xi \end{pmatrix}.$$

Die Funktionen $G(x,\xi)$, $G_\xi(x,\xi)$, $G_x(x,\xi)$, $G_{x\xi}(x,\xi)\xi$ sind im Punkt (0, 0) stetig ergänzbar. Damit ist $\mathfrak{P}$ ein linearer Operator, der die Menge $R = C[0,1] \times C[0,1]$ in sich abbildet und bezüglich der Maximumnorm vollstetig ist. Da die Funktion H nichtnegativ ist, bildet $\mathfrak{P}$ den Kegel

$$K_2 = \{\, \mathfrak{y} = (y_3, y_6)^T \in R \mid y_3(x) \geqslant 0, \;\; y_6(x) \leqslant 0 \;\; \text{in } 0 \leqslant x \leqslant 1 \,\}$$

in sich ab. Der Fall $c > 0$ läßt sich auf diese Weise nicht erfassen, da die Funktion H_γ mit $\gamma = \frac{c}{1 + c\eta}$, die dann an die Stelle der Funktion H tritt, das Vorzeichen wechselt.

Es wurden zwei Iterationsschritte gemäß (11) durchgeführt: Der erste ausgehend von $v_o(x) = 235\,200\,(1 - x)^2\,(1 + 2x)$, der zweite ausgehend von einem Vielfachen des im ersten Schritt gewonnenen $v_1(x) = (1 - x)^2\,(18061 + 36\,122\,x + 8\,004\,x^2 - 20\,114\,x^3 - 457\,x^4 + 384\,x^5)$. Nach Satz 3. 5 ergaben sich für den betragskleinsten EW λ_o der EWA (12) die Einschließungen: $12.42 < \lambda_o < 16.80$ und $12.79 < \lambda_o < 13.30$.

Der Verfasser dankt Herrn Prof. Albrecht für seine Ratschläge beim Anfertigen der Arbeit.

Literatur

[1] ALBRECHT, J.: Verallgemeinerung eines Einschließungssatzes von L. Collatz. Z. Angew. Math. Mech. 48 (1968), T 43 - T 46

[2] ALBRECHT, J.: Zur optimalen Wahl der Norm beim Iterationsverfahren für Randwertaufgaben. ISNM 31, Birkhäuser Verlag, Basel und Stuttgart, 1976, 263 - 276

[3] BIOLLAY, Y.: Problèmes de Sturm-Liouville: Bornes pour les valeurs propres et les zéros des fonctions propres. Z. Angew. Math. Phys. 24 (1973), 525 - 536

[4] BOHL, E.: Die Theorie einer Klasse linearer Operatoren und Existenzsätze für Lösungen nichtlinearer Probleme in halbgeordneten Banach-Räumen. Arch. Rational Mech. Anal. 15 (1964), 263 - 288

[5] COLLATZ, L.: Eigenwertaufgaben mit technischen Anwendungen. Leipzig: Akad. Verlagsges. Geest & Portig K.G. 1963

[6] COLLATZ, L.: The numerical treatment of differential equations. Berlin, Göttingen, New York: Springer Verlag 1966

[7] HARTMAN, P.: Ordinary differential equations. New York, London, Sydney: John Wiley & Sons, Inc. 1964

[8] KRASNOSELSKII, M. A.: Positive solutions of operator equations. Groningen: P. Noordhoff Ltd. 1964

[9] STIEFEL, E. und ZIEGLER, H.: Natürliche Eigenwertprobleme. Z. Angew. Math. Phys. 1 (1950), 111 - 138

[10] WIELANDT, H.: Das Iterationsverfahren bei nicht selbstadjungierten linearen Eigenwertaufgaben. Math. Z. 50 (1944), 93 - 143

Dr. Peter P. Klein
Institut für Mathematik der TU Clausthal
Erzstraße 1
D-3392 Clausthal-Zellerfeld

PERIODIC SOLUTIONS OF NONLINEAR DISPERSIVE WAVE EQUATIONS

Jean Mawhin

We prove the existence of generalized solutions 2π-periodic in t and x for nonlinear wave equations of the form

$$u_{tt} - u_{xx} = f(t,x,u)$$

under an asymptotic nonresonance condition of the form

$$\mu < p \leqslant u^{-1}f(t,x,u) \leqslant q < \nu$$

for a.e. $(t,x) \in [0,2\pi]\times[0,2\pi]$ and large values of $|u|$, where μ and ν are consecutive elements of the spectrum of the linear part. It is moreover assumed that, for a.e. (t,x), the function

$$\text{sign } p.f(t,x,u)$$

is nondecreasing in u. The approach is a combination of recent results on Hammerstein equations and Leray-Schauder's theory.

1. INTRODUCTION

The existence of generalized 2π-periodic solutions in t and x for nonlinear wave equations of the form

(1) $$u_{tt} - u_{xx} = f(t,x,u)$$

has been considered by various authors (see e.g.[6] and the references therein). The aim of this paper is to use a theorem on Hammerstein equations recently proved by the author and M. Willem [8] to replace the nonresonance Lipschitz type conditions on f given in [6,7] by weaker asymptotic nonresonance conditions, familiar for the case of ordinary and elliptic partial differential equations (see e.g. [6]), together with some monotonicity assumptions.

As shown in a subsequent paper, the same approach can be used to unify and generalize recent results of Brézis-Nirenberg [1] , Rabinowitz [12] , Mancini [4,5] and McKenna [9]dealing with both resonant and non-resonant situations.

2. REDUCTION OF THE PROBLEM TO A HAMMERSTEIN EQUATION

Let $J = [0,2\pi]\times [0,2\pi]$, let

$$f : J \times \mathbb{R} \to \mathbb{R} , \ (t,x,u) \mapsto f(t,x,u)$$

be a mapping satisfying the Caratheodory conditions and such that $f(.,.,u)$ belongs to $L^2(J)$ for each u in $L^2(J)$. We consider the nonlinear dispersive wave equation

(1) $$u_{tt} - u_{xx} = f(t,x,u) .$$

If (u,v) denotes the usual inner product of u and v in $L^2(J)$, we define a generalized 2π-periodic solution of (1) (shortly GPS) to be a function $u \in L^2(J)$ such that

$$(u,v_{tt} - v_{xx}) = (f(.,.,u),v)$$

for every $v \in C^2(J)$ which is 2π-periodic in both variables. It has been shown previously (see e.g.[7]) that if

$$f(t,x,u) = cu + h(t,x)$$

with $c\in \mathbb{R}$ and $h\in L^2(J)$, equation (1) has a unique GPS for every $h \in L^2(J)$ if and only if $c \in \Sigma$, with $\Sigma = (2\mathbb{Z} + 1) \cup 4\mathbb{Z}$ the spectrum of the associated homogeneous problem. Moreover, for such a value of c, the linear mapping defined by

$$T_c : L^2(J) \to L^2(J), \ h \mapsto u ,$$

with u the corresponding unique GPS, is bounded, with

$$T_c = (\mathrm{dist}(c,\Sigma))^{-1} ,$$

but is not compact. The noncompactness comes from the fact that zero is an eigenvalue of the associated linear homogeneous problem of infinite multiplicity. It is also known that the other elements of Σ have a finite multiplicity (see e.g. [7]). Finally, it is shown in [2,12] that the eigenspace relative to zero is the range of the orthogonal projector P in

$L^2(J)$ defined by

$$(Pu)(t,x) = (2\pi)^{-1}\int_0^{2\pi}[u(t+x-s,s) + u(t-x+s,s)]\,ds - (2\pi)^{-2}\int_J u ,$$

and that $PT_c = T_cP$.

Let then $c \notin \Sigma$ be given and let us write equation (1) in the equivalent form

$$u_{tt} - u_{xx} - cu = f(t,x,u) - cu .$$

If we define the (continuous) mapping $G_c : L^2(J) \to L^2(J)$ by

$$G_c(u) = f(.,.,u) - cu ,$$

then the GPS of (1) are given by the solutions of the Hammerstein equation

(2) $$u = T_cG_c(u)$$

in $L^2(J)$. The difficulty in analyzing (2) is that T_cG_c is not a compact mapping. But equation (2) is equivalent to equation

(3) $$u = T_cPG_c(u) + T_c(I-P)G_c(u)$$

and, because of the properties of the spectrum mentioned earlier, $T_c(I-P)$ is a compact linear mapping in $L^2(J)$, so that $T_c(I-P)G_c$ is compact on each bounded subset of $L^2(J)$. Now, if $g \in \text{Im } P$, it is easily checked that the GPS of the equation

$$u_{tt} - u_{xx} - cu = g$$

is given by $u = -c^{-1}g$, so that $T_cP = -c^{-1}P$ and equation (4) can be written equivalently as

(4) $$u + c^{-1}PG_c(u) = T_c(I-P)G_c(u) ,$$

and has the form of the Hammerstein equations recently studied in [8] where the following result has been proved among others.

Let H be a real Hilbert space with inner product (,) and let $M : H \to H$, $N : H \to H$, and $C : H \times [0,1[\to H$ be possibly nonlinear mappings. One has the following

PROPOSITION 1. *Assume that there exists a real number $c > 0$ such that the following conditions hold for all u and v in H.*

1. $(M(u) - M(v), u - v) \geq c\,|M(u) - M(v)|^2$.
2. $(N(u) - N(v), u - v) \geq -c|u - v|^2$.
3. N *is demi-continuous and bounded.*

4. $M(0) = 0$.

5. C *is compact on bounded subsets of* $H \times [0,1[$.

Then, for each $\lambda \in [0,1[$, *the mapping* $I + \lambda MN : H \to H$ *is one-to-one and onto, and the mapping*

$$R : H \times [0,1[\;\to H, \; (u,\lambda) \mapsto (I + \lambda MN)^{-1} C(u,\lambda)$$

is compact on bounded subsets of $H \times [0,1[$.

3. THE EXISTENCE OF A GPS FOR AN ASSOCIATED FAMILY OF EQUATIONS

Let now $0 \leqslant \mu < \nu$ be two consecutive elements of Σ and let us assume that there exist reals $\mu < p \leqslant q < \nu$, $r \geqslant 0$, and a function $g \in L^2(J)$ such that

$$|f(t,x,u)| \leqslant g(t,x) \tag{5}$$

when $|u| \leqslant r$, and

$$p \leqslant u^{-1} f(t,x,u) \leqslant q \; , \tag{6}$$

when $|u| > r$. This implies that, for each $c \in \mathbb{R}$, the mapping G_c is defined, continuous and takes bounded sets into bounded sets. Let us assume moreover that, for a.e. $(t,x) \in J$, $f(t,x,u)$ is nondecreasing in u, and let $c \in \mathbb{R}$ be defined by

$$c = (1/2)(p + q),$$

which implies that $c \notin \Sigma$. Let us consider the family of equations, with $\lambda \in [0,1[$,

$$u + \lambda c^{-1} PG_c(u) = \lambda T_c(I-P)G_c(u) \; . \tag{7}$$

If we put

$$M = c^{-1}P \; , \; N = G_c \; , \; C(u,\lambda) = \lambda T_c(I-P)G_c(u) \; ,$$

we can check easily that those mappings satisfy the conditions of Proposition 1 above, and hence each equation (7) is equivalent to

$$u = (I + \lambda c^{-1} PG_c)^{-1}(\lambda T_c(I-P)G_c(u)) = R(u,\lambda), \tag{8}$$

where R defined in this way is compact on bounded subsets of $H \times [0,1[$ and such that $R(.,0) = 0$.

By the Leray-Schauder's theorem [3] applied to (8) we shall obtain the existence of a solution of (8) for each $\lambda \in [0,1[$ if we can find a priori bounds for the possible solutions of (8), i.e. of (6), which is in turn equivalent to the equation

(9) $$u = \lambda T_c G_c(u) .$$

Now, letting

$$d = (1/2)(q-p) = q-c = c-p ,$$

we obtain, for a.e. $(t,x) \in J$ and all $u \in \mathbb{R}$,

$$|f(t,x,u) - cu| \leq d|u| + dr + g(t,x) ,$$

and then, for all $u \in L^2(J)$,

$$|G_c(u)| \leq d|u| + e ,$$

where $e \geq 0$ is some constant. Consequently, for all $u \in L^2(J)$ and $\lambda \in [0,1[$, we have

$$|T_c G_c(u)| \leq (\min(\nu - c, c - \mu))^{-1}(d|u| + e)$$

$$= \max(\frac{q-c}{\nu-c}, \frac{c-p}{c-\mu})(|u| + \breve{e}) = \gamma(|u| + \tilde{e}) ,$$

with $0 \leq \gamma < 1$. Therefore, each possible solution of (9) is such that

(10) $$|u| \leq (1-\gamma)^{-1}\gamma \breve{e} = K ,$$

which is the required a priori bound. We thus have proved the following

PROPOSITION 2. *Under assumptions listed at the beginning of this section, equation (9) has, for each $\lambda \in [0,1[$, at least one solution u_λ which satisfies (10).*

We shall show in the next section how to use those solutions u_λ to obtain a GPS of equation (1).

4. EXISTENCE OF A GENERALIZED PERIODIC SOLUTION

Let us assume that the conditions of Section 3 hold, so that, for each $\lambda \in [0,1[$, we have a solution u_λ of (9) verifying (10) or, using the equivalent form (6), verifying the system of equations

(11) $$Pu_\lambda + \lambda c^{-1} PG_c(u_\lambda) = 0 ,$$

(12) $$(I-P)u_\lambda = \lambda T_c (I-P) G_c(u_\lambda) ,$$

and the inequalities

(13) $$|u_\lambda| \leq K , \; |Pu_\lambda| \leq K , \; |(I-P)u_\lambda| \leq K .$$

By (12), (13), the boundedness of G_c and the compactness of $T_c(I-P)G_c$, there exist sequences (λ_k), (u_{λ_k}) such that, with $\rightharpoonup$ denoting the weak convergence in $L^2(J)$, one has, for k going to infinity,

(14) $\lambda_k \to 1,\ Pu_{\lambda_k} \rightharpoonup v,\ (I-P)u_{\lambda_k} \to w,\ G(u_{\lambda_k}) \rightharpoonup y$,

with $y \in H$, $v \in \operatorname{Im} P$ and $w \in \operatorname{Im}(I-P)$. On the other hand, by a result of Section 3, we have, for every $z \in H$,

$$(G_c(u_{\lambda_k}) + cu_{\lambda_k} - G_c(z) - cz,\ u_{\lambda_k} - z) \geq 0 ,$$

and hence, using (11),

$$(c(1-\lambda_k^{-1})Pu_{\lambda_k} - PG_c(z) - cz,\ Pu_{\lambda_k} - Pz) +$$

$$+ (G_c(u_{\lambda_k}) + cu_{\lambda_k} - G_c(z) - cz,\ (I-P)u_{\lambda_k} - (I-P)z) \geq 0 .$$

Therefore, going to the limit and using (13) and (14), we get

$$((I-P)y + cw - G_c(z) - cz,\ (v+w) - z) \geq 0 ,$$

so that, using Minty's trick [10] we have, with $u = v+w$,

$$(I-P)y + cw = G_c(u) + cu,$$

i.e.

(15) $$PG_c(u) + cPu = 0 ,$$

(16) $$(I-P)y = (I-P)G_c(u) .$$

By (12) we have, for k going to infinity,

$$T_c(I-P)G_c(u_{\lambda_k}) \longrightarrow w = (I-P)u ,$$

and by (14), (16) and the weak continuity of (I-P), we get

$$(I-P)G(u_{\lambda_k}) \rightharpoonup (I-P)y = (I-P)G_c(u) .$$

The graph of T_c being weakly closed, this implies that

(17) $$(I-P)u = T_c(I-P)G_c(u),$$

and then, together with (15),

$$u + c^{-1}PG_c(u) = T_c(I-P)G_c(u) .$$

We have thus proved the following

PROPOSITION 3. *If the conditions listed at the beginning of Section 3 hold, then equation (1) has at least one GPS* .

Now it is immediate to check that the above approach equally holds, under the same assumptions, for the equation

(18) $$-(u_{tt} - u_{xx}) = f(t,x,u) .$$

Therefore, if $\mu < \nu \leqslant 0$ are now consecutive non-positive elements of and if, for some reals $\mu < p \leqslant q < \nu$, $r \geqslant 0$ and some $g \in L^2(J)$, the conditions (5) and (6) hold, and if, moreover, for a.e. $(t,x) \in J$, the function $f(t,x,u)$ is non-increasing in u, we can write equation (1) in the form

(19) $$-(u_{tt} - u_{xx}) = - f(t,x,u)$$

where now $-f$ verifies all the assumptions of Proposition 3 relatively to the two consecutive non-negative elements $-\nu$ and $-\mu$ of Σ . Therefore, by Proposition 3, equation (1) has at least one GPS, so that summarizing, we have proved the following final

THEOREM. *Let* $\mu < \nu$ *be consecutive elements of* Σ *and assume that there exist reals* $\mu < p \leqslant q < \nu$, $r \geqslant 0$ *and a function* $g \in L^2(J)$ *such that for a.e.* $(t,x) \in J$, *one has*

$$|f(t,x,u)| \leqslant g(t,x)$$

when $|u| \leqslant r$, *and*

$$p \leqslant u^{-1} f(t,x,u) \leqslant q \,,$$

when $|u| > r$. *Then, if*

$$\operatorname{sign} p \, . \, f(t,x,u)$$

is nondecreasing in u *for a.e.* $(t,x) \in J$, *equation* (1) *has at least one generalized* 2π-*periodic solution*.

REFERENCES

1. Brézis, H., and L. Nirenberg : Characterizations of the ranges of some nonlinear operators and applications to boundary value problems, Ann. Scuola Norm. Sup. Pisa Cl. Sci. (4) 5 (1978) 225-326.
2. De Simon, L., and G. Torelli: Soluzione periodiche di equazioni a derivate parziali di tipo iperbolico nonlineari, Rend. Sem. Mat. Univ. Padova 40 (1968) 380-401.
3. Leray, J., and J. Schauder : Topologie et équations fonctionnelles, Ann. Sci. Ecole Norm. Sup. (3) 51 (1934) 45-78.
4. Mancini, G.: Periodic solutions of semilinear wave equations via generalized Leray-Schauder degree, to appear.
5. Mancini, G. : Periodic solutions of some semilinear autonomous wave equations, to appear.

6. Mawhin, J. : Recent trends in nonlinear boundary value problems, in VII. Internationale Konferenz über nichtlineare Schwingungen, Band I.2, Berlin, Akademie-Verlag, 1977, 52-70.

7. Mawhin, J. : Solutions périodiques d'équations aux dérivées partielles hyperboliques non linéaires, in Mélanges "Théodore Vogel", Bruxelles, Université Libre de Bruxelles, 1978, 301-315.

8. Mawhin, J., and M. Willem : Compact perturbations of some nonlinear Hammerstein equations, Riv. Mat. Univ. Parma, to appear.

9. McKenna, P.J. : On the reductions of a semilinear hyperbolic problem to a Landesman-Lazer type problem, to appear.

10. Minty, G. : Monotone (nonlinear) operators in a Hilbert space, Duke Math. J. 29 (1962) 341-346.

11. Rabinowitz, P. : Periodic solutions of nonlinear hyperbolic partial differential equations, Comm. Pure Appl. Math. 20 (1967) 145-205.

12. Rabinowitz, P. : Some minimax theorems and applications to nonlinear partial differential equations, in Nonlinear Analysis, New York, Academic Press, 1978, 161-178.

Université de Louvain
Institut Mathématique
Chemin du Cyclotron, 2,
B-1348 Louvain-la-Neuve,
Belgique.

EINE FEHLERSCHRANKE FÜR GALERKINAPPROXIMATIONEN LOKALER NAVIER-STOKES-LÖSUNGEN

Reimund Rautmann

Zur Aufgabenstellung

In der vorliegenden Arbeit wird die Konvergenzrate von Galerkinapproximationen für Lösungen Navier-Stokesscher Anfangs-Randwertaufgaben mit Hilfe der Eigenwerte entsprechender (linearer) Stokesscher Randwertaufgaben abgeschätzt. Wie wir sehen werden, lassen sich Fehlerabschätzungen, die im stationären Fall für Entwicklungen nach den Eigenfunktionen einer Stokesschen Randwertaufgabe gelten, in einfacher Weise auf Galerkinapproximationen instationärer Navier-Stokes-Lösungen übertragen.

Die Fehlerschranken für Entwicklungen nach Eigenfunktionen hängen wesentlich von L^2-Normschranken für die ersten und zweiten partiellen Ableitungen der darzustellenden Funktionen ab. Für eine Navier-Stokes-Lösung und ihre Galerkinnäherungen lassen sich solche Normschranken, wie Heywood in einer neuen Arbeit [3] gezeigt hat, sehr elegant herleiten, wenn die Galerkinnäherungen auf der Basis der Eigenfunktionen der entsprechenden Stokesschen Randwertaufgabe gebildet werden. Die gesuchte Fehlerabschätzung ergibt sich dann aus einer Gleichung für die L^2-Norm der Differenz zweier Galerkinnäherungen. Die Schlußweise verläuft ähnlich wie Serrin's Konstruktion zur Eindeutigkeit von Navier-Stokes-Lösungen in [1o].

Im Abschnitt 1. stellen wir bekannte Eigenschaften der Stokesschen Randwertaufgabe zusammen, soweit wir sie benötigen. Eine für uns wesentliche Folgerung, die Fehlerschranken für Entwicklungen nach Eigenfunktionen, bringen wir im Abschnitt 2. mit einer kurzen Herleitung. Unter Verwendung der (im Abschnitt 3. zitierten) Normschranken aus [3] leiten wir im Abschnitt 4. die versprochene Fehlerabschätzung her (Satz 4.1.).

1. Die Stokessche Randwertaufgabe und ihre Eigenfunktionen.

Es sei Ω eine offene Menge im R^3 mit Rand $\partial\Omega$, $x = (x^1, x^2, x^3) \in R^3$. Der Kürze halber setzen wir voraus, daß Ω beschränkt und $\partial\Omega$ eine C_3-Untermannigfaltigkeit des R^3 ist. In neueren Arbeiten hat es sich als zweckmäßig erwiesen, (zeitlich lokale) Lösungen der Navier-Stokesschen Anfangsrandwertaufgabe in Ω aus einem Galerkinansatz zu gewinnen, dessen Näherungslösungen auf der Basis der Eigenfunktionen der Randwertaufgabe der Stokesschen Gleichungen

$$(1.1)\qquad \begin{aligned} -\Delta v + \nabla q &= h \;, \\ \nabla\cdot v &= o \quad \text{in } \Omega, \\ v &= o \quad \text{auf } \partial\Omega \end{aligned}$$

gebildet werden.

Zur genauen Formulierung der Randwertaufgabe verwenden wir den Hilbertraum H_m aller (reellen) Vektorfunktionen $f = (f^1, f^2, f^3)$ auf Ω, die mit ihren verallgemeinerten partiellen Ableitungen bis zur Ordnung m einschließlich zu $L^2(\Omega)$ gehören. Die Norm auf H_m ist

$$|f|_m = \Big(\sum_{o \le \alpha_1+\alpha_2+\alpha_3 \le m} \int_\Omega \Big(\frac{\partial^{\alpha_1+\alpha_2+\alpha_3}}{(\partial x^1)^{\alpha_1}(\partial x^2)^{\alpha_2}(\partial x^3)^{\alpha_3}} f\Big)^2 dx\Big)^{1/2}.$$

Ferner sei D die Menge aller divergenzfreien C_∞-Vektorfunktionen mit kompaktem Träger in Ω. Mit $\mathcal{L}^2$ bzw. $\mathcal{H}_1$ bezeichnen wir den Abschluß von D in L^2 bzw. H_1.

Die Orthogonalprojektion

$$P : L^2 \to \mathcal{L}^2$$

annulliert nach dem Weylschen Satz [14] genau alle verallgemeinerten Gradientenfelder. Die Stokessche Randwertaufgabe nimmt dann die folgende Gestalt an: Zu gegebenem $h \in \mathcal{L}^2$ ist eine Lösung $v \in H_2 \cap \mathcal{H}_1$ von

$$(1.2) \qquad -P\Delta v = h$$

gesucht. Es gilt

Hilfssatz 1.1.:

Die Abbildung $-P\Delta : H_2 \cap \mathcal{H}_1 \to \mathcal{L}^2$ definiert auf $\mathcal{H}_1 \subset \mathcal{L}^2$ einen symmetrischen positiv definiten Operator mit kompaktem Inversen $(-P\Delta)^{-1}: \mathcal{L}^2 \to \mathcal{L}^2$;

[7, S. 44-45], [5 , S. 115-116],[3 , S. 17], [12 , S. 2o ff].

Der Beweis des Hilfssatzes ergibt sich aus den folgenden, auch für die nächsten Abschnitte nützlichen Bemerkungen: Als linearer Operator in $\mathcal{L}^2$ ist $P\Delta$ symmetrisch, da sein Definitionsbereich $H_2 \cap \mathcal{H}_1$ dicht in $\mathcal{L}^2$ liegt und für $f \in H_2 \cap \mathcal{H}_1$, $g \in \mathcal{H}_1$ stets

$$(1.3) \qquad \int_\Omega (-P\Delta f)g = \int_\Omega (\nabla f)\cdot(\nabla g) \qquad {}^{1)}$$

erfüllt ist, also die Gleichung $\int_\Omega (-P\Delta f)\cdot g = \int_\Omega f\cdot(-P\Delta g)$ gilt, falls g auch zu H_2 gehört.

1)Das Volumendifferential dx schreiben wir hier und im folgenden nicht mit.

Die Gleichung (1.3) folgt zunächst für $f_k \in C_2(\bar{\Omega})$ statt f und $g_k \in D$ statt g mit dem Gaußschen Integralsatz und überträgt sich auf f und g, wenn wir f_k in der Norm von H_2 und g_k in der Norm von H_1 gegen f bzw. g konvergieren lassen. Dabei verwenden wir, daß H_2 (wegen der Glattheit von $\partial\Omega$) die Vervollständigung von $C_2(\bar{\Omega})$ in der Norm $|\cdot|_2$ ist, [2 , S. 18]. Die Gleichung (1.3) definiert zugleich den Operator $-P\Delta$ auf $\mathcal{H}_1$.

Die positive Definitheit von $-P\Delta$ ist gleichbedeutend damit, daß auf der beschränkten offenen Menge Ω die Poincarésche Ungleichung

$$(1.4) \qquad |f|_{L^2} \leq \alpha \cdot |\nabla f|_{L^2}$$

mit einer Konstanten $\alpha > o$ für alle Funktionen $f \in \mathcal{H}_1$ gilt. Aus (1.4) folgt auch bereits, daß für jedes gegebene $h \in \mathcal{L}^2$ die Gleichung

$$(1.5) \qquad \int_\Omega \nabla v \cdot \nabla g = \int_\Omega h \cdot g ,$$

wenn sie für jedes $g \in \mathcal{H}_1$ besteht, höchstens eine Lösung $v \in \mathcal{H}_1$ haben kann. Die Existenz mindestens einer Lösung in $\mathcal{H}_1$ ergibt sich in bekannter Weise mit einem Galerkinansatz unter Verwendung der Poincaréschen Ungleichung sowie der Kompaktheit der Einbettung von $\mathcal{H}_1$ in $\mathcal{L}^2$. Folglich besitzt $-P\Delta$ den auf $\mathcal{L}^2$ definierten inversen Operator $(-P\Delta)^{-1} : \mathcal{L}^2 \to \mathcal{H}_1$. Er ist in $\mathcal{L}^2$ kompakt, da aus (1.5) zusammen mit (1.4) die Abschätzung $|v|_1 \leq c \cdot |h|_{L^2}$ mit einer Konstanten $c > o$ folgt.

Eine unmittelbare Folgerung ist

<u>Hilfssatz 1.2.:</u>

$-P\Delta$ besitzt eine Folge (λ_i) positiver Eigenwerte $\lambda_i > o$, $\lambda_1 \leq \lambda_2 \leq \ldots$, $\lambda_i \to \infty$ mit $i \to \infty$, und die zugehörigen

Eigenfunktionen (e_i) bilden ein vollständiges Orthonormalsystem in $\mathcal{L}^2$. Die Funktionen $(\frac{e_i}{\lambda_i^{1/2}})$ sind orthonormal in $\mathcal{H}_1$ bezüglich des Skalarproduktes $\int_\Omega (\nabla f)(\nabla g)$.

Der Beweis des ersten Teils ergibt sich mit bekannten funktionalanalytischen Schlußweisen aus Hilfssatz 1.1. Wegen

$$-P\Delta e_i = \lambda_i e_i$$

und (1.3) folgt damit auch die zweite Behauptung des Hilfssatzes.

Die Regularitätseigenschaften der Eigenfunktionen beschreibt

Hilfssatz 1.3.:

Ist $\partial\Omega$ eine C_m-Untermannigfaltigkeit des R^n $(m \geq 2)$, so gehören die Eigenfunktionen e_i von (1.2) zu $H_m(\Omega)$, [12 , S.39].

2. Zwei Fehlerschranken für die Entwicklung nach Eigenfunktionen der Stokesschen Randwertaufgabe.

Im folgenden sei

$$f_m = \sum_{i=1}^{m} e_i \cdot \int_\Omega (f \cdot e_i)$$

die m-te Fourierapproximation von $f \in \mathcal{L}^2$.
Es gilt

Hilfssatz 2.1.:

Im Falle $f \in H_2 \cap \mathcal{H}_1$ erfüllt f_m die Fehlerabschätzung

(2.1) $$|f-f_m|^2_{L^2} \leq \frac{1}{\lambda^2_{m+1}} |P\Delta f|^2_{L^2} ,$$ [6 , S. 38].

Zum Beweis betrachten wir für die Funktion $f_m^* = f - f_m$ die Parsevalsche Gleichung

$$(2.2) \qquad |f_m^*|_{L^2}^2 = \sum_{i=m+1}^{\infty} \left(\int_\Omega f \cdot e_i\right)^2 .$$

Wegen $-P\Delta e_i = \lambda_i e_i$ und $\lambda_i \geq \lambda_{m+1}$ für $i \geq m+1$ folgt für den i-ten Fourierkoeffizienten von f die Abschätzung

$$\left(\int_\Omega f e_i\right)^2 = \frac{1}{\lambda_i^2}\left(\int_\Omega (-P\Delta f) e_i\right)^2$$

$$\leq \frac{1}{\lambda_{m+1}^2}\left(\int_\Omega (-P\Delta f) e_i\right)^2 \text{ für } m+1 \leq i$$

unter Verwendung der Symmetrie von $P\Delta$. Damit folgt aus (2.2)

$$|f_m^*|_{L^2}^2 \leq \frac{1}{\lambda_{m+1}^2} \sum_{i=m+1}^{\infty} \left(\int_\Omega (-P\Delta f) e_i\right)^2$$

und daraus die Behauptung mit einer Anwendung der Besselschen Ungleichung auf die Funktion $-P\Delta f \in \mathcal{L}^2$.

Ebenso einfach erhalten wir

Hilfssatz 2.2.:

Im Falle $f \in \mathcal{H}_1$ erfüllt f_m die Fehlerabschätzung

$$(2.3) \qquad |f - f_m|_{L^2}^2 \leq \frac{1}{\lambda_{m+1}} |\nabla f|_{L^2}^2 , \qquad [6, S. 39]$$

Zum Beweis beachten wir die Abschätzung

$$\left(\int_\Omega f e_i\right)^2 = \frac{1}{\lambda_i^2}\left(\int_\Omega f \cdot (-P\Delta e_i)\right)^2 = \frac{1}{\lambda_i^2}\left(\int_\Omega (\nabla f)(\nabla e_i)\right)^2$$

$$\leq \frac{1}{\lambda_m}\left(\int_\Omega (\nabla f)\left(\nabla \frac{e_i}{\lambda_i^{1/2}}\right)\right)^2 \qquad \text{für } m+1 \leq i,$$

die sich aus (1.3) ergibt. Damit erhalten wir aus (2.2)

$$|f_m^*|_{L^2}^2 \leq \frac{1}{\lambda_{m+1}} \sum_{i=m+1}^{\infty} \left(\int_\Omega (\nabla f)(\nabla \frac{e_i}{\lambda_i^{1/2}})\right)^2 .$$

Da die $\frac{e_i}{\lambda_i^{1/2}}$ ein Orthonormalsystem bezüglich des Skalarproduktes $\int_\Omega (\nabla f)(\nabla g)$ in $\mathcal{H}_1$ bilden, folgt aus der letzten Abschätzung die Behauptung (2.3) mit einer Anwendung der Besselschen Ungleichung für f bezüglich dieses Skalarproduktes.

3. Normschranken für lokale Navier-Stokes-Lösungen und ihre Galerkinapproximationen.

Das Geschwindigkeitsfeld $u(t,x) = (u^1,u^2,u^3)$ einer inkompressiblen zähen, am Rande haftenden Strömung in Ω zur Zeit $t \geq o$ erfüllt mit der Druckfunktion $p(t,x)$ (bei geeigneter Normierung der Strömungsgrößen) die Navier-Stokessche Anfangs-Randwertaufgabe

$$(3.1) \quad \begin{aligned} u_t + u\cdot\nabla u - \Delta u &= - \nabla p \;, \\ \nabla\cdot u &= o \quad \text{in } \Omega \quad \text{für } t > o. \\ u = o \text{ auf } \partial\Omega,\; u &= u_o \quad \text{für } t = o. \end{aligned}$$

Im folgenden legen wir die schwache Formulierung

$$(3.2) \quad \begin{aligned} &\int_\Omega \{(u_t + u\cdot\nabla u)\cdot\varphi + \nabla u\cdot\nabla\varphi\} = o \text{ für jedes } \varphi \in \mathcal{H}_1, \\ &\lim_{t \downarrow o} |u(t,\cdot) - u_o|_{L^2} = o \end{aligned}$$

von (3.1) zu Grunde.

Mit den Eigenfunktionen (e_i) der Stokesschen Randwertaufgabe bilden wir die k-te Galerkinnäherung

$$(3.3) \quad u_k(t,x) = \sum_{i=1}^{k} a_{ki}(t)e_i(x)$$

einer Lösung u von (3.2). Die Koeffizienten

$$a_{ki}(t) = \int_\Omega u_k(t,\cdot)\cdot e_i,$$

die stetig differenzierbar sein sollen, werden durch die Anfangswertaufgabe

$$(3.4) \quad \int_\Omega \{(u_{kt} + u_k\cdot\nabla u_k)\cdot e_i + \nabla u_k \cdot \nabla e_i\} = o,$$

$$\int_\Omega u_k(o,\cdot)\cdot e_i = \int_\Omega u_o\cdot e_i\ , \quad i = 1,\dots,k$$

für k gewöhnliche Differentialgleichungen festgelegt. Dieses System ist quadratisch in den gesuchten Funktionen a_{ki}, also lokal Lipschitz-stetig. Die globale eindeutige Lösbarkeit von (3.4) folgt nach einem bekannten Satz über gewöhnliche Differentialgleichungen aus der Energiegleichung

$$(3.5) \quad \int_\Omega ((u_k)^2)_t + 2\int_\Omega (\nabla u_k)^2 = o,$$

die aus (3.4) durch Multiplikation mit a_{ki} und Summation über $i = 1,\dots,k$ hervorgeht, [4 , S. 226]. Hierbei fällt der nichtlineare Term heraus wegen

Hilfssatz 3.1.:

Das Integral $\int_\Omega (f\cdot\nabla g)\cdot h$ ist eine auf $\mathcal{H}_1$ beschränkte, in g und h antisymmetrische Trilinearform, [12 , S. 162-163].

Über die Lösbarkeit der Navier-Stokesschen Aufgabe gilt der grundlegende

Satz 3.1.:

Es sei $u_o \in \mathcal{H}_1$.

a) Dann gibt es für hinreichend kleine Zeiten $T > o$ genau eine Lösung $u \in L^\infty([o,T],\mathcal{H}_1)$ von (3.1) mit $u_t \in L^2([o,T], L^2(\Omega))$, $u_{x^i x^j} \in L^2([o,T], L^2(\Omega))$,

$\nabla p \in L^2([o,T], L^2(\Omega))$, $\lim_{t \downarrow o} |u(t,\cdot) - u_o|_{H_1} \to o$.

b) Darüberhinaus gelten mit stetigen, durch die Dirichletnorm von u_o festgelegten Funktionen F,G,H für alle Galerkinapproximationen u_k (gleichmäßig in k) und für u selbst die Abschätzungen

$$(3.6) \qquad |\nabla u(t,\cdot)|_{L^2(\Omega)} \le F(t),$$

$$(3.7) \qquad \int_o^t |u_t|^2_{L^2(\Omega)} \, d\tau \le G(t),$$

$$(3.8) \qquad \int_o^t |u|^2_{H_2} \, d\tau \le H(t), \quad t \in [o,T] \qquad , \quad [3\ , \text{S. } 3o, \text{S. } 63].$$

Kiselev und Ladyženskaja hatten die Existenz eindeutiger starker Lösungen von (3.1) unter der Voraussetzung $u_o \in H_2 \cap \mathcal{H}_1$ bewiesen, [7, S. 143, 161]. Existenzbeweise für starke Lösungen zu Anfangswerten $u_o \in \mathcal{H}_1$ haben Prodi in [8] und Kaniel und Shinbrot gegeben [11 , S. 193-212].

Eine unmittelbare Folgerung ist

Korollar 3.1.:

Es gibt eine Teilfolge $(u_{k'})$ der (u_k) aus (3.3), (3.4), die in der $L^2(\Omega)$-Norm gleichmäßig auf [o,T] gegen die Navier-Stokes-Lösung u konvergiert.

Zum Beweis zeigen wir zunächst mit einer Anwendung des Satzes von Ascoli-Arzelà, daß eine gleichmäßig auf $[o,T]$ konvergente Teilfolge $(u_{k'})$ existiert: Wegen (3.6) für u_k und der Kompaktheit der Einbettung von $\mathcal{H}_1$ in $\mathcal{L}^2$ ist die Wertemenge $\{u_k(t,\cdot)\}$ für jedes $t \in [o,T]$ relativ kompakt in $\mathcal{L}^2$, und die $\{u_k(t,\cdot)\}$ bilden eine in der $L^2(\Omega)$-Norm gleichgradig stetige Funktionenmenge; denn aus der Cauchy-Schwarzschen Ungleichung erhalten wir für $t,s \in [o,T]$ die Abschätzung

$$(u_k(t,x)-u_k(s,x))^2 = (\int_s^t u_{kt}(\tau,x)d\tau)^2 \leq |t-s| \, |\int_s^t (u_{kt})^2 d\tau| ,$$

und daraus durch Integration über Ω

$$(3.9) \quad |u_k(t,\cdot) - u_k(s,\cdot)|^2_{L^2(\Omega)} \leq |t-s| \cdot G(T)$$

wegen (3.7).

Es sei $u^* \in C_o([o,T], \mathcal{L}^2(\Omega))$ der Grenzwert der $u_{k'}$. Aus (3.6) - (3.8) und den Eigenschaften der schwachen Konvergenz in Sobolevräumen [2 , S. 16] folgt wie in [3 , S. 31], daß u^* und allgemein jeder Häufungspunkt der u_k in $L^2([o,T], \mathcal{L}^2(\Omega))$ eine Lösung von (3.1) mit den im Satz 3.1. genannten Eigenschaften ist. Wegen der Eindeutigkeit dieser Lösung gilt $u^* = u$ in $L^2(\Omega)$, und die Folge (u_k) kann in $L^2([o,T], \mathcal{L}^2(\Omega))$, somit auch in $C_o([o,T], \mathcal{L}^2(\Omega))$ höchstens einen Häufungspunkt besitzen. Damit folgt sogar die gleichmäßige Konvergenz der *ganzen* Folge $(u_k(t,\cdot))$ in $L^2(\Omega)$.

4. Eine Fehlerschranke für die Galerkinnäherungen.

Die Zeitschranke $T > o$ sei so klein gewählt, daß die Existenzaussage und die Abschätzungen aus Satz 3.1. gelten. Wie bisher bezeichnet e_i eine zum Eigenwert λ_i, $i = 1,2,\ldots$ der Stokesschen Randwertaufgabe (1.2) gehörige Eigenfunktion. Wir beweisen

Satz 4.1.:

Die Galerkinnäherung u_k aus (3.3), (3.4) der Lösung u von (3.1) erfüllt die Fehlerabschätzung

$$(4.1) \qquad |u(t,\cdot) - u_k(t,\ )|^2_{L^2(\Omega)} \le \frac{F^*(t)}{\lambda_{k+1}}$$

für $t \in [o,T]$ mit einer nur von T und der Dirichletnorm von u_o abhängigen stetigen Funktion F^*.

Zum Beweis schreiben wir die Differentialgleichungen für zwei Galerkinnäherungen in einer zu (3.4) äquivalenten Form, aus der sich eine nichtlineare Integralrelation für

$$\varphi(t) = |u_l(t,\cdot) - u_k(t,\cdot)|^2_{L^2(\Omega)}$$

ergibt. Einige Normabschätzungen mit den Schranken aus den letzten beiden Abschnitten führen dann auf eine lineare Integralungleichung für φ und damit, wie wir sehen werden, auf (4.1).

Zunächst scheint bei einem Vergleich von u_k mit einer l-ten Galerkinapproximation u_l für $l > k$ anhand von (3.4) die Schwierigkeit zu bestehen, daß u_k die Gleichungen (3.4) nur für $i = 1,\ldots,k$ erfüllt. Mit der Hilfsfunktion

$$\varepsilon_{ik} = \begin{cases} o & \text{für } i \le k \\ 1 & \text{für } i > k \end{cases}$$

schreiben wir deshalb (3.4) in der Form

$$\int_\Omega \{(u_{kt} + u_k\cdot\nabla u_k)\cdot e_i + \nabla u_k\cdot\nabla e_i\} = \varepsilon_{ik}\cdot\int_\Omega(u_k\cdot\nabla u_k)\cdot e_i\ ,$$

$$(4.2)\qquad \int_\Omega u_k(o,\cdot)\cdot e_i = (1-\varepsilon_{ik})\cdot\int_\Omega u_o\cdot e_i$$

für *jedes* $i = 1,2,\ldots$.

Für $i = 1,\ldots,k$ stimmen diese Gleichungen offensichtlich mit (3.4) überein. Für $i = k+1, k+2, \ldots$ sind sie nach der Definition (3.3) von u_k und wegen

$$\int_\Omega \nabla u_k\cdot\nabla e_i = -\int_\Omega u_k\cdot P\Delta e_i = \lambda_i\int_\Omega u_k\cdot e_i = o$$

identisch erfüllt.

Multiplizieren wir die für u_l gebildete Gleichung (4.2) mit a_{ki} bzw. (4.2) mit a_{li} und summieren über $i = 1,\ldots,k$ bzw. $i = 1,\ldots,l$ so folgen die Gleichungen

$$\int_\Omega\{u_{lt}u_k + (u_l\cdot\nabla u_l)u_k + \nabla u_l\cdot\nabla u_k\} = o$$

und

$$\int_\Omega\{u_{kt}u_l + (u_k\cdot\nabla u_k)u_l + \nabla u_k\cdot\nabla u_l\} = \int_\Omega\{(u_k\cdot\nabla u_k)\cdot\sum_{i=k+1}^{l} a_{li}e_i\}.$$

Subtraktion der mit 2 multiplizierten Summe dieser beiden Gleichungen von der Summe der Energiegleichungen (3.5) für u_k und u_l liefert für

$$w = u_l - u_k$$

die Gleichung

$$\int_\Omega((w)^2)_t + 2\int_\Omega(\nabla w)^2 = 2\int_\Omega(w\cdot\nabla w)u_k - 2\int_\Omega\{(u_k\cdot\nabla u_k)\cdot\sum_{i=k+1}^{l} a_{li}e_i\}.$$

Bei der Umformung des ersten nichtlinearen Terms rechts wurde wieder Hilfssatz 3.1. benutzt. Es gilt also

$$(4.3)\qquad \int_\Omega (w(t,\cdot))^2 + 2\int_{[o,t]\times\Omega} (\nabla w)^2 = \begin{cases} \int_\Omega (w(o,\cdot))^2 + 2\int_{[o,t]\times\Omega} (w\cdot\nabla w)\,u_k \\ \\ -\,2\int_{[o,t]\times\Omega} \{(u_k\cdot\nabla u_k)\cdot\sum_{i=k+1}^{l} a_{li}\,e_i\} \end{cases}$$

für $t \in [o,T]$.

Die drei Terme auf der rechten Seite schätzen wir einzeln ab.

Für $t = o$, $i = 1,\dots,k$ haben wir

$$a_{ki}(o) = a_{li}(o) = \int_\Omega u_o\cdot e_i.$$

Aus dem Hilfssatz 2.2. mit $f = u_l$ und $f_m = u_k$ erhalten wir deshalb die Schranke

$$(4.4)\qquad \int_\Omega (w(o,\cdot))^2 \le \frac{F(o)}{\lambda_{k+1}}$$

mit F aus (3.6).

Für das räumliche Integral $2\,|\int_\Omega (w\cdot\nabla w)u_k|$ im zweiten Term erhalten wir mit der Cauchy-Schwarzschen und der Hölderschen Ungleichung die Majorante

$$2|u_k|_{L^6}\cdot |w|_{L^3}\cdot|\nabla w|_{L^2} \quad \text{bei festem } t,$$

die mit Rücksicht auf die Sobolev-Ungleichungen

$$|f|_{L^6(\Omega)} \le c_o\cdot|\nabla f|_{L^2(\Omega)} \quad \text{für } f\in \mathcal{H}_1\,, \quad [7, \text{S. 10}],$$

und

$$|f|_{L^3(\Omega)} \le c_1\cdot\{|\nabla f|^{1/2}_{L^2(\Omega)}\cdot|f|^{1/2}_{L^2(\Omega)} + |f|_{L^2(\Omega)}\}$$

für $f \in H_1$, [3], [2, S. 27], durch das Produkt

$$c_2 \cdot |\nabla u_k|_{L^2} \cdot \{ |\nabla w|^{3/2}_{L^2} \; |w|^{1/2}_{L^2} + |w|_{L^2} \cdot |\nabla w|_{L^2} \}$$

beschränkt wird. Eine Anwendung der Youngschen Ungleichung (mit Exponenten 4 und 4/3) auf den ersten Summanden und der Cauchyschen Ungleichung auf den zweiten ergibt die Schranke

$$(4.5) \quad 2 \; |\int_\Omega (w \cdot \nabla w) u_k| \leq h(t) \cdot \varphi(t) + \varepsilon \cdot |\nabla w|^2_{L^2(\Omega)}$$

mit $h(t) = c_\varepsilon \cdot \{F^2(t) + F(t)\}$,

F aus (3.6) und dem Parameter $\varepsilon > o$, durch den $c_\varepsilon > o$ festgelegt wird. Hier und im folgenden bezeichnet $c_.$ jeweils eine positive, von den betrachteten Funktionen unabhängige Konstante.

Aus dem Hilfssatz 2.1. mit $f = u_l$ und $f_m = \sum_{i=1}^{k} a_{li} e_i$ folgt die Ungleichung

$$|\sum_{i=k+1}^{l} a_{li}(t) \cdot e_i|_{L^2(\Omega)} \leq \frac{1}{\lambda_{k+1}} \cdot |P\Delta u_l(t,\cdot)|_{L^2(\Omega)} \quad .$$

Hiermit und mit der Sobolev-Ungleichung

$$|u_k(t,\cdot)|_{L^\infty} \leq c_3 \cdot |u_k(t,\cdot)|_{H_2}$$

erhalten wir für das räumliche Integral

$$2 \quad |\int_\Omega (u_k \cdot \nabla u_k) \cdot \sum_{i=k+1}^{l} a_{li}(t) \cdot e_i|$$

im dritten Term zunächst bei festem t die Majorante

$$\frac{c_3}{\lambda_{k+1}} \cdot |u_k(t,\cdot)|_{H_2} \cdot |P\Delta u_l(t,\cdot)|_{L^2} \cdot |\nabla u_k(t,\cdot)|_{L^2}$$

durch Anwenden der Cauchy-Schwarzschen Ungleichung.
Wegen $|P\Delta u_1|_{L^2(\Omega)} \leq |u_1|_{H^2}$ liefert eine Anwendung der Cauchyschen Ungleichung die Schranke

$$(4.6) \quad 2\left|\int_{[o,t]\times\Omega} \{(u_k \cdot \nabla u_k) \cdot \sum_{i=k+1}^{l} a_{li} \cdot e_i\}\right| \leq \frac{g(t)}{\lambda_{k+1}}$$

mit $g(t) = c_4 \cdot (\max_{\tau \in [o,T]} F^{1/2}(\tau))H(t)$, F aus (3.6), H aus (3.8).

Die Ungleichungen (4.4) - (4.6) lassen erkennen, daß für $\varepsilon = 2$ aus (4.3) die lineare Integralungleichung

$$\varphi(t) \leq \frac{1}{\lambda_{k+1}} (F(o)+g(t)) + \int_o^t h(\tau)\varphi(\tau)d\tau$$

folgt, $t \in [o,T]$. Wegen der Stetigkeit der Funktionen φ, g und $h \geq o$ ergibt das Gronwallsche Lemma [13, S. 14-15] die Abschätzung (4.1) zunächst für $|u_1(t,\cdot) - u_k(t,\cdot)|^2_{L^2}$ mit

$$F^*(t) = F(o) + g(t) + \int_o^t (F(o) + g(\tau))h(\tau) \cdot e^{\tilde{H}(t)-\tilde{H}(\tau)}d\tau,$$

$$\tilde{H}(t) = \int_o^t h(\tau)d\tau .$$

Die rechte Seite in dieser Abschätzung ist unabhängig von der speziellen Galerkinnäherung u_1. Da wir nach Korollar 3.1. die u_1 aus einer gleichmäßig bezüglich t in $L^2(\Omega)$ gegen u konvergierenden Folge wählen können, folgt die Behauptung (4.1).

Adresse:

Prof. Dr. R. Rautmann
Fachbereich Mathematik-Informatik
Gesamthochschule Paderborn
Warburger Straße 1oo

D-479o Paderborn

West-Germany

Literatur

[1] Cattabriga, L., Su un problema al contorno relativo al sistema di equazioni di Stokes, Rend. Mat. Sem. Univ. Padova 31 (1961), 3o8-34o.

[2] Friedman, A., Partial Differential Equations, Holt, Rinehart and Winston, New York 1969.

[3] Heywood, J.G., The Navier-Stokes equations: On the existence, regularity and decay of solutions, Preprint. Univ. of British Columbia, Vancouver 1978.

[4] Hopf, E., Über die Anfangswertaufgabe für die hydrodynamischen Grundgleichungen, Math. Nachr. 4 (1951), 213-231.

[5] Ito, S., The existence and the uniqueness of regular solution of non-stationary Navier-Stokes equation, J. Fac. Sci. Univ. Tokyo Sect. I A, 9 (1961), 1o3-14o.

[6] Jörgens, K., Rellich, F., Eigenwerttheorie gewöhnlicher Differentialgleichungen, Springer Berlin 1976.

[7] Ladyženskaja, O.A., The Mathematical Theory of Viscous Incompressible Flow, Second Edition, Gordon and Breach, New York 1969.

[8] Prodi, G., Teoremi di tipo locale per il sistema di Navier-Stokes e stabilità delle soluzione stazionarie. Rend. Sem. Mat. Univ. Padova 32 (1962), 374-397.

[9] Rautmann, R., On the convergence of a Galerkin method to solve the initial value problem of a stabilized Navier-Stokes equation. Internat. Schriftenreihe zur Num. Math., Birkhäuser Basel 1975, 255-264.

[1o] Serrin, J., The initial value problem for the Navier-Stokes equations, Nonlinear Problems, edited by R.E. Langer, The University of Wisconsin Press Madison, 1963.

[11] Shinbrot, M., Lectures on Fluid Mechanics, Gordon and Breach, New York 1973.

[12] Temam, R., Navier-Stokes Equations, North-Holland Publ. Comp., Amsterdam 1977.

[13] Walter, W., Differential and Integral Inequalities, Springer, Berlin 197o.

[14] Weyl, H., The method of orthogonal projection, Duke Math. J. 7 (194o), 411-444.

CONTINUA OF PERIODIC SOLUTIONS OF THE LIÉNARD EQUATION

Rolf Reißig

Some conditions for the existence, non-uniqueness or uniqueness and iterative construction of periodic solutions of the non-autonomous Liénard equation are considered. Especially, the problem of continua of oscillations is discussed, under conditions suggested by Bebernes-Martelli. It is shown that all periodic solutions result from one by adding a constant, and that the restoring term must be of a special degenerate type. If this term is not explicitly depending on the time an existence and uniqueness theorem can be formulated.

The main purpose of this paper is to consider the problem of non-uniqueness of periodic solutions for the generalized Liénard equation

(1) $x'' + f(x)\,x' + g(t,x) = e(t)$

where $f,e \in C^0(\mathbb{R},\mathbb{R})$, $g \in C^0(\mathbb{R}^2,\mathbb{R})$ and $g(t+2\pi,x) \equiv g(t,x)$, $e(t+2\pi) \equiv e(t)$ as well as $\int_0^{2\pi} e(t)\,dt = 0$.

EXISTENCE

It is a well-known fact(see [9]) that equation (1) admits a 2π - periodic solution when $f(x)$ is arbitrary whereas $g = g(x)$ describes a restoring force the characteristic of which is within the resonance angle, at least for large $|x|$. This result was proved by means of Leray-Schauder fixed point technique making use of certain simple oscillatory properties of the solutions.

Without any modification, the argumentation in [9] can be extended to the more general case $g = g(t,x)$. A recent paper of Martelli [4] is devoted to this case, however, under more restrictive assumptions. It is based on some new results concerning nonlinear equations and mapping degree.

THEOREM 1 . [9] Suppose that for all $|x| \geqq h$

(i) $0 \leqq x\ g(t,x) \leqq q\ x^2\ (0 < q < 1)$

or

(ii) $0 \geqq x\ g(t,x)$.

Then there is at least one 2π - periodic solution of equation (1).

NOTE. Condition (i) can be relaxed as

$$0 \leqq x\ g(t,x) < x^2$$

provided that

$$\lim_{|x| \to \infty} (|x| - |g(t,x)|) = \infty \text{ (uniformly in } t) .$$

The proof will be slightly different from the previous one ([9]).

$\int_0^{2\pi} e(t)dt$ may be arbitrary when in (i) or (ii), respectively, $x\ g(t,x) \geqq 0$ ($\leqq 0$) is replaced by $x\ g(t,x) \geqq p\ x^2$ ($\leqq q\ x^2$) where p positive (q negative).

Let P be the range of all periodic solutions, and let P_t be its restriction to a fixed $t \in [0,2\pi]$, $P = \cup \{P_t : 0 \leqq t \leqq 2\pi\}$. If $x\ g(t,x) \neq 0\ \forall |x| \geqq h$ then P is bounded : $|x(t)| \leqq H$ for all solutions $x(t) \equiv x(t + 2\pi)$ of equation (1).

CONTINUA OF PERIODIC SOLUTIONS

Now let us discuss the more special case f(x) = c (constant):

(2) $x'' + c\ x' + g(t,x) = e(t),\ \int_0^{2\pi} e(t)dt = 0$.

Assume that, in addition to (i) or (ii), for $\inf P_t \leqq x \leqq y \leqq \sup P_t$

(i') $0 \leqq (x-y)\ [g(t,x) - g(t,y)] < (x-y)^2$

or

(ii') $0 \geqq (x-y)\ [g(t,x) - g(t,y)]$.

Following an elementary analytic approach we shall find that the difference between two periodic solutions is constant. If $\xi(t)$ denotes a periodic solution then $P_t=\{\xi(t)+u \mid u\in i\}$, $i\in\mathbb{R}$ an interval which is compact when P is bounded. Hence the set of all periodic solutions is a simple type of continuum.

The question of continua of periodic solutions under conditions similar to (i'), (ii') was posed by Bebernes-Martelli, in connection with certain nonlinear mappings and related theorems.

As a consequence of our result, the additional conditions (i') or (ii') turn out to be equivalent to

(3) $\quad g(t,\xi(t) + u) \equiv g(t,\xi(t)) \;\forall\; u\in i$.

Whenever $|i| > 0$ a restoring term with this property seems to be of a minor importance for applications. It exhibits an insensibility giving rise to an indefinite behavior of the dynamical system under external forcing. In general, the problem of continua of oscillations is an autonomous systems problem.

PROOF

Consider two periodic solutions $\xi(t)$ and $\xi(t) + u(t)$, $u(t)\not\equiv 0$. Then

(4) $\quad u'' + c\;\; u' + [g(t,\xi(t) + u(t)) - g(t,\xi(t))] = 0$.

Condition (i'):

There is no interval $[a,b]$, $0 < b-a \leq \pi$ where $u(a) = u(b) = 0$, $u(t) \neq 0$ for $a < t < b$.

Of course, if such an interval exists we derive from (4)

$$\int_a^b u'^2(t)\,dt = \int_a^b u(t) \quad [g(t,\xi(t) + u(t)) - g(t,\xi(t))]\,dt$$
$$< \int_a^b u^2(t)\,dt \leqq \left(\frac{b-a}{\pi}\right)^2 \int_a^b u'^2(t)\,dt$$

by virtue of Wirtinger's inequality. But this is a contradiction.

Consequently, there must be a $\tau \in [0,2\pi]$ such that

$u(t) \neq 0$ for $\tau < t < \tau + 2\pi$.

We obtain by periodicity

$$\int_\tau^{\tau+2\pi} [\,g(t,\xi(t) + u(t)) - g(t,\xi(t))]\,dt = 0 \ ,$$

and we derive from monotony:

$$g(t,\xi(t) + u(t)) \equiv g(t,\xi(t)) \ .$$

Therefore

$$u'' + c\,u' = 0 \ , \ u(t) \text{ constant.}$$

Moreover for every θ , $0 \leqq \theta \leqq 1$:

$$g(t,\xi(t) + \theta u) \equiv g(t,\xi(t)) \ ;$$

thus, $\xi(t) + \theta u$ is another periodic solution.

Condition (ii')

This time we have

$$\int_0^{2\pi} u'^2(t)\,dt = \int_0^{2\pi} u(t)\,[g(t,\xi(t) + u(t)) - g(t,\xi(t))]\,dt \leqq 0 \ ,$$

i.e.

$$u'(t) \equiv 0 \ , \ u(t) \text{ constant,}$$

and the same conclusion as before.

Special case $g(x)$:

Let us evaluate condition (3) when $|i| > 0$. We may assume, without loss of generality, that there is a positive $u \in i$.

Let

$$m = \min_{[0,2\pi]} \xi(t) \ , \ M = \max_{[0,2\pi]} \xi(t) \ , \ \frac{M-m}{k} \leq u \ (k \in \mathbb{N}^+) \ ;$$

$$\xi(t_\kappa) = \frac{\kappa}{k} (M-m) + m \quad (0 \leqq \kappa \leqq k)$$

Then

$$g(\xi(t_\kappa)) = g(\xi(t_\kappa) + \frac{M-m}{k}) = g(\xi(t_{\kappa+1})) \ , \quad 0 \leqq \kappa < k$$

and

$$g(m) = g(M) \ , \text{ i.e. } \ g(\xi(t)) \ \text{ constant.}$$

Integrating differential equation (2) for $\xi(t)$ over one period we find

$$g(\xi(t)) \equiv 0 \ , \ g(x) = 0 \ \ \forall \ x = \mu + u \ (m \leqq \mu \leqq M \ , \ u \in i) \ .$$

THEOREM 2. Assume that

$0 \leqq (x-y)(g(x) - g(y)) \leqq q\,(x-y)^2 \ , \ 0<q<1$

or

$0 \geqq (x-y)(g(x) - g(y)) \ ;$

moreover, let $g^{-1}(0) \neq \emptyset$.

Then there is a periodic solution which is unique if and only if there is no interval $i \subset g^{-1}(0)$, $|i| > M-m$.

NOTE. Since

$$\xi'' + c\,\xi' = e(t) \quad \text{if } g(\xi(t)) \equiv 0$$

a simple calculation yields:

$$M-m = \max_{0 \leqq s,t \leqq 2\pi} \int_s^t [\,\phi(c) + \int_0^\tau e^{c\sigma} e(\sigma) d\sigma\,] \, e^{-c\tau} \, d\tau$$

where

$$\phi(c) = \begin{cases} (e^{2\pi c} - 1)^{-1} \int_0^{2\pi} e^{c\tau} \, e(\tau) \, d\tau \ , & c \neq 0 \\ (2\pi)^{-1} \int_0^{2\pi} \tau \, e(\tau) \, d\tau \ , & c = 0 \ . \end{cases}$$

CONSTRUCTION

Finally, let us discuss differential equation (2) where

$\int_0^{2\pi} e(t)\,dt$ arbitrary,

$p\,(x-y)^2 \leqq (x-y)\,[g(t,x) - g(t,y)] \leqq q(x-y)^2 \quad \forall\, x,y \in \mathbb{R}$.

Following an idea of Mawhin [6] we can show that there is a unique periodic solution provided that the constants c, p, q satisfy a suitable condition. This solution can be constructed by means of iterations in the real Hilbert space $H = L^2\,[0,2\pi]$.

Let $\nu = \frac{p+q}{2}$, $L\,x \equiv x'' + c\,x' + \nu\,x$, $N\,x \equiv \nu\,x - g(t,x)$.

We note that

$$L : D \to H\ ,\ x \mapsto L\,x$$

is a bijection if

$c \neq 0$ or $c = 0$, $m^2 < p \leqq q < (m+1)^2$, $m \in \mathbb{N}$ or $c = 0$, $q < 0$.

The domain $D \subset H$ is the subspace of those functions which are differentiable twice (in Lebesgue's sense) the derivatives belonging to H. Moreover these functions are subject to periodic boundary conditions: $x^{(i)}\,\big|_0^{2\pi} = 0 \quad (i = 0,1)$.

Admitting, for a moment, that H is complex and using the ON-basis $\left(\frac{e^{ikt}}{\sqrt{2\pi}}\right)_{k \in \mathbb{Z}}$ we obtain:

$$L\,e^{ikt} = (-k^2 + i\,k\,c + \nu)\,e^{ikt} .$$

As a consequence we have

$$\|L^{-1}\| = 2 \sup_{k \in \mathbb{N}} [\,(p+q-2\,k^2)^2 + 4\,c^2\,k^2]^{-1/2} .$$

Furthermore, we note that

$$N : H \to H\ ,\ x \mapsto N\,x \quad \text{where} \quad \|N\,x\| \leqq \frac{p-q}{2}\,\|x\| .$$

A generalization of the periodic boundary value problem of differential equation (2) is

(5) $x \in \mathbb{D} : L\,x - N\,x = e \in H$,

$$\text{i.c. } x - L^{-1}\,N\,x + L^{1}\,e\ .$$

The operator

$$H \to H\ ,\ x \mapsto L^{-1}\,N\,x$$

will be a contraction if

(6) $(k^2 - p)\,(q - k^2) < k^2\,c^2 \;\forall\; k \in \mathbb{N}$

which implies $(k = 0) : p\,q > 0$.

Then equation (5) can be solved by means of successive approximations; if $e \in C^0$ we obtain the classical solution. Hence, condition (6) is sufficient for equation (5) to possess a unique 2π - periodic solution.

It is fulfilled when

c arbitrary, $p \leqq q < 0$

or

$$p > 0\ ,\ c^2 > \frac{(q-k^2)(k^2-p)}{k^2} \;\forall\; k \in \mathbb{N}^+ : \sqrt{p} \leqq k \leqq \sqrt{q}\ .$$

If $0 < p < q$ arbitrary then it results from

$$|c| > \sqrt{q} - \sqrt{p}\ .$$

Special cases are:

$k^2 < p \leqq q < (k+1)^2$, $k \in \mathbb{N}$; $c = 0$

$k^2 = p$, $(k+1)^2 = q$, $k \in \mathbb{N}$; $c \neq 0$.

REFERENCES

[1] Ahmad, S.: An existence theorem for periodically perturbed conservative systems. Michigan Math.J. 20(1973), 385-392.

[2] Lazer, A.C.: On Schauder's fixed point theorem and forced second order nonlinear oscillations. J.Math. Analysis Appl. 21(1968), 421-425.

[3] Lazer, A.C.: Application of a lemma on bilinear forms to a problem in nonlinear oscillations. Proc. Amer. Math. Soc. 33(1972), 89-94.

[4] Martelli, M.: Spectral theory for nonlinear operators and forced second order nonlinear oscillations. Proceedings "Equadiff 78", 501-512, Firenze 1978.

[5] Mawhin, J.: An extension of a theorem of A.C. Lazer on forced nonlinear oscillations. J.Math. Analysis Appl. 40 (1972), 20-29.

[6] Mawhin, J.: Contractive mappings and periodically perturbed conservative systems. Inst.Math.Pure Appl., Uni. Cath. Louvain, Rapport 80(1974).

[7] Reissig, R.: Extension of some results concerning the generalized Liénard equation. Ann.Mat.Pura Appl.(IV) 104 (1975), 269-281.

[8] Reissig, R.: Contractive mappings and periodically perturbed non-conservative systems. Acc.Nac.Lincei, Rend. Cl. Sci. fis.mat.nat., Ser. VIII, vol. 58(1975), 696-702.

[9] Reissig, R.: Schwingungssätze für die verallgemeinerte Liénardsche Differentialgleichung. Math. Abh. Hamburg 44 (1975), 45-51.

Ruhr-Universität
Institut für Mathematik
Universitätsstraße 150
D - 4630 Bochum 1

ÜBER DIE KONSTRUKTION INVARIANTER TORI, WELCHE VON EINER STATIONÄREN GRUNDLÖSUNG EINES REVERSIBLEN DYNAMISCHEN SYSTEMS ABZWEIGEN

Jürgen Scheurle

An existence theorem for invariant tori near equilibria of reversible dynamical systems is presented. It is assumed that the linearized vector field has exactly n pairs of simple conjugate eigenvalues moving along the imaginary axis with non-vanishing velocities corresponding to certain external parameters. The remaining part of the spectrum may be arbitrary. The motion on the tori turns out to be quasi-periodic. Finally a generalized Newton method is described which enables one to construct the tori inspite of the arising difficulty with small divisors.

1. Reversible Systeme

Reversible Systeme sind eine Klasse von Differentialgleichungen, welche eine nicht-dissipative Bewegung beschreiben. Wir beschränken uns hier auf gewöhnliche Differentialgleichungen und betrachten eine Schar von Systemen

$$(1.1) \qquad \dot{\underline{x}} = \underline{X}(\underline{\lambda},\underline{x}),$$

wobei $\underline{X} : \mathbb{R}^e \times \mathbb{R}^m \to \mathbb{R}^m$, $\underline{x}$ eine Funktion der unabhängigen Variablen t mit Werten in $\mathbb{R}^m$ und die Komponenten von $\underline{\lambda} \in \mathbb{R}^e$ die Scharparameter seien.

Definition 1.1 (J. Moser [3]). (1.1) heißt reversibel, falls eine lineare Reflektion R des $\mathbb{R}^m$ existiert mit

(1.2) $R^2 = \mathrm{id}$

so daß

(1.3) $\underline{X}(\underline{\lambda},R\underline{x}) = -R\underline{X}(\underline{\lambda},\underline{x})$

gilt für alle $\underline{\lambda} \in \mathbb{R}^e$, $\underline{x} \in \mathbb{R}^m$.

Offensichtlich ist in diesem Fall mit $\underline{x}(t)$ auch die reflektierte Funktion $R\underline{x}(-t)$ eine Lösung von (1.1). (1.2) impliziert, daß die Reflektion R nur die Eigenwerte $\pm$ 1 besitzt und nach Wahl einer geeigneten Basis des $\mathbb{R}^m$ als Diagonalmatrix dargestellt werden kann. Die Zukunft ist bei einem reversiblen System also gewissermaßen ein Spiegelbild der Vergangenheit.

Ein Beispiel ist das System schwachgekoppelter Schwingungen

(1.4) $\ddot{q}_k + \lambda_k q_k = Q_k(\underline{q},\underline{p})$, $1 \leq k \leq n$,

$Q_k(\underline{q},\underline{p}) = o(\|\underline{q}\| + \|\underline{p}\|)$, $\lambda_k > 0$. Hier bezeichne $\|\cdot\|$ irgendeine Norm des $\mathbb{R}^n$. Das äquivalente System 1. Ordnung

(1.5)
$$\begin{aligned} \dot{q}_k &= p_k \\ \dot{p}_k &= -\lambda_k q_k + Q_k(\underline{q},\underline{p}) \end{aligned}$$

ist reversibel, falls die nicht-linearen Terme Q_k eine der beiden folgenden Symmetrieeigenschaften erfüllen:

(1.6) $Q_k(\underline{q},-\underline{p}) = Q_k(\underline{q},\underline{p})$

oder

$Q_k(\underline{q},-\underline{p}) = -Q_k(\underline{q},\underline{p})$

(1.7)

$$Q_k(-\underline{q},-\underline{p}) = Q_k(\underline{q},\underline{p})$$

Im ersten Fall ist die zugehörige Reflektion des $\mathbb{R}^{2n}$ gegeben durch

$$R\underline{x} = \begin{pmatrix} \underline{q} \\ -\underline{p} \end{pmatrix}, \quad \underline{x} = \begin{pmatrix} \underline{q} \\ \underline{p} \end{pmatrix}$$

und im zweiten Fall durch

$$R\underline{x} = \begin{pmatrix} -q \\ \underline{p} \end{pmatrix}, \quad \underline{x} = \begin{pmatrix} \underline{q} \\ \underline{p} \end{pmatrix}.$$

Ist das Vektorfeld $\underline{X}$ bezüglich $\underline{x}$ differenzierbar, so überträgt sich die Eigenschaft (1.3) natürlich auch auf die Jakobimatrix $\frac{\partial \underline{X}}{\partial \underline{x}}$ in jedem Punkt $(\underline{\lambda},\underline{x})$. Es gilt dann

(1.7) $$\frac{\partial \underline{X}}{\partial \underline{x}} R = -R \frac{\partial \underline{X}}{\partial \underline{x}} .$$

(1.7) hat eine bemerkenswerte Konsequenz für das Spektrum von $\frac{\partial \underline{X}}{\partial \underline{x}}$. Man sieht unmittelbar, daß dieses notwendigerweise punktsymmetrisch zum Ursprung der komplexen Zahlenebene liegt, d.h. mit ν ist stets auch $-\nu$ ein Eigenwert. Ist $\nu,\bar{\nu}$ ein Paar einfacher, konjugiert komplexer Eigenwerte von $\frac{\partial \underline{X}}{\partial \underline{x}}$ welche, für festes $\underline{x}$, stetig von den Parametern λ_k abhängen, so befindet sich dieses Paar entweder für alle Werte der Parameter auf der imaginären Achse oder für gar keinen. Andernfalls würde nämlich beim Überqueren der imaginären Achse infolge der Symmetrieeigenschaft des Spektrums eine Aufspaltung in mindestens 4 Eigenwerte erfolgen, was wegen der Einfachheit ausgeschlossen ist. Darin besteht der Grund, weshalb sich die Theorie der Hopfverzweigung einschließlich ihrer konstruktiven Methoden auf reversible dynamische Systeme nicht anwenden läßt. Es werden dort bekanntlich nur isolierte kritische Punkte untersucht, wohingegen die Betrachtung reversibler Systeme zwangsläufig auf Verzweigungsphänomene führt, welche durch ein kontinuierliches Spektrum erzeugt werden.

2. Existenz invarianter Tori

Eine bzgl. (1.1) invariante Mannigfaltigkeit ergibt sich als Projektion einer Schar von Trajektorien in den Zustandsraum $\mathbb{R}^m$. Befindet sich die Lösung $\underline{x} = \underline{x}(t)$ zu einem Zeitpunkt t_o auf einer solchen Mannigfaltigkeit, so gilt dies für alle Zeiten t. Die Invarianzeigenschaft bezieht sich also auf den von (1.1) erzeugten Fluß. Man beachte, daß bei einem reversiblen System mit der Mannigfaltigkeit M auch ihr Bild bezüglich der zugehörigen Reflektion R eine invariante Mannigfaltigkeit ist.

Wir betrachten hier Mannigfaltigkeiten, welche von sogenannten quasiperiodischen Lösungen erzeugt werden. Die Funktion $\underline{x} = \underline{x}(t)$ heißt quasiperiodisch mit den Frequenzen $\omega_1, \ldots, \omega_n$, falls diese Zahlen rational unabhängig sind und falls $\underline{x}$ eine Darstellung der Form

$$\underline{x}(t) = \underline{f}(\omega_1 t, \ldots, \omega_n t)$$

besitzt, wobei $\underline{f}(u_1, \ldots, u_n)$ stetig und 2π-periodisch in den Variablen u_k ist. Quasiperiodische Funktionen beschreiben somit Schwingungen, bei welchen die Anzahl unabhängiger Grundfrequenzen endlich ist. Wir setzen dabei stets voraus, daß $n < m$ und $\underline{f} : [0,2\pi]^n \to \mathbb{R}^m$ ein Diffeomorphismus der Klasse C^1 ist mit rank $\frac{\partial \underline{f}}{\partial \underline{u}}(\underline{u}) \geq n$ für alle $\underline{u} = (u_1, \ldots, u_n)$. Dann beschreibt die Gleichung

$$\underline{v} = \underline{f}(u_1, \ldots, u_n)$$

offensichtlich die Einbettung einer n-dimensionalen Mannigfaltigkeit M in den m-dimensionalen $\underline{v}$-Raum, welche diffeomorph ist zum

Torus $T^n = T^1 x \ldots x T^1$. T^1 bezeichne den Einheitskreis in $\mathbb{R}^2$. M ist daher ein n-dimensionaler Torus. $u_1, \ldots, u_n$ sind Koordinaten auf M, falls sie mod 2π identifiziert werden (Winkelvariable). Der Fluß auf M wird beschrieben durch die Gleichungen $u_k = \omega_k t$. Diese stellen im $\underline{u}$ - Raum eine Gerade dar, welche mod 2π identifiziert den Torus dicht überdeckt.

Es ist bekannt, daß ein lineares dynamisches System

(2.1) $\dot{\underline{x}} = A\underline{x}$

eine n-parametrige Schar invarianter Tori

(2.2) $\underline{v} = \sum_{k=1}^{n} c_k \mathrm{Re}(\underline{v}_k e^{iu_k})$, $c_k \in \mathbb{R}$

besitzt, falls die Systemmatrix A wenigstens n Paare rein imaginärer Eigenwerte $\pm i\omega_k$ hat. Hierbei ist $\underline{v}_k$ jeweils ein zu $i\omega_k$ gehörender Eigenvektor. Die Lösungen auf den Tori sind quasiperiodisch und gegeben durch

$$u_k = \omega_k t + d_k \quad , \quad d_k \in \mathbb{R} .$$

Im Folgenden wird ein (nichtlineares) System der Form (1.1) behandelt. Es sei reversibel und $\underline{x} = 0$ sei ein Gleichgewichtszustand für alle Werte der Parameter λ_k. Das Vektorfeld $\underline{X}$ sei in beiden Variablen stetig differenzierbar. Bei der Suche nach invarianten Tori quasiperiodischer Lösungen beschränken wir uns auf eine Umgebung dieses Grundzustandes. Wir gehen davon aus, daß das in der Grund-Lösung linearisierte System

(2.3) $\dot{\underline{x}} = \frac{\partial \underline{X}}{\partial \underline{x}}(\underline{\lambda},\underline{0})\underline{x}$

für einen gewissen Wert $\underline{\lambda} = \underline{\lambda}_o$ eine Schar invarianter Tori besitzt. Infolge der am Ende von Abschnitt 1 erwähnten Spektraleigenschaften reversibler Systeme existieren dann im allgemeinen sogar für sämtliche $\underline{\lambda}$ in der Nähe von $\underline{\lambda}_o$ solche invarianten Mannigfaltigkeiten quasiperiodischer Lösungen von (2.3). Man hat also ein ganzes Kontinuum kritischer Punkte auf der Grundlösung von (1.1). Dies erschwert natürlich in beträchtlichem Maße die Beantwortung der Frage, welche der Tori des linearisierten Systems - bis auf "kleine Störungen" - auch bei (1.1) vorhanden sind.

Mit den Methoden in [1] folgt, daß sich über jeder Lösung der Linearisierung (bzgl. eines geeigneten Projektionsoperators), welche auf der gesamten reellen Achse beschränkt ist, lokal allenfalls eine einzige derartige Lösung von (1.1) befindet. Dies besagt, daß höchstens die Lösungen einer Zentrumsmannigfaltigkeit für alle Zeiten t in einer Umgebung des stationären Grundzustandes verbleiben. Zentrumsmannigfaltigkeiten sind lokal invariant bzgl. (1.1) und verlaufen, für festes $\underline{\lambda}$, in $\underline{x} = \underline{0}$ tangential zu jenem verallgemeinerten Eigenraum der Linearisierung, welcher zu den Eigenwerten mit verschwindendem Realteil gehört.

Im allgemeinen sind jedoch nicht so viele "kleine" Lösungen vorhanden. Die meisten invarianten Tori des linearisierten Systems werden durch die nichtlinearen Terme zerstört. Es treten Resonanzeffekte ein. Im wesentlichen bleiben nur die quasiperiodischen Lösungen übrig, deren Frequenzen ω_k einer Unabhängigkeitsbedingung

$$\left|\sum_{k=1}^{n} j_k\omega_k\right| \geq \gamma\|\underline{j}\|^{-\tau} \tag{2.4}$$

genügen, wobei γ,τ positive Konstanten sind und $\underline{j} = (j_1, \ldots, j_n)$. Die Erhaltung einer solchen Eigenschaft ist allerdings nur dann möglich, wenn genügend viele externe Parameter zur Verfügung stehen um die einzelnen Frequenzen zu kontrollieren. Man sieht leicht, daß die Menge aller $\underline{\omega} \in \mathbb{R}^n$, deren Komponenten (2.4) für kein γ und τ erfüllen, von 2. Kategorie ist.

Wir setzen hier voraus, daß es für jede Grundfrequenz wenigstens einen Kontrollparameter gibt. In diesem Fall lassen sich die Grundfrequenzen längs einzelner Lösungszweige sogar konstant halten. Hinsichtlich einer Reduzierung dieser Parameterzahl siehe [5].

Hypothese 2.1. Der Parametervektor $\underline{\lambda}$ habe n Komponenten und die Jakobi-Matrix $\frac{\partial \underline{X}}{\partial \underline{x}}(\underline{\lambda},\underline{0})$ habe genau n Paare einfacher Eigenwerte $\pm\, i\, \omega_k(\underline{\lambda})$ für alle $\underline{\lambda}$. Die Realteile der anderen Eigenwerte seien von 0 verschieden und es gelte

$$(2.5) \qquad \det \frac{\partial \underline{\omega}}{\partial \underline{\lambda}}(\underline{\lambda}_o) \neq 0 \quad ,$$

wobei $\underline{\omega} = (\omega_1, \ldots, \omega_n)$.

Satz 2.2. Das System (1.1) sei reversibel. Das Vektorfeld $\underline{X} : \mathbb{R}^n \times \mathbb{R}^m \to \mathbb{R}^m$ sei für kleine $\|\underline{\lambda} - \underline{\lambda}_o\|$ und $\|\underline{x}\|$ reell analytisch und $\underline{X}(\underline{\lambda},\underline{0}) = \underline{0}$. Ferner sei die Hypothese 2.1 erfüllt und für die Frequenzen $\omega_k = \omega_k(\underline{\lambda}_o)$ gelte (2.4).

Dann existiert für alle $\underline{c} = (c_1, \ldots, c_n) \in \mathbb{R}^n$ mit $\|\underline{c}\| = 1$ eine Schar invarianter Tori

$$\underline{v}(\epsilon,\underline{u}) = \epsilon \sum_{k=1}^{n} c_k \operatorname{Re}(\underline{v}_k e^{iu_k}) + \epsilon\, \underline{\psi}(\epsilon,\underline{u}), |\epsilon| < \epsilon_o(\underline{c}),$$

wobei $\underline{\psi} = O(\epsilon)$ 2π-periodisch in $u_1, \ldots, u_n$ ist und $\underline{\lambda} = \underline{\lambda}(\epsilon) = \underline{\lambda}_o + O(\epsilon)$. Die Dimension der Tori stimmt mit der Anzahl nichtverschwindender Komponenten von $\underline{c}$ überein, i.e. $\underline{v}$ hängt nicht explizit von u_k ab falls $c_k = 0$ ist. Die Funktionen $\underline{\psi} : \mathbb{R} \times \mathbb{R}^n \to \mathbb{R}^m$ und $\underline{\lambda} : \mathbb{R} \to \mathbb{R}^n$ sind analytisch in $|\epsilon| < \epsilon_o$. Die Lösungen auf den

Tori sind quasiperiodisch:

$$u_k = \omega_k t + d_k , \quad d_k \in \mathbb{R} .$$

Die Hypothese 2.1 impliziert insbesondere, daß die Voraussetzungen von Satz 2.2 für alle $\underline{\lambda}$ nahe $\underline{\lambda}_o$, außerhalb einer Menge vom Lebesgue-Maß 0, erfüllt sind. Für die Mehrheit der Parameterwerte besitzt das System (1.1) daher in der Nähe des Gleichgewichtszustandes $\underline{x} = \underline{0}$ invariante Tori quasiperiodischer Lösungen.

3. Bemerkungen zur Konstruktion der Tori

Die Schwierigkeit eines konstruktiven Beweises von Satz 2.2 besteht im sogenannten "Problem der kleinen Nenner": man sieht leicht, daß sich die Funktionen $\underline{\psi}$ und $\underline{\lambda}$ rekursiv als formale Potenzreihen in ϵ bestimmen lassen. Die Koeffizienten der Entwicklung für $\underline{\psi}$ ergeben sich als formale Fourierreihen in $u_1, \dots, u_n$. In den Nennern der Fourierkoeffizienten treten hierbei beliebige ganzzahlige Linearkombinationen der Grundfrequenzen ω_k auf. Diese können natürlich trotz Bedingung (2.4) sehr klein werden. Daher ist ein Konvergenzbeweis der formalen Entwicklungen mit klassischen Methoden wie etwa dem Cauchy'schen Majorantenkriterium nicht möglich.

Im Fall $m = 2n$ und $c_k \neq 0$ für alle k reduziert sich der Beweis von Satz 2.2 nach Einführung von Normalkoordinaten auf ein Beispiel von J. Moser in [4]. Er begegnet dort dem "Problem der kleinen Nenner" mittels Transformationstechniken der Differentialgleichung. Die Anwendung solcher Methoden ist jedoch nur unter ziemlich einschränkenden Voraussetzungen auch an jene Eigenwerte der Linearisierung möglich, welche nicht auf der imaginären Achse liegen. Man beachte, daß der Satz über die Zentrumsmannigfaltigkeit nicht dazu geeignet ist, den allgemeinen Fall auf den Fall rein imaginärer Eigenwerte zurückzuführen. Zentrumsmannigfaltigkeiten sind bekanntlich selbst bei analytischen Vektorfeldern im allgemeinen nicht analytisch.

Andererseits existiert seit A.N. Kolmogorov [2] die Idee, solche Probleme mittels eines verallgemeinerten Newtonverfahrens zu lösen. Man hat dabei die berechtigte Hoffnung, daß sich das "Wachstum" der kleinen Nenner durch die hohe Konvergenzgeschwindigkeit dieser Verfahren in den Griff bekommen läßt. Newtonverfahren erfordern allerdings - zumindest näherungsweise - die Invertierung der Ableitung in einer vollen Umgebung der Lösung. Stellt man die Bestimmungsgleichung für die invarianten Tori von (1.1) als Funktionalgleichung $F(\underline{\lambda},z) = 0$ in einem geeigneten Raum dar, so stellt sich heraus, daß die Größen $i\sum_{k=1}^{n} j_k\omega_k$ als Eigenwerte der Linearisierung in der Grundlösung $z = 0$ auftreten, d.h. gemäß (2.4) liegt das Spektrum dicht auf der imaginären Achse. Die Invertierbarkeit der Einschränkung auf das Komplement des Kerns kann daher bereits durch die kleinste Störung zerstört werden. Die Pseudoinverse ist unbeschränkt.

Zur Überwindung dieser Schwierigkeiten benötigt man ein schnell konvergentes Verfahren, welches die Invertierung der Ableitung höchstens in einem einzigen Punkt erfordert. In [6] wird ein derartiges Newtonverfahren beschrieben, wobei die Inversen der Ableitungen in der Newton'schen Iterationsvorschrift formal durch geeignete lineare Operatoren K_n ersetzt sind:

$$(3.1)_{n+1} \qquad z_{n+1} = z_n - K_nF(z_n) \ , \ n = 0,1, \ldots$$

Die Operatoren K_n werden parallel zu den sukzessiven Newtonschritten gemäß folgendem Iterationsschema rekursiv konstruiert ($K_o = L_o^{-1}$, $\Gamma_o = id$):

$$(3.2)_{n+1} \quad \begin{aligned} \Lambda_n &= DF(z_{n+1})\Gamma_n - L_n \\ L_{n+1} &= L_n M_n + L_n + \Lambda_n \\ \Gamma_{n+1} &= \Gamma_n(\mathrm{id} + M_n) \\ K_{n+1} &= \Gamma_{n+1} L_{n+1}^{-1} \end{aligned} \quad , \; n = 0,1, \ldots$$

Hierbei hat $\| L_o - DF(z_o) \| << 1$ und $\| M_n \| \leq C \| \Lambda_n \|$, $C > 0$, in geeigneten Operatornormen zu gelten. Die Operatoren M_n sind durch diese Iterationsvorschrift offensichtlich nicht eindeutig festgelegt. Durch $(3.1)_{n+1}$, $(3.2)_{n+1}$ wird eine ganze Klasse von Iterationsverfahren definiert. Im einfachsten Fall $M_n = 0$ ergibt sich $\Gamma_{n+1} = \mathrm{id}$, $L_{n+1} = DF(z_{n+1})$ und $K_{n+1} = DF(z_{n+1})^{-1}$, also das klassische Newtonverfahren. Ein weiteres Beispiel ist $M_n = -L_n^{-1}\Lambda_n$. Dies führt zu $L_{n+1} = L_o$ für alle n, so daß L_o der einzige Operator ist, der während der gesamten Iteration zu invertieren ist.

4. Literatur

[1] Kirchgässner K. und Scheurle J.: On the bounded solutions of a semilinear elliptic equation in a strip, erscheint in J. Diff. Equat.

[2] Kolmogorov A.: On conservation of conditionally periodic motions for a small change in Hamilton's function. Dokl. Akad. Nauk. SSSR 98 (1954), 527 - 530.

[3] Moser J.: Stable and random motions in dynamical systems. Ann. Math. Studies 77, Princeton New Jersey, Princeton Univ. Press 1973.

[4] Moser J.: Convergent series expansions for quasiperiodic motions. Math. Ann. 169 (1967), 136 - 176.

[5] Scheurle J.: Bifurcation of a stationary solution of a dynamical system into n-dimensional tori of quasi-periodic solutions. Proceedings der FDE- und AFP-Konferenz Bonn 1978, erscheint in Springer lecture notes.

[6] Scheurle J.: Newton iterations without inverting the derivative. Praeprint 1978.

Jürgen Scheurle
Math. Institut A der
Universität Stuttgart
Pfaffenwaldring 57
7000 Stuttgart 80

DEUX METHODES NUMERIQUES SIMPLES DANS LE DOMAINE DES OSCILLATIONS NON LINEAIRES

Bruno V. Schmitt*

Les équations de Duffing :

$$\ddot{x} + a\,x + b\,x + c\,x^3 = d\,\cos(\omega t) \tag{1}$$

de Liénard forcée :

$$\ddot{x} + f(x)\dot{x} + a\,x = b\,\cos(\omega t) \tag{2}$$

du pendule simple forcé :

$$\ddot{x} + k\,\sin x = \ell\,\cos(\omega t) \tag{3}$$

sont des exemples caractéristiques d'équations différentielles du 2me ordre, ou systèmes différentiels de dimension 2, non linéaires, et dont les coefficients varient périodiquement avec le temps; ce type d'équation se rencontre dans tous les domaines de la technique.

La préoccupation principale, lorsque l'on étudie ces équations, est l'obtention de solutions périodiques, de préférence stables. Or l'intégration analytique de ces équations n'est pas possible, et les seuls renseignements que peut éventuellement fournir la théorie mathématique sont des théorèmes d'existence de solutions périodiques qui ne permettent pas d'obtenir ces solutions de manière effective. On en est alors réduit à utiliser des techniques d'analyse numérique. Mais si on consulte la littérature spécialisée, on constate qu'à part les méthodes de perturbation (méthode du premier harmoni-

* Département de Mathématiques Université de Metz, et Institut de Recherche de Mathématique Avancée, Université Louis Pasteur, Strasbourg, France.

que, méthode de la moyenne, méthode de Newton), dont le domaine d'application est limité en particulier au cas faiblement non linéaire, on ne rencontre que des méthodes très élaborées, difficiles à mettre en oeuvre (voir par exemple Cesari [1] et Urabe et Reiter [7]) à tel point que la localisation des solutions périodiques d'équations du type (1), (2) ou (3) est fort peu avancée.

Le problème est en fait le suivant : les méthodes d'intégration numérique d'une équation différentielle (méthode de Runge-Kutta, méthodes à pas liés, ...) permettent d'obtenir avec une certaine approximation, et après discrétisation des valeurs approchées de $x(t,t_o,x^o)$, solution de l'équation qui prend la valeur x^o au temps t_o. Or si le système différentiel

$$\frac{dx}{dt} = f(t,x), \quad t \in \mathbb{R}, \quad x \in \mathbb{R}^2 \tag{4}$$

est tel que $f(t+p,x) = f(t,x)$, $(t,x) \in \mathbb{R} \times \mathbb{R}^2$, la solution $x(t,t_o,x^o)$ est périodique de période p si et seulement si

$$x(t_o+p,t_o,x^o) = x^o$$

Mais si $x(t_o+p,t_o,x^o)$ est obtenu de manière approchée, on ne peut pas affirmer que la solution $x(t,t_o,x^o)$ est p-périodique, ni même qu'elle est proche d'une telle solution. Une méthode numérique de localisation des solutions p-périodiques doit donc s'appuyer obligatoirement sur un argument d'existence d'une solution p-périodique issue d'un point voisin de x^o.

Les deux méthodes ci-dessous (méthode des symétries et méthode de l'index de Seifert) valorisent les méthodes numériques traditionnelles (Runge-Kutta, etc...) dans la détermination des solutions périodiques, en ce sens qu'elles les complètent par un théorème d'existence :

A. Méthode des symétries : Cette méthode s'applique si et seulement si le système différentiel admet certaines symétries; l'idée de la méthode est dûe à S. Mazzanti [3].

Soit le système différentiel (4) où $f(t+p,x) = f(t,x)$, $(t,x) \in \mathbb{R} \times \mathbb{R}^2$; on suppose que la solution $x(t,t_o,x^o)$ est définie pour tout t, et dépend continûment de (t,t_o,x^o). On pose $f = (f_1,f_2)$ et $x = (x_1,x_2)$.

1. Lemme [2,3,4] S'il existe $\alpha \in \mathbb{R}$ tel que la condition de symétrie

$$\begin{cases} f_1(\alpha-t,\ x_1,-x_2) = -f_1(\alpha+t,\ x_1,\ x_2) \\ f_2(\alpha-t,\ x_1,-x_2) = f_2(\alpha+t,\ x_1,\ x_2) \end{cases} \qquad (5_1)$$

soit satisfaite, alors si $(x_1(\alpha+t),\ x_2(\alpha+t))$ est solution de (4), $(x_1(\alpha-t),\ -x_2(\alpha-t))$ est aussi solution. De même, si

$$\begin{cases} f_1(\alpha-t,-x_1,x_2) = f_1(\alpha+t,\ x_1,\ x_2) \\ f_2(\alpha-t),\ -x_1,x_2) = f_2(\alpha+t,x_1,x_2) \end{cases} \qquad (5_2)$$

alors, $(-x_1(\alpha-t),\ x_2(\alpha-t))$ est aussi solution de (4).

2. Théorème [2,3,4] Soit $T : \mathbb{R}^2 \to \mathbb{R}^2$ l'application définie par :

$$T(x^o) = x(\alpha+p/2,\ \alpha,x^o)$$

et soit D_1 la droite portée par Ox_1, D_2 la droite portée par Ox_2.
Si alors (4) satisfait l'hypothèse de symétrie (5_i), et si $x^o \in D_i$ est tel que $T(x^o) \in D_i$, alors la solution $x(\alpha+t,\ \alpha,x^o)$ est périodique de période p, et sa trajectoire est symétrique par rapport à D_i (i=1 ou i=2).

3. Corrollaire [3]. Si (4) satisfait l'hypothèse de symétrie (5_i), et si $x_1^o \in D_i$, $x_2^o \in D_i$ sont tels que $T(x_1^o)$ et $T(x_2^o)$ sont de part et d'autre de D_i, alors il existe $x^o \in I$, $I = [x_1^o,\ x_2^o] \subset D_i$, tel que $x(\alpha+t,\ \alpha,x^o)$ est p-périodique, de trajectoire symétrique par rapport à D_i.

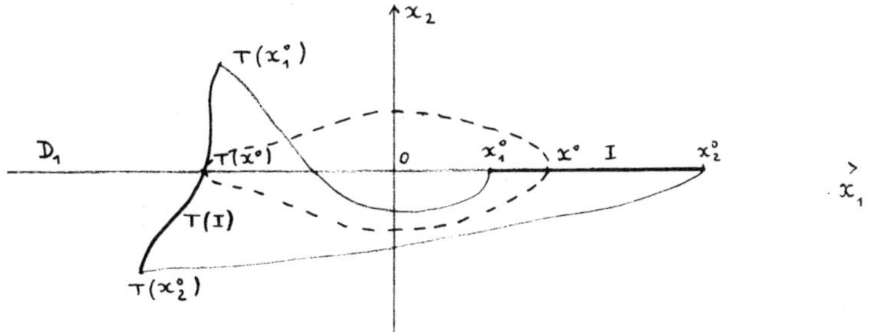

4. Méthode numérique des Symétries : Si (4) admet la symétrie (5_i), on l'intègre numériquement, par exemple avec la méthode de Runge-Kutta, avec la condition initiale $x^o \in D_i$, $t_o = \alpha$, et on détermine approximativement le point $T(x^o) \in \mathbb{R}^2$, pour différents points $x^o \in D_i$; Si deux tels points x_1^o et x_2^o ont leur image par T de part et d'autre de D_i, sur le segment qui les joint il existe une condition initiale x^o de solution p-périodique; en cherchant l'image par T du milieu $x_3^o = (x_1^o + x_2^o)/2$, donc par dichotomie, si le calcul de $T(x_j^o)$ est suffisamment précis, on peut localiser x^o avec la précision désirée.

5. Remarques a. Cette méthode est valable même si le système est autonome; la valeur de p n'est alors pas déterminée à l'avance.

b. La période p n'est pas nécessairement la période minimale; on peut donc ainsi déterminer les solutions sous-harmoniques de (4).

c. Si (4) dépend de paramètres, on peut fixer x^o sur D_i, faire varier le ou les paramètres, et déterminer ainsi les paramètres de l'équation pour lesquels (4) a une solution p-périodique issue de x^o.

d. L'équation (4) peut admettre simultanément deux types de symétrie; ainsi

$$\ddot{x} + b\,x + c\,x^3 = d\cos(\omega t) \qquad (6)$$

admet la symétrie (5_1) avec $\alpha = o$, et la symétrie (5_2) avec $\alpha = \frac{\pi}{2}$. L'équation (6) peut donc admettre des solutions $2\pi/\omega$-périodiques, de trajectoire symétrique par rapport à D_1, ou par rapport à D_2, ou par rapport à D_1 et D_2.

B. Méthode de l'Index de Seifert : Elle s'applique à tout système différentiel p-périodique (4); elle est aussi simple que la méthode des symétries, mais les calculs pour obtenir des solutions p-périodiques sont plus longs. Pour un exposé de la méthode, voir [5] ou [6].

Références

1. L. Cesari, Functionnal analysis and periodic solutions of non-linear differential equations, Contrib. to. Diff. Eq. Vol.1 (1963).

2. H. Ehrmann, Uber Existenzsätze für periodische Lösungen bei nichtlinearen Schwingungsdifferentialgleichungen, Z. ang. Math. und Mech. 35, 9-10, 326-327 (1955).

3. S. Mazzanti, Familles de solutions périodiques symétriques d'un système différentiel à coefficients périodiques avec symétries, Thèse, Univ. Louis-Pasteur, Strasbourg, (Sept. 1978).

4. G.R. Morris, A differential equation for undamped forced non linear oscillations I, Pr. Camb. Phil. Soc. 51, 297-312 (1955).

5. B.V. Schmitt, Détermination à l'aide d'index des solutions périodiques de l'équation de Duffing $x'' + 2x^3 = \lambda \cos t$, Lect.Notes in Math. n° 280, Springer, 330-334 (1972).

6. B.V. Schmitt et R. Brzezinski, Localisation numérique de solutions périodiques, Int. Conf. Equadiff 78, Florence (1978).

7. M. Urabe and A. Reiter, Numerical computations of non-linear forced oscillations by Galerkin's procedure, J. Math. An. Appl. 14, 107-140, (1966).

OBERE SCHRANKEN FÜR DIE AUSBREITUNGSGESCHWINDIGKEIT BEI PARABOLISCHEN FUNKTIONALDIFFERENTIALGLEICHUNGEN

Konrad Schumacher

A method for the computation of upper bounds for the speed of generalized travelling front – solutions of parabolic functional-differential equations is given. It depends on the construction of majorizing functions of exponential type.

1. Fragestellung

Die Beschreibung von Ausbreitungsvorgängen in der Populationsgenetik und Epidemietheorie führt häufig auf nichtlineare parabolische Differential- bzw. Funktionaldifferentialgleichungen. Der Einfachheit wegen beschränken wir uns auf den Fall eines 1-dimensionalen Areals. Wir setzen voraus, daß die unbekannte Funktion $u:\mathbb{R}\times\mathbb{R}\mapsto\mathbb{R}_+$ die Ungleichung

(1) $\quad u_t \leq f(x,u_{xx},u,\mu^1 * g^1(u),\dots,\mu^k * g^k(u))$

für alle $t>0$ und $x\in\mathbb{R}$ erfüllt. Hierbei bedeuten die μ^i endliche Borel-Maße auf $(-\infty,0]\times\mathbb{R}$, $g^i:\mathbb{R}_+\mapsto\mathbb{R}$ sind gegebene stetige Funktionen und $\mu^i * g^i(u)$ bedeuten die Faltungsprodukte

(2) $\quad (\mu^i * g^i(u))(t,x) := \int_{-\infty}^{0}\int_{\mathbb{R}} g^i(u(t+\lambda,x+\xi))\,\mu^i d(\lambda,\xi)$.

Die μ^i seien normiert, d.h. es gilt

(3) $\quad \mu^i((-\infty,0]\times\mathbb{R}) = \int_{-\infty}^{0}\int_{\mathbb{R}} \mu^i\, d(\lambda,\xi) = 1$.

Damit (1) sinnvoll ist, nehmen wir an, daß

(4) $\quad u \in C_t^1 \cap C_x^2$ für $t>0, x\in\mathbb{R}$, sowie
$\quad u \in C_b((-\infty,t]\times\mathbb{R},\mathbb{R}_+)$ für alle $t>0$

erfüllt ist ($C_b(M,N)$:=Menge der stetigen und beschränkten Funktionen $M\mapsto N$). Auf die Existenz der 2. Ableitungen nach x kann verzichtet werden, wenn $f:\mathbb{R}^{k+3}\mapsto\mathbb{R}$ im 2. Argument konstant ist.

Zusätzlich zu (1) erfülle u für ein $\alpha\in(0,\infty]$ die Anfangsbedingung

(5) $\quad u(t,x)=u_o(t,x)$, $t\leq 0$, $x\in\mathbb{R}$, $\quad u_o \in E_\alpha$,

wobei E_α eine vorgegebene Klasse von Anfangsfunktionen ist,die

(6) $\emptyset \neq E_\alpha \subset M_\alpha := \{v \in C_b((-\infty,0]\times\mathbb{R}, \mathbb{R}_+) \mid v(t,x)e^{\alpha x}$ ist beschränkt in $(-\infty,0]\times\mathbb{R}\}$ im Falle $\alpha < \infty$

erfüllt.Falls $\alpha = \infty$,so gelte $E_\alpha \subset \bigcap_{\delta>0} M_\delta$, $E_\alpha \neq \emptyset$.

Man interessiert sich für die Frage,unter welchen Voraussetzungen aus (1) und (5) folgt,daß die durch u beschriebene Größe für wachsendes t sich nur mit endlicher Geschwindigkeit in Richtung der positiven x-Achse ausbreiten kann,d.h. daß die Ausbreitungsgeschwindigkeit

(7) $c_\alpha := \sup_{u_0 \in E_\alpha} \inf\{c>0 \mid \lim_{t\to\infty} u(t,x+ct) = 0$ für alle $x \in \mathbb{R}\}$

existiert.Die Supremumbildung in(7) ist so zu verstehen,daß das Supremum über alle Lösungen der Ungleichung (1) gebildet wird,die zu einer Anfangsfunktion $u_0 \in E_\alpha$ gehören.

Für die praktische Anwendung ist es bedeutsam,ein einfaches Verfahren zur Berechnung von guten oberen Schranken für c zu kennen. Außerdem möchte man die Ordnung abschätzen können,mit der u(t,x+ct) für $t \to \infty$ nach 0 strebt.Wie man dies erreichen kann,soll in diesem Artikel gezeigt werden.

2. Spezialfälle

2.I Die Fisher´sche Gleichung

Sie lautet

(8) $u_t = D\, u_{xx} + u(1-u)h(u) \quad ,t > 0,\ x \in \mathbb{R}$.

Hierbei gilt $D > 0$ und $h:\mathbb{R}\mapsto\mathbb{R}$ ist in $[0,1]$ stetig und positiv.Aus Arbeiten von Aronson&Weinberger[1],Kanel[5],Kolmogorov [6]und Rothe[9]ist folgendes bekannt:(Nach Normierung D:=1)

a) Es gibt eine minimale Geschwindigkeit $c^*>0$,so daß für alle $c \geq c^*$ eine Pulslösung $u(t,x)=z_c(x-ct) \in (0,1)$ mit den Eigenschaften $\lim_{y\to\infty} z_c(y) = 0$ und $\lim_{y\to-\infty} z_c(y) = 1$ existiert.

b) Es gilt $2\sqrt{h(0)} \leq c^* \leq 2\sqrt{\max_{0\leq u\leq 1} (1-u)h(u)}$.

c) Für jede Pulslösung z_c existiert $\gamma>0$,so daß

$$\lim_{y\to\infty} \frac{z_c(y)}{e^{\lambda_0(c)y}} = \gamma \quad , \text{ wobei } \lambda_0(c) := \begin{cases} -c^*/2 - \sqrt{c^{*2}/4 - h(0)} & ,c=c^* \\ -c/2 + \sqrt{c^2/4 - h(0)} & ,c>c^* \end{cases} .$$

d) Jede Anfangsfunktion $u_0(x) \in [0,1]$,für die $u_0(t,x):=u_0(x)$ zu E_α gehört,konvergiert für $t\to\infty$ gegen eine Pulslösung.Anfangsfunktionen mit kompakten Trägern konvergieren gegen Pulslösungen mit minimaler Geschwindigkeit.($E_\alpha := \{v \in M_\alpha ,\ 0 \leq v \leq 1\}$)

Aus a)-d) ergibt sich für die Gleichung (8) mit D:=1 die Aussage

$$(9)\qquad c_\alpha \geq \begin{Bmatrix} \max\{c^*, \alpha + \alpha^{-1}h(o)\} & , 0 < \alpha \leq \sqrt{h(o)} \\ c^* & , \sqrt{h(o)} < \alpha \leq \infty \end{Bmatrix} .$$

Insbesondere wächst die Ausbreitungsgeschwindigkeit,wenn die Abklingrate α abnimmt.

2.II Das Epidemiemodell von Kendall

Eine von Aronson [2] durchgeführte Transformation führt auf die Gleichung

$$(10)\qquad u_t = -\lambda u + \lambda(1 - e^{-\frac{1}{\lambda}\hat{k} * u}) + \lambda v_o(x),\ x \in \mathbb{R}, t \geq 0 .$$

Hierbei bedeuten $\lambda>0$ einen reellen Parameter, $\hat{k}: \mathbb{R} \mapsto \mathbb{R}_+$ eine Dichtefunktion,die $\hat{k}(y)=\hat{k}(-y)$ und $\int_{\mathbb{R}}\hat{k}(y)dy=1$ erfüllt,sowie $v_o: \mathbb{R} \mapsto \mathbb{R}_+$ eine vorgegebene stetige Funktion,die für große Argumente identisch verschwindet. $\hat{k} * u$ bedeutet die Faltung von $\hat{k}$ und u im Ortsraum

$$(11)\qquad (\hat{k} * u)(t,x) := \int_{\mathbb{R}} \hat{k}(y)u(t,x+y)dy .$$

Wählt man $E_\infty := \{0\}$ (u beschreibt im Modell die Dichte der Individuen,die ins Stadium R (= removed) gelangt sind) und setzt man die Existenz einer reellen Zahl $\nu>0$ voraus,so daß

$$(12\qquad \int_{\mathbb{R}} \hat{k}(y)\, e^{\nu y}dy < \infty \text{ und}$$

$$(13)\qquad \inf_{\mu\in(0,\nu)} \frac{1}{\mu}\left(\int_{\mathbb{R}} \hat{k}(y)\, e^{\mu y}dy - \lambda\right) = \frac{1}{\bar{\mu}}\left(\int_{\mathbb{R}} \hat{k}(y)e^{\bar{\mu} y}dy - \lambda\right) := c^*(\lambda)$$

für ein $\bar{\mu}\in(0,\nu)$ gilt,so wurden für die Lösung u von (10) mit den Anfangsdaten $u_o = 0$ die folgenden Aussagen bewiesen :

a) Gilt $\lambda \geq 1$,so folgt $\lim_{t\to\infty} u(t,x+ct)=0$ für alle $c>0$ und $x \in \mathbb{R}$.

b) Gilt $0<\lambda<1$,so folgt für alle $x\in \mathbb{R}$

$$\lim_{t\to\infty} u(t,x+ct) = \begin{cases} 0 & ,\text{falls } c > c^*(\lambda) \\ >0 & ,\text{falls } 0 < c < c^*(\lambda) \end{cases} .$$

Nach Definition (6) folgt aus a) und b) für $\lambda>0$ die Aussage

$$(14)\qquad c_\infty(\lambda) \geq c^*(\lambda) \qquad\qquad (c^*(\lambda) := 0 \text{ falls } \lambda \geq 1).$$

3. Grundidee

Zur Erläuterung des Prinzips zur Gewinnung von oberen Schranken für c_α nehmen einmal an,es gäbe reelle Zahlen $\delta_\alpha>0$ und $\beta_\alpha>0$,so daß für jede Lösung u von (1) zu einer Anfangsfunktion $u_o \in E_\alpha$ eine reelle Zahl $M=M(u_o, \delta_\alpha, \beta_\alpha) > 0$ existiert,so daß

$$(15)\qquad u(t,x) \leq M\, e^{-\delta_\alpha x + \beta_\alpha t} \qquad \text{für alle } t \geq 0 \text{ und } x\in \mathbb{R}$$

gilt.Hieraus folgt für $c > \beta_\alpha/\delta_\alpha$ die Abschätzung

(16) $u(t,x+ct) \leq M e^{-\delta_\alpha x} e^{(-\delta_\alpha c+\beta_\alpha)t} \longrightarrow 0$ für $t \to \infty$,

also $c_\alpha \leq \beta_\alpha / \delta_\alpha$ .Somit findet man

(17) $c_\alpha \leq \inf\{\beta_\alpha/\delta_\alpha \mid (15)$ ist mit positiven $M, \beta_\alpha, \delta_\alpha$ erfüllbar$\}$.

Um eine Abschätzung vom Typ (15) nachzuweisen,benötigt man weitere Voraussetzungen an f, g^i und μ^i .

4. Voraussetzungen

(i) Monotonie von f

Es gilt $f(x,a\uparrow,b,d_1\uparrow,\dots,d_k\uparrow)$,wobei $f(\dots,d\uparrow,\dots)$ bedeutet, daß f eine nichtfallende Funktion von d bei festgehaltenen übrigen Argumenten ist.

(ii) Regularität von f

Zu jedem $r>0$ existiert ein $L>0$,so daß für alle reellen Zahlen $x,a,b,d_1,\dots,d_k,\sigma$ und ρ mit den Eigenschaften $|b| \leq r$, $|d_i| \leq r$ $(i=1,\dots,k)$, $0 \leq \rho \leq r$ und $0 \leq \sigma \leq \rho$ die folgende Ungleichung gilt:

$$f(x,a,b+\sigma,d_1+\rho,\dots,d_k+\rho)-f(x,a,b,d_1,\dots,d_k) \leq L\rho \quad .$$

(iii) Monotonie und Regularität der g^i

Für jedes $i \in \{1,\dots,k\}$ gilt $g^i(0)=0$ und zu jedem $r>0$ existieren reelle Zahlen $q_r^i \geq 0$,so daß für alle $a,b \in [0,r]$

$$g^i(a)-g^i(b) \leq q_r^i \max\{0,a-b\} \qquad \text{erfüllt wird.}$$

(iv) Abklingbedingung für die Borel-Maße

Für alle $i \in \{1,\dots,k\}$ gibt es $\alpha_i > 0$,so daß $\int_{-\infty}^{0}\int_{\mathbb{R}} e^{-\alpha_i \xi} \mu^i d(\lambda,\xi) < \infty$.

(v) Exponentielle Beschränktheit der "Inhomogenität" von f

Es gibt reelle Zahlen $R_o > 0$ und $\alpha_o > 0$,so daß

$$\sup_{x \in \mathbb{R}} f(x,0,0,0,\dots,0) \max\{1,e^{\alpha_o x}\} \leq R_o \quad .$$

(vi) Wachstumsbeschränkung für f

Es gilt $\sup_{\substack{x \in \mathbb{R}, \rho>0 \\ 0 \leq \sigma \leq \rho}} \rho^{-1}(f(x,\rho,\sigma,\rho,\dots,\rho)-f(x,0,0,0,\dots,0)) < \infty$.

(vii) Wachstumsbeschränkung der g^i

Für alle $i \in \{1,\dots,k\}$ gilt $\varkappa_i := \sup_{\rho>0} \rho^{-1} g^i(\rho) < \infty$.

6. Lemmata

Die Voraussetzungen (i)-(iii) implizieren die Gültigkeit des folgenden Vergleichsprinzips, dessen Beweis mit Hilfe der üblichen Techniken (vgl. [7][8]) durchgeführt werden kann. Bei der Formulierung verwenden wir die folgende Abkürzung:

DEFINITION: Eine Funktion $w: \mathbb{R} \mapsto \mathbb{R}$ heißt nach unten regulär an der Stelle x, falls es $z \in C^2(\mathbb{R},\mathbb{R})$ gibt, so daß $w \geq z$ in $\mathbb{R}$ und $w(x)=z(x)$ gilt.

LEMMA 1: u sei eine Lösung von (1) mit $u_o \in E_\alpha$ und $w: \mathbb{R}\times\mathbb{R} \mapsto \mathbb{R}_+$ habe folgende Eigenschaften:

1) In $(-\infty,0]\times\mathbb{R}$ gilt $0 \leq u_o \leq w_o$.
2) Für alle $t \geq 0$ gilt $w \in C_b((-\infty,t]\times\mathbb{R},\mathbb{R}_+)$.
3) Die linksseitige Ableitung w_t existiert für alle $t>0$ und $x\in\mathbb{R}$. Falls $w(t,.)$ an der Stelle x nach unten regulär ist, so existiert $w_{xx}(t,x)$ und es gilt

$$f(x,w_{xx},w,\mu^1 * g^1(w),\ldots,\mu^k * g^k(w)) \leq w_t \quad .$$

Dann gilt $u \leq w$ in $\mathbb{R}\times\mathbb{R}$.

Aus den Voraussetzungen (i),(iv),(vi) und (vii) ergibt sich die folgende Aussage:

LEMMA 2: Die Laplace-Transformierten der Borel-Maße μ^i

$$(18) \qquad p_i(\delta,\beta) := \int_{-\infty}^{0}\int_{\mathbb{R}} e^{-\delta\xi+\beta\lambda}\mu^i d(\lambda,\xi) \quad ,i=1,\ldots,k,$$

sind im Bereich $\delta\in[0,\alpha_i]$, $\beta\geq 0$, wohldefiniert. Für $\delta\in[0,\hat{\alpha}]$, $\hat{\alpha}:=\min\{\alpha_1,\ldots,\alpha_k\}$, und für $\beta\geq 0$ existiert

$$(19) \qquad H(\delta,\beta) := \sup_{x\in\mathbb{R},\rho>0} \rho^{-1}(f(x,\delta^2\rho,\rho,\varkappa_1 p_1(\delta,\beta)\rho,\ldots,\varkappa_k p_k(\delta,\beta)\rho) - f(x,0,0,0,\ldots,0))$$

und es gilt $H(\delta,\beta\downarrow)$, d.h. H ist eine nichtwachsende Funktion von β bei festgehaltenem δ.

Aus Lemma 2 schließt man, daß zu jedem $\delta\in[0,\hat{\alpha}]$ ein $\beta\geq 0$ existiert, welches $\beta > H(\delta,\beta)$ erfüllt.

LEMMA 3: $\beta\geq 0$ und $\delta\in(0,\bar{\alpha}]$, $\bar{\alpha}:=\min\{\alpha,\alpha_o,\hat{\alpha}\}$ seien so gewählt, daß $\beta > H(\delta,\beta)$ gilt. Ferner seien $K_o \geq 0$ und $K_1 > 0$ bestimmt, so daß

$$\sup_{x\in\mathbb{R}}\{u_o(t,x) \mid t\leq 0, x\in\mathbb{R}\} \leq K_o, \quad \sup_{x\in\mathbb{R}}\{u_o(t,x)e^{\delta x} \mid t\leq 0, x\in\mathbb{R}\} \leq K_1$$

erfüllt wird. Dann existieren reelle Zahlen $\beta_1>0$ und $q>1$, die nur von $f,\delta,\beta,g^i (i=1,\ldots,k)$ und K_1 abhängen, so daß für jede Lösung u von (1) mit $u_o \in E_\alpha$ die folgende Abschätzung gilt:

$$(20) \qquad u(t,x) \leq \begin{cases} \min\{K_o, K_1 e^{-\delta x}\} & ,t\leq 0 \\ \min\{K_o(1-q+qe^{\beta_1 t}), K_1 e^{-\delta x}(1-q+qe^{\beta t})\}, & t>0 \end{cases} \quad ,x\in\mathbb{R} .$$

Beweis: Wähle $R_1 > 0$, so daß $\beta \geq H(\delta,\beta)+R_o/R_1$ (vgl. (v)). Nach Definition von H (vgl. (19)) folgt hieraus

$$\beta \geq \sup_{x\in\mathbb{R},\rho>0} \frac{f(x,\delta^2\rho,\varkappa_1 p_1(\delta,\beta)\rho,\ldots,\varkappa_k p_k(\delta,\beta)\rho)-f(x,0,0,0,\ldots,0)}{\rho + R_1 e^{-\delta x}} + \frac{R_o}{R_1}$$

$$\geq \sup_{\substack{x\in\mathbb{R}\\ \rho>0}} \left\{ \frac{f(x,\delta^2\rho,\varkappa_1 p_1(\delta,\beta)\rho,\ldots,\varkappa_k p_k(\delta,\beta)\rho)}{\rho + R_1 e^{-\delta x}} + \frac{R_o e^{-\delta x} - f(x,0,0,0,\ldots,0)}{\rho + R_1 e^{-\delta x}} \right\} ,$$

wobei nach Voraussetzung (v) der zweite Term nicht negativ ist. Es gilt somit für alle $x \in \mathbb{R}$ und $\rho>0$ die Ungleichung

$$(21) \quad \beta(\rho+R_1 e^{-\delta x}) \geq f(x,\delta^2\rho,\varkappa_1 p_1(\delta,\beta)\rho,\ldots,\varkappa_k p_k(\delta,\beta)\rho) \quad .$$

Wähle $\beta_o > \beta$ und definiere $q:=1+R_1/K_1$. Nach Voraussetzung (i), (v) und (vi) existiert zu

$$r_o := \max_{t\geq 0} \delta^{-1} \ln \frac{K_1(1-q+qe^{\beta t})}{K_o(1-q+qe^{\beta_o t})}$$

eine Konstante $B > 0$, so daß für alle $\rho \geq K_o$

$$(22) \quad \sup_{x\leq r_o} f(x,0,\rho,\varkappa_1\rho,\ldots,\varkappa_k\rho) \leq B\rho$$

erfüllt wird. Definiere $\beta_1 := \max\{B,\beta_o\}$.

$w(t,x)$ bezeichne nun die mit diesen Konstanten q und β_1 gebildete rechte Seite der Ungleichung (20). Offensichtlich gelten die Voraussetzungen 1) und 2) von Lemma 1. Um die Voraussetzung 3) zu zeigen, sei $t > 0$ fest vorgegeben. Lediglich an der Stelle

$$x_o := \delta^{-1} \ln \frac{K_1(1-q+qe^{\beta t})}{K_o(1-q+qe^{\beta_1 t})} \leq r_o$$

ist w nicht nach unten regulär.

1.Fall $\quad x < x_o$

Man findet $w=K_o(1-q+qe^{\beta_1 t})$, $w_t=K_o q\beta_1 e^{\beta_1 t}$, $w_{xx}= 0$ und

$$(\mu^i * g^i(w))(t,x) \leq \varkappa_i(\mu^i * w)(t,x) = \varkappa_i K_o(1-q)+\varkappa_i K_o q\, p_i(0,\beta_1)e^{\beta_1 t} ,$$

also nach (i) und (22) (beachte $p_i(0,\beta_1) \leq 1$)

$$f(x,w_{xx},w,\mu^1 * g^1(w),\ldots,\mu^k * g^k(w)) \leq f(x,0,w,\varkappa_1 w,\ldots,\varkappa_k w) \leq$$
$$\leq B\, w \leq \beta_1\, w < w_t \quad .$$

2.Fall $\quad x > x_o$

Man findet (beachte $q > 1$ und $p_i(\delta,\beta) \leq p_i(\delta,0)$)

$$w=K_1 e^{-\delta x}(1-q+qe^{\beta t}), \quad w_t=K_1 q\beta\, e^{-\delta x+\beta t}, \quad w_{xx} =\delta^2 w \quad ,$$

$$(\mu_i * g^i(w))(t,x) \le \varkappa_i (\mu^i * w)(t,x) =$$
$$= K_1(1-q)\, p_i(\delta,0)e^{-\delta x} + K_1 q\, p_i(\delta,\beta)\, e^{-\delta x+\beta t} \le p_i(\delta,\beta)\, w\ ,$$

also nach (i),(21) und der Definition von q

$$f(x,w_{xx},w,\mu^1 * g^1(w),\ldots,\mu^k * g^k(w)) \le$$
$$\le f(x,\delta^2 w,w,p_1(\delta,\beta)w,\ldots,p_k(\delta,\beta)w) \le \beta(w+R_1 e^{-\delta x}) = w_t\ .$$

Die Behauptung folgt nun aus Lemma 1.

7. Sätze

Mit Hilfe von Lemma 3 läßt sich eine obere Schranke für c_α herleiten $(0<\alpha\le\infty)$. Man findet:

SATZ 1 Es seien die Voraussetzungen (i)-(vii) erfüllt. Dann gilt für $0<\alpha\le\infty$

$$(23)\qquad c_\alpha \le \bar{c}_\alpha := \inf\left\{ \frac{\beta}{\delta} \,\middle|\, 0<\delta\le\bar{\alpha},\ \beta\ge 0,\ \beta > H(\delta,\beta) \right\}\ ,$$

wobei $\bar{\alpha} := \min\{\alpha,\alpha_0,\alpha_1,\ldots,\alpha_k\}$. Zu jeder Lösung u von (1) mit $u_0 \in E_\alpha$ und zu jedem $\varepsilon>0$ existiert eine Konstante $K>0$, so daß

$$(24)\qquad \sup_{x\ge x_0} u(t,x+ct) \le K\, e^{-\delta x_0}\, e^{-\delta(c-\bar{c}_\alpha-\varepsilon)t}$$

für alle $t\ge 0$, $x_0\in\mathbb{R}$ und $c\in\mathbb{R}$ gilt. Hierbei ist $\delta\in(0,\bar{\alpha}]$ so bestimmt, daß

$$(25)\qquad \bar{c}_\alpha \le \frac{\beta}{\delta} \le \bar{c}_\alpha+\varepsilon \quad \text{und} \quad \beta\ge 0,\ \beta>H(\delta,\beta)$$

erfüllt werden.

Beweis: Es reicht aus, die zweite Behauptung zu zeigen. Aus (24) folgt nämlich für jede Lösung u von (1) mit $u_0\in E_\alpha$

$$\lim_{t\to\infty} u(t,x+ct)=0 \qquad \text{für alle } x\in\mathbb{R}$$

sofern $c\ge\bar{c}_\alpha+\varepsilon$, also $c_\alpha\le\bar{c}_\alpha+\varepsilon$ nach Definition (7). Weil $\varepsilon>0$ beliebig war, folgt hieraus $c_\alpha\le\bar{c}_\alpha$.

Sei nun $\varepsilon>0$ und eine Lösung u von (1) mit $u_0\in E_\alpha$ gegeben. Aus der Abschätzung (20) von Lemma 3 folgt mit $K := K_1 q$ (beachte $q>1$)

$$u(t,x)\le K\, e^{-\delta x+\beta t} \qquad \text{für alle } x\in\mathbb{R} \text{ und } t\ge 0\ ,$$

also

$$u(t,x+ct)\le K\, e^{-\delta x}\, e^{(-\delta c+\beta)t}\ ,\quad x\in\mathbb{R},\ t\ge 0.$$

Wegen $-\delta c+\beta = -\delta(c-\bar{c}_\alpha) - \delta\bar{c}_\alpha + \beta \le -\delta(c-\bar{c}_\alpha-\varepsilon)$ folgt hieraus (24).

Aus (23) erkennt man,daß $\bar{c}_\alpha$ eine nichtwachsende Funktion von α ist.Im Spezialfall der Fisher'schen Gleichung weiß man,daß auch c_α das gleiche Verhalten aufweist.Offensichtlich wird

$$(26)\qquad \bar{c}_\alpha = \bar{c}_\infty \quad \text{für } \alpha \geq \min\{\alpha_0,\alpha_1,\ldots,\alpha_k\} ,$$

wobei $\bar{c}_\infty$ im allgemeinen noch von $\alpha_0,\alpha_1,\ldots,\alpha_k$ abhängt.Vergrößert man diese Konstanten solange als die Voraussetzungen (iv) und (v) erfüllt bleiben,so nimmt $\bar{c}_\infty$ höchstens ab.Somit wird

$$(27)\qquad \bar{c}_* := \inf\{\bar{c}_\alpha | \alpha>0, \text{(iv) und (v) gelten mit } \alpha_0,\alpha_1,\ldots,\alpha_k\}$$

eine obere Schranke für die minimale Ausbreitungsgeschwindigkeit.

Die Bestimmung von $\bar{c}_\alpha$ bzw. $\bar{c}_*$ erfordert die Lösung eines Optimierungsproblems.Für die praktische Anwendung ist es bedeutsam,etwas über die Struktur dieses Problems zu wissen.Insbesondere möchte man hinreichende Bedingungen für $\bar{c}_\alpha=0$ angeben können,da in diesem Fall keine Ausbreitung stattfindet.Hierüber macht der folgende Satz eine Aussage:

SATZ 2 Zusätzlich zu den Voraussetzungen (i)-(vii) werde angenommen,daß $H:[0,\bar{\alpha}]\times\mathbb{R}_+ \mapsto \mathbb{R}$ stetig ist.Dann gilt:

1) Für $\bar{c}_\alpha=0$ ist notwendig,daß $H(\delta,0)\leq 0$ für mindestens ein $\delta\in[0,\bar{\alpha}]$ gilt.
2) Für $\bar{c}_\alpha=0$ ist hinreichend,daß $H(0,0)<0$ oder $H(\delta,0)\leq 0$ für mindestens ein $\delta\in(0,\bar{\alpha}]$ erfüllt ist.
3) Es gelte nun $H(\delta,0)>0$ für $0\leq\delta\leq\bar{\alpha}$.Dann besitzt die Gleichung $\varkappa=H(\delta,\varkappa)$ für alle $\delta\in[0,\bar{\alpha}]$ genau eine in δ stetige Lösung $\varkappa(\delta)>0$ und es gilt

$$(28)\qquad \bar{c}_\alpha = \min\left\{\frac{\varkappa(\delta)}{\delta} , 0<\delta\leq\bar{\alpha}\right\}.$$

Beweis: 1) Es gelte $\bar{c}_\alpha=0$.Dann existieren Folgen $\{\beta_n\}$ und $\{\delta_n\}$, so daß

$$\beta_n \geq 0,\ \delta_n\in(0,\bar{\alpha}],\ \beta_n > H(\delta_n,\beta_n) \quad \text{und} \lim_{n\to\infty} \beta_n/\delta_n = 0.$$

Durch Übergang zu einer Teilfolge kann man annehmen,daß die Folge der δ_n gegen $\delta\in[0,\bar{\alpha}]$ konvergiert.Weil H stetig ist,folgt hieraus $H(\delta,0)\leq 0$.

2) Es gelte nun $H(0,0)<0$ oder $H(\delta,0)\leq 0$ für mindestens ein $\delta\in(0,\bar{\alpha}]$.Im ersten Fall gilt $H(\delta,0)<0$ auch noch für hinreichend kleines $\delta>0$,so daß man sich auf den zweiten Fall beschränken kann. Wegen $H(\delta,\beta\downarrow)$ folgt aus $H(\delta,0)\leq 0$ die Ungleichung

$$(29)\qquad H(\delta,1/n) < 1/n \quad \text{für alle } n\in\mathbb{N} .$$

Wegen $\delta\in(0,\bar{\alpha}]$ folgt aus (29) $\bar{c}_\alpha\leq 1/n\delta$,also $\bar{c}_\alpha=0$.

3) Aus $H(\delta,\beta\downarrow)$,$H(\delta,0)>0$ und der Stetigkeit von H folgt,daß die Gleichung $\varkappa=H(\delta,\varkappa)$ genau eine positive Lösung $\varkappa(\delta)$ besitzt.Sei $\delta\in(0,\bar{\alpha}]$ fest vorgegeben.Für jedes $\delta'\in[0,\bar{\alpha}]$, $\delta'\neq\delta$,findet man im

Fall $\varkappa(\delta') \geq \varkappa(\delta)$

$$0 \leq \varkappa(\delta') - \varkappa(\delta) = H(\delta', \varkappa(\delta')) - H(\delta, \varkappa(\delta)) \leq H(\delta', \varkappa(\delta)) - H(\delta, \varkappa(\delta))$$

und im Fall $\varkappa(\delta') \leq \varkappa(\delta)$ analog

$$0 \geq \varkappa(\delta') - \varkappa(\delta) \geq H(\delta', \varkappa(\delta)) - H(\delta, \varkappa(\delta)) \quad ,$$

also in jedem Fall

$$|\varkappa(\delta') - \varkappa(\delta)| \leq |H(\delta', \varkappa(\delta)) - H(\delta, \varkappa(\delta))| \quad .$$

Dies zeigt die Stetigkeit von $\varkappa$ für $0 \leq \delta \leq \bar{\alpha}$.

Aus dem bereits bewiesenen ersten Teil des Satzes folgt $\bar{c}_\alpha > 0$. Es existieren Folgen $\{\beta_n\}$ und $\{\delta_n\}$, so daß

$$\beta_n \geq 0, \delta_n \in (0, \bar{\alpha}], \delta_n \to \delta \in [0, \bar{\alpha}], \beta_n > H(\delta_n, \beta_n), \beta_n / \delta_n \to \bar{c}_\alpha \quad .$$

Wäre $\delta = 0$, so würde dies $\beta_n \to 0$ und somit $0 \geq H(0,0)$ nach sich ziehen im Widerspruch zur Voraussetzung. Also gilt $\delta > 0$ und $\beta_n \to \beta := \bar{c}_\alpha \delta > 0$ sowie $\beta \geq H(\delta, \beta)$. Wäre $\beta > H(\delta, \beta)$, so fände man ein $\varepsilon > 0$, so daß ebenfalls noch $\beta - \varepsilon > 0$ und $\beta - \varepsilon > H(\delta, \beta - \varepsilon)$ erfüllt wäre. Hieraus bekäme man jedoch den Widerspruch $\bar{c}_\alpha \leq (\beta - \varepsilon)/\delta < \bar{c}_\alpha$. Also gilt $\beta = \varkappa(\delta)$ und $\bar{c}_\alpha = \varkappa(\delta)/\delta$. Dies zeigt 3).

8. Beispiele

8.I $u: \mathbb{R} \times \mathbb{R} \mapsto \mathbb{R}_+$ genüge der Ungleichung

$$(30) \quad u_t \leq u_{xx} + a(x,u)u + b(x) \qquad , \; t > 0, \; x \in \mathbb{R}.$$

Hierbei seien $a: \mathbb{R} \times \mathbb{R}_+ \mapsto \mathbb{R}$ und $b: \mathbb{R} \mapsto \mathbb{R}$ nach oben beschränkte Funktionen, wobei b zusätzlich die Bedingung

$$(31) \quad \sup_{x \in \mathbb{R}} b(x)\, e^{\alpha_0 x} < \infty$$

für ein $\alpha_0 > 0$ erfüllt. Für die Anfangsfunktionen gelte $u_0 \in E_\alpha := M_\alpha$. Die Voraussetzungen (i)-(vii) sind erfüllt. Man findet für $0 < \delta \leq \bar{\alpha}$ mit $\bar{\alpha} := \min\{\alpha_0, \alpha\}$,

$$(32) \quad H(\delta, \beta) = \delta^2 + q \quad , \; q := \sup_{x \in \mathbb{R}, \rho > 0} a(x, \rho) \quad ,$$

also nach Satz 1 (23)

$$(33) \quad \bar{c}_\alpha = \begin{cases} 0 & , \text{falls } q \leq 0 , \\ \bar{\alpha} + q/\bar{\alpha} & , \text{falls } \bar{\alpha} \leq \sqrt{q} , \\ 2\sqrt{q} & , \text{falls } \sqrt{q} \leq \bar{\alpha} \end{cases} \quad .$$

Nach Definition (27) findet man mit $\tilde{\alpha} := \sup\{\alpha_0 \geq 0 \mid (31) \text{ gilt}\}$

$$(34) \quad \bar{c}_* = \begin{cases} 0 & , \text{falls } q \leq 0 , \\ \tilde{\alpha} + q/\tilde{\alpha} & , \text{falls } \tilde{\alpha} \leq \sqrt{q} , \\ 2\sqrt{q} & , \text{falls } \sqrt{q} \leq \tilde{\alpha} \end{cases} \quad .$$

Für die Fisher'sche Gleichung gilt $q = \max\{(1-\rho)h(\rho) \mid 0 \leq \rho \leq 1\} > 0$,

$\bar{\alpha} = \alpha$, $\tilde{\alpha} = \infty$, so daß die nach (34) berechnete obere Schranke $\overline{c}_*$ in diesem Fall mit der in 2 I b) angegebenen oberen Schranke für die Minimalgeschwindigkeit übereinstimmt. Gilt außerdem $h(0)=q$, so ist diese Schranke scharf.

8.II $u: \mathbb{R} \times \mathbb{R} \mapsto \mathbb{R}_+$ genüge der Ungleichung

$$(35)\qquad u_t \leq -\lambda u + \lambda(1 - e^{-\frac{1}{\lambda}\mu_1 * u}) + \lambda v_0(x), \quad x \in \mathbb{R}, t \geq 0 .$$

Hierbei bedeuten $\lambda > 0$ einen reellen Parameter, μ_1 ein normiertes Borel-Maß auf $(-\infty, 0] \times \mathbb{R}$, so daß $p_1(\alpha_1, 0) < \infty$ für ein $\alpha_1 > 0$ gilt (vgl. (18)), und $v_0: \mathbb{R} \mapsto \mathbb{R}_+$ eine nach oben beschränkte Funktion, die

$$(36)\qquad \sup_{x \in \mathbb{R}} v_0(x)\, e^{\alpha_0 x} < \infty$$

für ein $\alpha_0 > 0$ erfüllt. Die Ungleichung (35) verallgemeinert die zum Epidemiemodell von Kendall gehörende Gleichung (10). Die Voraussetzungen (i)-(vii) sind für

$$f(x,a,b,d_1) := -\lambda b + \lambda(1 - e^{-\frac{1}{\lambda} d_1}) + \lambda v_0(x), \quad g_1(u) := u,$$

erfüllt. Für $0 < \delta \leq \bar{\alpha}$, $\bar{\alpha} := \min\{\alpha_0, \alpha_1\}$ und für $\beta > 0$ bekommt man nach (19)

$$(37)\qquad H(\delta,\beta) = \sup_{\rho > 0} \rho^{-1}(-\lambda\rho + (1 - e^{-\frac{1}{\lambda} p_1(\delta,\beta)\rho})) = p_1(\delta,\beta) - \lambda .$$

Wählt man formal $\alpha = \infty$ und $E_\infty = \{0\}$, so folgt aus (37), Satz 1 und Satz 2 mit der Abkürzung $\tilde{\lambda} := \min\{p_1(\delta,0) \mid 0 \leq \delta \leq \bar{\alpha}\} \leq 1$

$$(38)\qquad \overline{c}_\infty(\lambda) = \begin{cases} 0 & , \text{falls } \lambda > 1 \text{ oder } \lambda \geq \tilde{\lambda} \text{ sofern } 0 < \tilde{\lambda} < 1 \\ \min\limits_{0 < \delta \leq \bar{\alpha}} \varkappa(\delta,\lambda)/\delta & , \text{falls } 0 < \lambda < \tilde{\lambda} \end{cases},$$

wobei $\varkappa(\delta,\lambda)$ die eindeutig bestimmte reelle Lösung der Gleichung $\varkappa = p_1(\delta,\varkappa) - \lambda$ ist. In dem von Aronson betrachteten Spezialfall ohne Zeitverzögerung [2] hängt p_1 nicht von β ab und es gilt $\tilde{\lambda} = 1$ (Symmetrie von k !), so daß in diesem Fall sogar $\overline{c}_\infty(\lambda) = c^*(\lambda)$ für $\lambda \neq 1$ gilt, sofern α_0 und α_1 hinreichend groß sind.

In diesem Zusammenhang werde noch darauf hingewiesen, daß Ausbreitungsvorgänge, die durch Integralgleichungen beschrieben werden, welche die in [2] betrachtete Gleichung verallgemeinern, in Arbeiten von Diekmann [3,4] und Thieme [10] betrachtet wurden. In diesen Arbeiten werden auch Formeln für die asymptotische Ausbreitungsgeschwindigkeit angegeben. Jedoch umfassen die in [3,4] [10] gemachten Ansätze keineswegs sämtliche Ausbreitungsvorgänge, die durch eine Relation vom Typ (1) erfaßt werden. Allerdings enthält (1) wiederum nicht die in [3,4] [10] betrachteten Integralgleichungen als Spezialfall.

Die Beispiele 8.I und 8.II zeigen, daß die nach Satz 1 bzw. Satz 2 berechneten oberen Schranken für die asymptotische Ausbreitungsgeschwindigkeit ziemlich gut sind. Für Fälle mit $k > 1$ sind bisher noch keine unteren Schranken für die asymptotische Ausbreitungsgeschwindigkeit bekannt, so daß in diesen Fällen die Genauigkeit der in Satz 1 angegebenen oberen Schranke noch nicht nachprüfbar ist.

Literaturverzeichnis

[1] D.G.Aronson,H.F.Weinberger,Nonlinear diffusion in population genetics,combustion and nerve propagation,Proceedings of the Tulane Program in partial differential equations,Lecture Notes in Mathematics,Springer 1975.

[2] D.G.Aronson,The asymptotic speed of propagation of a simple epidemic,W E Fitzgibbon(III) & H F Walker,Nonlinear diffusion,Research Notes in Mathematics,Pitman 1977.

[3] O.Diekmann,Thresholds and travelling waves for the geographical spread of infection,J.Math.Biology,Vo.6(2),1978.

[4] O.Diekmann,Run for your life.A note on the asymptotic speed of propagation of an epidemic,Preprint 1978.

[5] Ja.I.Kanel,Stabilization of the solution of the Cauchy problem for equations encountered in combustion theory. Mat.Sbornik(N.S.)59(101)1962,supplement,245-288.

[6] A.N.Kolmogorov,I.G.Petrovskij and N.S.Piskunov,Investigation of a diffusion equation with mass production and its application to a biological problem,Bull.Moskovskogo gos.universiteto,1-25(1937).

[7] R.Redheffer,W.Walter,Das Maximumprinzip in unbeschränkten Gebieten für parabolische Ungleichungen mit Funktionalen, Math.Annalen 226,155-170(1977).

[8] R.Redheffer,W.Walter,Uniqueness,stability and error estimation for parabolic systems containing functionals,to appear.

[9] F.Rothe,Über das asymptotische Verhalten der Lösungen einer nichtlinearen parabolischen Differentialgleichung aus der Populationsgenetik,Dissertation,Tübingen 1975.

[10] H.R.Thieme,Asymptotic estimates of the solutions of nonlinear integral equations and asymptotic speeds for the spread of populations,to appear (J.f.d.reine u. angew.Math.)

Konrad Schumacher
Institut f.Biologie II
Abteilung Biomathematik
Universität Tübingen
Auf der Morgenstelle 28

D-7400 Tübingen

NUMERICAL COMPUTATION OF PRIMARY BIFURCATION POINTS IN ORDINARY DIFFERENTIAL EQUATIONS

Rüdiger Seydel

This paper is concerned in a class of bifurcation problems in ordinary differential equations. It is shown how some basic aspects of bifurcation can be handled by standard methods of numerical analysis. The procedure is illustrated by four examples.

1. Introduction

Consider the nonlinear two-point boundary value problem

(1) $y'(t) = f(t,y(t),\lambda) \ , \quad r(y(a),y(b)) = 0$

where $\lambda \in \mathbb{R}$, $a \le t \le b$, $y:[a,b] \to \mathbb{R}^n$, $D \subset \mathbb{R}^n$, $f:[a,b] \times D \times \mathbb{R} \to \mathbb{R}^n$, $r: \mathbb{R}^n \times \mathbb{R}^n \to \mathbb{R}^n$. Suppose f is continuous and has continuous first order partial derivatives with respect to y_i , $i = 1,\ldots,n$.

In [8], a numerical method for the computation of branch points is presented. This method deals with the general case of branching from a non-trivial solution, which is a-priori unknown. Supplementary to [8], the present paper is interested in the bifurcation from an explicitly known basic solution $y(\lambda)$ only. By means of an appropriate transformation, this special case is reducible to the bifurcation from the trivial solution. In the following, it is assumed that the trivial solution $y \equiv 0$ exists for all λ,

(2) $f(t,0,\lambda) \equiv 0 \ , \ r(0,0) = 0 \ .$

This assumption is wide-spread in the literature; it strongly facilitates the numerical handling of the corresponding bifurcation problems.

Definition (e.g. [6], [11] p.138). λ_0 is called a *(primary) bifurcation point* (PBP) of (1),(2), if for each positive γ and δ there exists a solution (y,λ) of (1) with $0 < \|y\| < \gamma$, $|\lambda - \lambda_0| < \delta$ ($\|\ \|$ is the norm in an appropriate function space).

2. Computation of Primary Bifurcation Points

It is well-known that the value λ_0 of a PBP is in the spectrum of the linearized problem. In many problems this necessary criterion is also sufficient, cf. [3] p.196. Thus, computation of the PBP's means first of all computation of the eigenvalues of the linearized problem.

Linearizing (1) about the trivial solution yields

$$h' = f_y(t,0,\lambda)\, h \quad , \quad A\, h(a) + B\, h(b) = 0 \ , \tag{3}$$

where $A := \frac{\partial r(0,0)}{\partial y(a)}$, $B := \frac{\partial r(0,0)}{\partial y(b)}$ are $(n{\times}n)$- matrices, $h : [a,b] \rightarrow \mathbb{R}^n$, $f_y(t,0,\lambda)$ is the Jacobian matrix of f with respect to y.

Our aim is to find eigenfunctions of (3). An additional normalizing condition forces the solutions of (3) to be nonzero. Two possibilities of realizing $h \neq 0$ are

$$\int_a^b h_j^2(t)\, dt = 1 \quad , \quad 1 \le j \le n \ , \quad \text{or} \tag{4}$$

$$h_k(a) = 1 \quad , \quad 1 \le k \le n$$

(see [12] or [10]). The eigenvalue problem (3), (4) consists of n differential equations and $n+1$ boundary conditions. It can be solved by introduction of a trivial differential equation for the parameter λ ([9] p.153). This leads to the following two methods for the computation of PBP's:

<u>Method 1</u> Solve the boundary value problem of dimension $n+2$

$$\begin{pmatrix} h \\ \lambda \\ \varphi^* \end{pmatrix}' = \begin{pmatrix} f_y(t,0,\lambda)h \\ 0 \\ h_1^2 \end{pmatrix} \ , \quad \begin{pmatrix} A\, h(a) + B\, h(b) \\ \varphi^*(a) \\ \varphi^*(b) - 1 \end{pmatrix} = 0 \ , \tag{5}$$

$$\varphi^*(t) := \int_a^t h_1^2(\tau)\, d\tau \ .$$

<u>Method 2</u> Choose $k \notin \mathfrak{M}$, $1 \le k \le n$,

$$\mathfrak{M} := \left\{ 1 \le j \le n \;\middle|\; \exists\, i,\ 1 \le i \le n,\ \exists\, \eta \in \mathbb{R} \text{ such that } r_i(y(a),y(b)) = y_j(a) - \eta \right\},$$

and solve the linear boundary value problem of dimension $n+1$

$$(6) \qquad \begin{pmatrix} h \\ \lambda \end{pmatrix}' = \begin{pmatrix} f_y(t,0,\lambda)h \\ 0 \end{pmatrix}, \quad \begin{pmatrix} A\ h(a) + B\ h(b) \\ h_k(a) - 1 \end{pmatrix} = 0 \ .$$

A solution of (5) or (6) yields the value λ_0 of a candidate for a PBP.

3. Computation of Nontrivial Solutions

Consider the nonlinear problem of investigating an emenating branch. Local information is obtained by the calculation of nontrivial solutions close to a PBP. For this purpose special methods have been used, see e.g. [4] or the selective iteration [7].

This nonlinear problem can be handled again by the use of suitable boundary value problems. Solving (1) for values of λ close to a PBP λ_0 one has to expect convergence to the trivial solution $y \equiv 0$. Therefore, normalizing conditions have to be added analogously as in (5) or (6), which leads to the boundary value problems (7) or (8).

$$(7) \qquad \begin{pmatrix} y \\ \lambda \\ \psi^* \end{pmatrix}' = \begin{pmatrix} f(t,y,\lambda) \\ 0 \\ y_1^2 \end{pmatrix}, \quad \begin{pmatrix} r(y(a),y(b)) \\ \psi^*(a) \\ \psi^*(b) - N^2 \end{pmatrix} = 0 \ , \quad N \in \mathbb{R} \ .$$

$$(8) \qquad \begin{pmatrix} y \\ \lambda \end{pmatrix}' = \begin{pmatrix} f(t,y,\lambda) \\ 0 \end{pmatrix}, \quad \begin{pmatrix} r(y(a),y(b)) \\ y_k(a) - \delta \end{pmatrix} = 0 \ , \quad k \in \mathbb{N}, \ \delta \in \mathbb{R} \ .$$

The choice of appropriate parameters N or δ causes no difficulties. Repeated solution of (7) or (8) with various values of N or δ yields information about an emenating branch. Such a homotopy chain is an instrument for the local and global study of an emenating branch, see e.g. example 4.

4. Testfunction

A testfunction $\tau(y,\lambda)$, which indicates a PBP λ_0 by $\tau(0,\lambda_0) = 0$, is given in [8]. Such a testfunction $\tau(\lambda) := \tau(0,\lambda)$ can be helpful if one is interested in parameters λ, $\lambda \in [\lambda_a, \lambda_b]$, where the interval $[\lambda_a, \lambda_b]$ contains several PBP's. The testfunctions are easy to calculate if the multiple shooting code [2,9] is used. The $(n \times n)$ iteration matrix of this code is denoted by E ; one evaluation of E at the trivial solution requires one numerical differentiation. A matrix E_{lk} is obtained if the l-th row of E is replaced by the k-th unit vector e_k of $\mathbb{R}^n$.

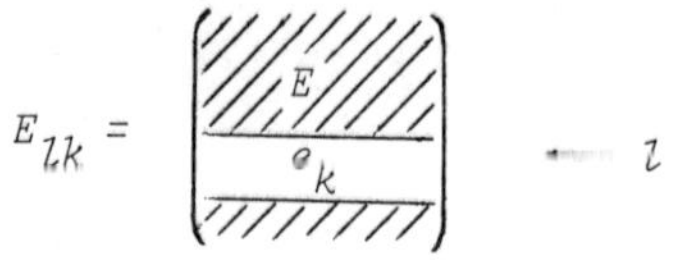

The indexes l and k have to be chosen such that E_{lk} is nonsingular. The matrix E_{lk} defines a testfunction τ_{lk} by

$$\tau_{lk} := e_l^T \, E \, E_{lk}^{-1} \, e_l \, .$$

Another simple testfunction is given by

$$\tau_o := det(E) \, .$$

In practice, the interval $[\lambda_a, \lambda_b]$ is subdivided

$$\lambda_a = \lambda_1 < \lambda_2 < \ldots < \lambda_m = \lambda_b$$

and a testfunction is evaluated at these points, $\tau(\lambda_j)$, $1 \leq j \leq m$. The behaviour of a testfunction will be demonstrated in example 1.

5. Summary

The numerical handling of many bifurcation problems only requires a solver for boundary value problems. Three tools will be illustrated by the examples of the next section:

a) boundary value problem (6) (alternatively (5)) for the computation of PBP's,
b) boundary value problems (7) or (8) for the local and global study of emenating branches,
c) testfunctions for a rough information about the location of PBP's.

6. Examples

In this section four examples will be discussed. All boundary value problems were solved by the multiple shooting code ([2], and [1], where further references are given). The computations were performed on the CYBER 175 of the Leibniz-Rechenzentrum der Bayerischen Akademie der Wissenschaften using single precision arithmetic.

Example 1

$$-y'' + y^3 = \lambda y \ , \ y(0) = y(\pi) = 0 \ .$$

The PBP's are known:

$$\lambda_{oi} = i^2 \quad , \quad i = 1,2,3,\dots \quad *)$$

The figur shows a testfunction which indicates the PBP's:

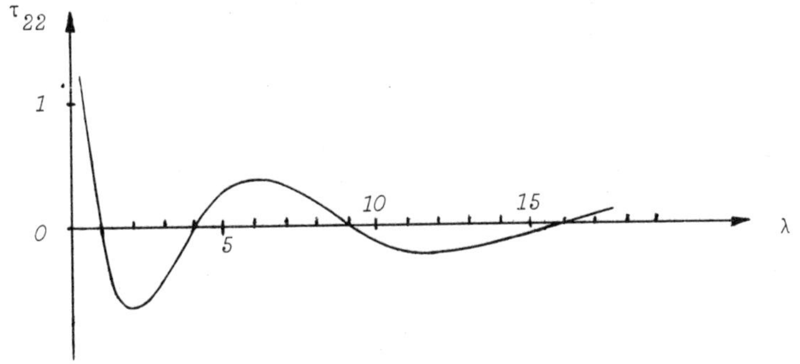

After each change of the sign of τ_{22} the boundary value problem (6)

$$\begin{aligned} y_1' &= y_2 & r_1 &= y_1(0) &&= 0 \\ y_2' &= -y_3\, y_1 & r_2 &= y_1(\pi) &&= 0 \\ y_3' &= 0 & r_3 &= y_2(0) - 1 &&= 0 \end{aligned}$$

($k = 2$, $y_3 := \lambda$) was solved in order to calculate the value λ_0 of a PBP. Subsequently, by (8), $\delta = 0.05$, a nontrivial solution of the emenating branch was calculated. The obtained values of λ show that each branch turns "to the right". After this, values of the testfunction were determined again. By this procedure, the bifurcation behaviour for e.g. $\lambda \in [0.,100.]$ could be investigated within 7 seconds, yielding all the PBP's.

---

*) The exact solutions of this problem are given in ZAMP 26, p. 717 (1975)

Example 2

$$-y'' + y^3 = \lambda y \quad , \quad y(0) = y(\pi) \quad , \quad y'(0) = y'(\pi) \ .$$

This example is similar to example 1 except that the boundary conditions are periodic. Solving (5), or (6) with $k=2$, five PBP's were calculated,

$$\lambda_{oi} = (2i)^2 \quad , \quad i = 1,\dots,5 \ .$$

The PBP's can be calculated, although the solutions of (5) or (6) are not unique in this example. In fact, different initial data yield different solutions h for the same value of a PBP.

Example 3

$$\lambda\varphi(s) = \frac{2}{\pi}\int_0^\pi (3\sin t \ \sin s + 2\sin 2t \ \sin 2s)(\varphi(t) + \varphi^3(t))\, dt \ .$$

This integral equation and the solutions are given in [6]. It can be transformed into a boundary value problem of type (7) by means of $y_1 := \varphi$, $y_6 := \lambda$,

$$y_1' = \frac{6\cos t}{\pi y_6}(y_2 + y_3) + \frac{8\cos 2t}{\pi y_6}(y_4 + y_5)$$

$$y_2' = (y_1 + y_1^3)\sin t \quad , \quad y_3' = -y_2'$$

$$y_4' = (y_1 + y_1^3)\sin 2t \quad , \quad y_5' = -y_4'$$

$$y_6' = 0 \quad , \quad y_7' = y_1^2 \quad ,$$

boundary conditions:

$$0 = y_1(0) = y_2(0) = y_3(\pi) = y_4(0) = y_5(\pi) = y_7(0) \ , \ y_7(\pi) = N^2.$$

The linearized equation (6) is

$$y_1' = \frac{6\cos t}{\pi y_6}(y_2 + y_3) + \frac{8\cos 2t}{\pi y_6}(y_4 + y_5)$$

$$y_2' = y_1 \sin t \quad , \quad y_3' = -y_2'$$

$$y_4' = y_1 \sin 2t \quad , \quad y_5' = -y_4' \quad , \quad y_6' = 0$$

$$0 = y_1(0) = y_2(0) = y_3(\pi) = y_4(0) = y_5(\pi) \quad , \quad y_k(0) = 1 \ .$$

This problem has two PBP's, $\lambda_0 = 2$ and $\lambda_0 = 3$. Both could be determined by (6) or (5).

Remark. In this artificial problem the index k of (6) changes with the bifurcation; for $\lambda_o = 2$ one has to choose $k = 5$, for $\lambda_o = 3$ the index is $k = 3$. The necessity of a change of k can be recognized by the behaviour of the testfunctions: There are two testfunctions suitable for this problem, τ_{33} and τ_{55} , which are determined by the matrices E_{33} and E_{55} respectively. If E_{55} becomes singular, one has to choose $k = 3$; if E_{33} becomes singular, one has to choose $k = 5$.

Example 4

$$u'' + \lambda \sin(u) \exp(F(\cos(u))) = 0 \ ,$$

$$F(z) := \frac{1}{5} \tanh(5(3 - 5z + 2z^2)) \ , \quad u'(0) = u'(2) = 0 \ .$$

This boundary value problem (from [5]) describes a particular case of buckling of a rod with a nonlinear compressibility property. The parameter λ is inversely proportional to the stiffness of the rod material.

This problem can be handled numerically in the same way as the previous examples. Some of the results are plotted in the branching diagram.

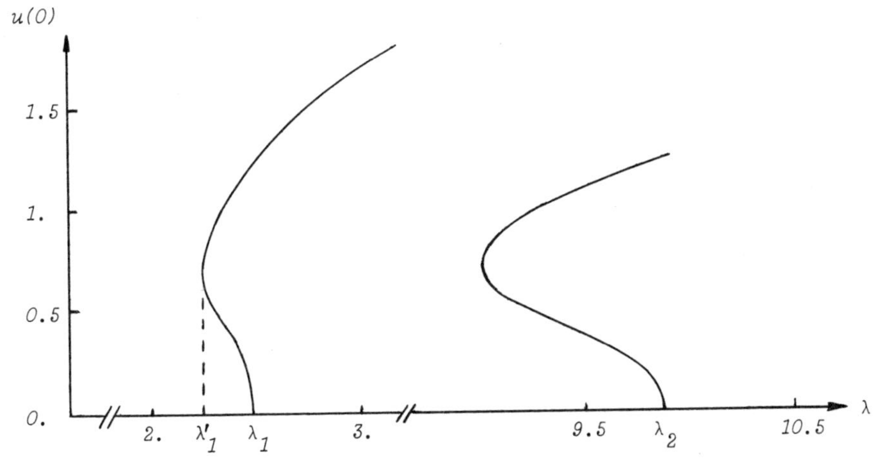

Remark. In [5] an interval is given for the value of the turning point at $\lambda = \lambda_1'$,

$$2.02 \leq \lambda_1' \leq 2.27 .$$

By homotopy with (8) and several values of $\delta = u(0)$, the value λ_1' can be determined approximately: $\lambda_1' = 2.24$. By the method of [8] the value

$$\lambda_1' = 2.24258$$

was obtained.

References

1. R. Bulirsch: Lecture on the Working Conference on Codes for Boundary Value Problems in ODE's. May 14 - 17, 1978 in Houston. To be published in Springer Lecture Notes.

2. R. Bulirsch, J. Stoer, P. Deuflhard: Numerical Solution of Nonlinear Two-Point Boundary Value Problems I. To appear in Numer. Math., Handbook Series Approximation.

3. M.A.Krasnosel'skii: Topological Methods in the Theory of Nonlinear Integral Equations. New York: Pergamon Press 1964

4. W.F. Langford: Numerical Solution of Bifurcation Problems for Ordinary Differential Equations. Numer. Math. 28, 171 - 190 (1977)

5. W.E. Olmstead: Extent of the Left Branching Solution to Certain Bifurcation Problems. SIAM J. Math.Anal. 8, 392 - 401 (1977)

6. G.H. Pimbley: Eigenfunction Branches of Nonlinear Operators, and their Bifurcations. Lecture Notes, Vol. 104. Berlin-Heidelberg-New York: Springer 1969

7. J. Scheurle: Ein selektives Projektions-Iterationsverfahren und Anwendungen auf Verzweigungsprobleme. Numer. Math. 29, 11 - 35 (1977)

8. R. Seydel: Numerical Computation of Branch Points in Ordinary Differential Equations. Numer. Math. 31 or 32

9. J. Stoer, R. Bulirsch: Einführung in die numerische Mathematik II. Heidelberger Taschenbuch, Band 114. Berlin-Heidelberg-New York: Springer 1973

10. H. Unger: Nichtlineare Behandlung von Eigenwertaufgaben. ZAMM 30, 281 - 282 (1950)

11. M.M. Vainberg: Variational Methods for the Study of Nonlinear Operators. San Francisco-London-Amsterdam: Holden-Day 1964

12. H. Wielandt: Das Iterationsverfahren bei nicht selbstadjungierten linearen Eigenwertaufgaben. Math. Zeitschrift 50, 93 - 143 (1944)

Rüdiger Seydel
Institut für Mathematik der
Technischen Universität München
Postfach 202420
D-8000 München 2

BOUNDS FOR THE CRITICAL VALUE OF A NONLINEAR CIRCULAR MEMBRANE UNDER NORMAL PRESSURE

Jürgen Sprekels and Heinrich Voss

In this note we use the finite dimensional iteration techniques developed in [3] to include the critical value of a circular membrane under constant normal pressure.

Let a circular membrane of radius $a > 0$ be subjected to a constant normal pressure $P > 0$. Let $u := \frac{\sigma_r}{c}$, where σ_r denotes the radial stress and $c = \left(\frac{Ea^2P^2}{16h^2}\right)^{1/3}$, with the Young's modulus E and the thickness h of the membrane.

Assuming axial symmetric displacement and neglecting small terms, we obtain the boundary value problem (see DICKEY [2], WEINITSCHKE [5]):

$$(1) \qquad Lu := -u'' - \frac{3}{x}u' = \frac{2}{u^2}, \qquad x \in (0,1),$$

$$u'(0) = 0, \qquad u(1) = \lambda.$$

Here we have set $x := \frac{r}{a}$, where r denotes the distance from the center of the membrane, and $\lambda := \frac{\sigma_r(a)}{c}$, where $\sigma_r(a)$ is the boundary stress.

For every $\lambda > 0$, (1) has a uniquely determined solution u_λ (see BOHL [1], WEINITSCHKE [5], in a more general setting). Moreover, to every given pressure P there exists a critical value λ^* for the boundary stress such that for $\lambda > \lambda^*$ the membrane is completely in tension whereas for $\lambda < \lambda^*$ circumferential compressions may occur.

By the criterion of STEIN-HEDGEPETH (see [4]) it follows that $\lambda < \lambda^*$ if there is an $x \in [0,1]$ such that

(2) $$Q(x) := x \cdot u_\lambda'(x) + u_\lambda(x) < 0.$$

Since Q decreases in x a necessary and sufficient condition for (2) to be the case is

(3) $$Q(1) = u_\lambda'(1) + u_\lambda(1) < 0.$$

We thus have to find a positive zero of the real-valued function

(4) $$F(\lambda) := u_\lambda'(1) + \lambda .$$

With the Green's function

(5) $$K(x,t) := \frac{1}{2} \begin{cases} t^3(x^{-2}-1), & t \le x \\ t - t^3, & x \le t \end{cases}$$

the solutions u_λ of (1) are exactly the fixed points of the integral operator $T_\lambda : C[0,1] \to C[0,1]$;

(6) $$T_\lambda u(x) := \lambda + \int_0^1 K(x,t) \frac{2}{u^2(t)} dt, \qquad x \in [0,1].$$

Hence

(7) $$F(\lambda) = \lambda - 2 \int_0^1 \frac{t^3}{u_\lambda^2(t)} dt,$$

and Lemma 5.1 in [2] implies that F is increasing in $\lambda > 0$. We thus can state

<u>LEMMA 1:</u>
Let $\lambda > 0$, and let $v_\lambda \in C[0,1]$ be positive on $[0,1]$. Then the following assertions hold:

Whenever

(i) $$v_\lambda(x) \le u_\lambda(x),\ 0 \le x \le 1, \text{ and } \lambda \ge 2 \int_0^1 \frac{t^3}{v_\lambda^2(t)} dt ,$$

then $\lambda \ge \lambda^*$,

whenever

(ii) $\qquad v_\lambda(x) \geq u_\lambda(x),\ o \leq x \leq 1, \text{ and } \lambda \leq 2 \int_o^1 \frac{t^3}{v_\lambda^2(t)}\, dt,$

then $\lambda \leq \lambda^*$.

Lemma 1 yields a method to include λ^*: For fixed $\lambda > o$ we have to determine upper or lower bounds for u_λ and to check whether (i) or (ii) holds.

To this end, we remark that T_λ is antitone with respect to the natural, i.e. pointwise, ordering $\leqq$ of $C[o,1]$. Moreover, if we set $K_o := \{u \in C[o,1]: u \geqq \Theta\}$, $K_1 := \{u \in K_o: u \text{ is decreasing}\}$, $K_2 := \{u \in K_1: u \text{ is concave}\}$, it is easy to see that $TK_o \subset K_1$ and $TK_1 \subset K_2$. Hence $u_\lambda \in K_2$, and we may apply the finite dimensional versions of the monotone iteration described in [3] in order to obtain pointwise bounds for u_λ.

To this end, let $Z : o = x_o < x_1 < \ldots < x_m := 1$ be a partition of $[o,1]$. For every $u \in K_o$ we define the piecewise continuous and bounded functions Au and Bu by

(8) $$Au(x) := \frac{x_i - x}{x_i - x_{i-1}}\, u(x_{i-1}) + \frac{x - x_{i-1}}{x_i - x_{i-1}}\, u(x_i)\ ,$$

$$x \in [x_{i-1}, x_i], \quad i = 1,\ldots,m,$$

(9) $$Bu(x) := \begin{cases} u(o) & , \quad x \in [o,x_1], \\ \dfrac{x_{i-1} - x}{x_{i-1} - x_{i-2}} u(x_{i-2}) + \dfrac{x - x_{i-2}}{x_{i-1} - x_{i-2}} u(x_{i-1}), & \\ x \in (x_{i-1}, x_i], & i = 2,\ldots,m\ . \end{cases}$$

Obviously, we have for every $u \in K_2$

(1o) $$Au(x) \leq u(x) \leq Bu(x), \qquad x \in [o,1].$$

Moreover, we can state

THEOREM 1:

Let $u_o(x) := \lambda$ and $v_o := B\, T_\lambda\, u_o$. Then for every $n \in \mathbb{N}_o$ the iterates

$$(11) \qquad u_{n+1} = A\, T_\lambda\, u_n, \qquad v_{n+1} := B\, T_\lambda\, u_n\ ,$$

are defined, and it follows that

$$(12) \qquad u_o \leqq u_n \leqq u_{n+1} \leqq u_\lambda \leqq v_{n+1} \leqq v_n \leqq v_o .$$

For a proof we note that u_o and $v_o(x) = \lambda + \frac{1}{4\lambda^2}(B\phi)(x)$, where $\phi(x) = 1-x^2$, constitute suitable initial functions for the application of a well-known result due to SCHRÖDER, see for instance Theorem 1.1 in [3].

We remark that Au and Bu carry only a finite dimensional amount of information about u. This means that (11) reduces to a finite dimensional iteration which can be performed in algorithmic form on a computer. For details we may refer to [3].

For the numerical computation we took an equidistant grid $x_i = i/m$, $i = o, \ldots, m$. The following tables indicate the bounds for λ^* which can be guaranteed for various choices of m.

In the first table we merely used that $u_\lambda \in K_1$, i.e. instead of the operators (8), (9) we used

$$(8)^* \qquad A^* u(x) := u(x_i),\quad x \in [x_{i-1}, x_i),\quad i = 1,\ldots,m\ ,$$

$$(9)^* \qquad B^* u(x) := u(x_{i-1}), x \in [x_{i-1}, x_i),\quad i = 1,\ldots,m\ .$$

The second table gives bounds obtained by the use of monotonicity in [o,1/2] and of concavity in [1/2,1]. The use of concavity over the whole interval turned out to be subjected to round-off errors and is not advisable.

Table 1:

m				Error
1o	o.7oo5		o.75oo	o.o495
2o	o.716o		o.74o4	24o
4o	o.7228	$\leq \lambda^{*} \leq$	o.735o	122
8o	o.726o		o.7322	62
16o	o.7276		o.73o7	31
32o	o.7284		o.73oo	16

Table 2:

m				Error
1o	o.72521		o.73o83	o.oo562o
2o	o.728o3		o.72973	17oo
4o	o.72882	$\leq \lambda^{*} \leq$	o.72938	56o
8o	o.729o5		o.72926	21o
16o	o.72912		o.72921	9o
32o	o.729152		o.729189	37

The inclusion $o.729152 \leq \lambda^{*} \leq o.729189$ for m = 32o shows that DICKEY's value $\lambda^{*} \approx$ o.7292 (see [2]) is inside the region of stability.

References

[1] E. Bohl: On Two Boundary Value Problems in Nonlinear Elasticity from a Numerical Viewpoint. In: Lecture Notes in Mathematics No. 679, Ed.: R. Ansorge, W. Törnig. Springer, Berlin-Heidelberg-New York 1977, 1-14

[2] R. W. Dickey: The Plane Circular Elastic Surface Under Normal Pressure. Arch. Rat. Mech. Anal. 26 (1967), 219-236

[3] J. Sprekels, H. Voss: Pointwise Inclusions of Fixed Points by Finite Dimensional Iteration Schemes. To appear in Numer. Math.

[4] H. J. Weinitschke: Endliche Deformationen elastischer Membranen. ZAMM 53 (1973), 89-91

[5] H. J. Weinitschke: Verzweigungsprobleme bei kreisförmigen elastischen Platten. Intern. Ser. Numer. Math. 38 (1977), 195-212

Dr. J. Sprekels
Institut für Angewandte Mathematik
Universität Hamburg
Bundesstrasse 55
D-2000 Hamburg 13

Dr. H. Voss
Fachbereich Mathematik der
Universität Essen - GHS
Universitätsstrasse 2
D-4300 Essen

Bundesrepublik Deutschland

NUMERISCHE BEHANDLUNG VON VERZWEIGUNGSPROBLEMEN BEI GEWÖHNLICHEN RANDWERTAUFGABEN *

Helmut Weber

We consider the numerical solution of bifurcation problems for ordinary differential equations in the case of simple eigenvalues. First we treat the case of bifurcation from the trivial solution. We also give a new method for the numerical treatment of secondary bifurcation. It consists in the accurate determination of the bifurcation point for which a convex unrestricted minimization problem is derived, and the computation of both branches by conventional methods after transforming the problem.

1. Problemstellung

Wir betrachten die Randwertaufgabe (RWA)

(1) $F(u,\lambda) = Lu - f(\lambda,u) = 0, \; B[u] = 0$

mit

(2)
$Lu(t) = u'(t) - A(t)u(t), \; a \leq t \leq b, \; A \in C_{n\times n}[a,b],$
$B_a, B_b \in \mathbb{R}^{n,n}, \; \text{Rang}[B_a \; B_b] = n, \; f: \mathbb{R}\times\Omega \to \mathbb{R}^n, \; 0 \in \Omega \subset \mathbb{R}^n,$
Ω offen, f dreimal stetig differenzierbar.

In den letzten Jahren sind eine Reihe von Arbeiten erschienen, die sich mit der numerischen Lösung von Verzweigungsproblemen des Typs (1) oder ähnlicher Gleichungen befassen, s. Langford [3], Weiss [8], Keller [2], Scheurle [5]. Diese befassen sich hauptsächlich mit der Verzweigung von der trivialen Lösung. Wir be-

*: Diese Arbeit enthält Teile meiner Dissertation, die unter der Anleitung von Prof. Dr. W. Börsch-Supan an der Johannes Gutenberg - Universität in Mainz entstand.

fassen uns hier auch mit dem Problem der sekundären Verzweigung. Für beide Aufgaben geben wir einen Weg an, der nach Transformation des Problems zu einer regulären RWA mit isolierten Lösungen führt und damit die numerische Behandlung mit Standardverfahren ermöglicht. Damit werden auch Konvergenzaussagen für die Verfahren unproblematisch.

2. Verzweigung von der trivialen Lösung

Hier setzen wir voraus

(3) $f(\lambda,0) = 0$ für alle $\lambda \in \mathbb{R}$.

Damit ist $u \equiv 0$ Lösung von (1) für alle reellen λ. Es gelte weiter

(4) $N(L_0) = \text{span}\{\varphi\}$, $\varphi \in C_n^1[a,b]$, $\|\varphi\| = 1$,

wobei

$$\|y\| = \max_{t\in[a,b]} \|y(t)\|_\infty , \quad y \in C_n[a,b].$$

L_0 sei der lineare Differentialoperator $L - f_u(\lambda_0,0)$ mit Definitionsbereich $D(L_0) = D(L) = \{y \in C_n^1[a,b] \mid B[y] = 0\}$. Damit erfüllt $(0,\lambda_0)$ die notwendige Bedingung für einen Verzweigungspunkt. Aus (4) folgt $\dim N(L_0^*) = 1$, wobei L_0^* den zu L_0 adjungierten Differentialoperator bezeichnet. Es sei $N(L_0^*) = \text{span}\{\psi\}$, $\|\psi\| = 1$. Wir haben ferner

$$R(L_0) = N(L_0^*)^\perp,$$

wobei die Orthogonalität durch das Skalarprodukt

$$\langle y,z\rangle := \int_a^b y(t)^T z(t)dt, \quad y,z \in C_n[a,b]$$

definiert ist.

Für die gesuchte, in $(0,\lambda_0)$ abzweigende nichttriviale Lösung von (1) machen wir den Störungsansatz ([1],[3])

$$(5)\quad \begin{aligned} u(\varepsilon) &= \varepsilon\varphi + \varepsilon^2 v(\varepsilon), \qquad v(\varepsilon) \in N(L_0)^{\perp} \\ \lambda(\varepsilon) &= \lambda_0 + \varepsilon\eta(\varepsilon). \end{aligned}$$

Taylorentwicklung von f um $(0,\lambda_0)$ liefert

$$(6)\qquad f(\lambda,u) = f_u^0 u + f_{u\lambda}^0 u(\lambda-\lambda_0) + Q(u) + R(\lambda,u).$$

Dabei ist $f_u^0 := f_u(\lambda_0,u)$, $Q(u) := \frac{1}{2} f_{uu}^0 uu$ und R ein Restgliedterm dritter Ordnung in u und $\lambda-\lambda_0$.
Einsetzen von (5) in $L_0 u = f(\lambda,u) - f_u^0 u$ liefert

$$(7)\quad \begin{aligned} &L_0 v = f_{u\lambda}^0(\varphi+\varepsilon v) + Q(\varphi+\varepsilon v) + \frac{1}{\varepsilon^2} R(\lambda_0+\varepsilon\eta, \varepsilon\varphi+\varepsilon^2 v) \\ &\langle v,\varphi\rangle = 0, \qquad B[v] = 0. \end{aligned}$$

Äquivalent zum Problem (7) ist folgende RWA der Dimension n+2

$$(8)\quad \begin{aligned} &L_0 v - \eta f_{u\lambda}^0 \varphi = \varepsilon\eta f_{u\lambda}^0 v + Q(\varphi+\varepsilon v) + \frac{1}{\varepsilon^2} R(\lambda_0+\varepsilon\eta, \varepsilon\varphi+\varepsilon^2 v) \\ &\eta' = 0 \\ &\mu' - \varphi^T v = 0, \qquad B[v] = 0,\ \mu(a) = \mu(b) = 0. \end{aligned}$$

Dabei ist η als (konstante) Variable eingeführt und die Orthogonalitätsbedingung an $v = v(\varepsilon)$ durch die RWA $\mu' - \varphi^T v = 0$, $\mu(a) = \mu(b) = 0$ ersetzt.
Über die Lösbarkeitseigenschaften der nichtlinearen RWA (8) und als Existenzaussage erhalten wir

SATZ 1

Für (1) gelte (2), (3), (4) und

$$(9)\qquad \langle f_{u\lambda}^0 \varphi, \psi\rangle \neq 0.$$

Dann gibt es ein $\varepsilon_0 > 0$, so daß eine auf $(-\varepsilon_0,+\varepsilon_0)$ definierte stetige Kurve von isolierten Lösungen $(v(\varepsilon),\eta(\varepsilon),\mu(\varepsilon))$ von (8) existiert, aus denen man mit Hilfe von (5) einen stetigen Zweig von nichttrivialen Lösungen von (1) konstruieren kann, der in $(0,\lambda_0)$ von der trivialen Lösung abzweigt.

Der Beweis mit Hilfe des Theorems über implizite Funktionen ist in [6], [7] ausgeführt. Dort sind auch numerische Beispiele für die Anwendung von Standardverfahren auf die RWA (8) unter Verwendung einer Homotopie mittels des Parameters ε zu finden. Zur Problematik der Bestimmung von λ_0 und φ sei ebenfalls auf [6] und [7] verwiesen.

3. Sekundäre Verzweigung

Das Problem der sekundären Verzweigung (Branching) läßt sich leicht auf den Fall der Verzweigung von der trivialen Lösung zurückführen, wenn man den primären Zweig genau kennt ([1]). Eben dies ist jedoch in der Praxis selten der Fall. Die Kondition der Bestimmung des primären Zweiges ist zudem in der Nähe des Verzweigungspunktes sehr schlecht. Die genaue Kenntnis des Verzweigungspunktes und des primären Zweiges in der Nähe des Verzweigungspunktes ist jedoch zur genauen Berechnung des sekundären Zweiges unerläßlich.

Wir schlagen deshalb einen anderen Weg ein, der von der prinzipiellen Gleichberechtigung beider Zweige Gebrauch macht.

4. Bestimmung beider Zweige in der Nähe des Verzweigungspunktes

Wir behandeln weiter (1),(2). Voraussetzung (3) kann nun wegfallen. $(u^*,\lambda^*) \in C_n^1[a,b] \times \mathbb{R}$ sei ein Verzweigungspunkt. Es wird nun ([1]) die volle Fréchet - Ableitung

$$F'(u,\lambda) = (F_u(u,\lambda), F_\lambda(u,\lambda)) = (L-f_u(\lambda,u), -f_\lambda(\lambda,u))$$

mit Definitionsbereich $D = D(L) \times \mathbb{R}$ betrachtet. Es gelte

$$\begin{aligned} &\dim N(F'(u^*,\lambda^*)) = 2, \quad N(F'(u^*,\lambda^*)) = \operatorname{span}\{p,q\}, \\ (10) \qquad &p = (p_1,p_2), \quad q = (q_1,q_2), \quad p_1,q_1 \in C_n^1[a,b], \quad p_2,q_2 \in \mathbb{R}. \end{aligned}$$

Wir stellen uns zunächst auf den Standpunkt, daß u^*, λ^*, p und q bekannt sind. Wie man diese genau berechnen kann, wird im nächsten Abschnitt gezeigt.

Zur Bestimmung der beiden sich in (u^*,λ^*) schneidenden Zweige (vgl. [1]) machen wir ähnlich wie in (5) einen Störungsansatz der Form

$$(11)\qquad \begin{pmatrix} u(\varepsilon) \\ \lambda(\varepsilon) \end{pmatrix} = \begin{pmatrix} u^* \\ \lambda^* \end{pmatrix} + \varepsilon\{\alpha(\varepsilon)p + \beta(\varepsilon)q\} + \varepsilon^2 v(\varepsilon), \quad v(\varepsilon) = \begin{pmatrix} v_1(\varepsilon) \\ v_2(\varepsilon) \end{pmatrix}$$
$$\langle\!\langle v,p \rangle\!\rangle = \langle\!\langle v,q \rangle\!\rangle = 0, \quad \alpha(\varepsilon)^2 + \beta(\varepsilon)^2 = 1,$$

mit

$$\langle\!\langle f,g \rangle\!\rangle := \langle f_1,g_1 \rangle + (b-a)\cdot f_2 g_2.$$

Die Einzelheiten sind in [6] beschrieben. Man ersetzt wieder F durch den Anfang seiner Taylorentwicklung um (u^*,λ^*) bis zum Restglied R dritter Ordnung, setzt (11) ein und vereinfacht unter Beachtung von $F'^*p = F'^*q = 0$, $p,q \in D$ $(F'^* := F'(u^*,\lambda^*))$. Division durch ε^2 liefert

$$(12)\qquad F'^*v + \frac{1}{2}F''^*[\alpha p + \beta q + \varepsilon v]^2 + \frac{1}{\varepsilon^2}R = 0, \quad B[v_1] = 0$$
$$\langle\!\langle v,p \rangle\!\rangle = \langle\!\langle v,q \rangle\!\rangle = 0, \quad \alpha^2+\beta^2 - 1 = 0.$$

Dabei ist bei R der Einfachheit halber das Argument $(u(\varepsilon),\lambda(\varepsilon))$ weggelassen. Ähnlich wie bei der Herleitung von (8) definieren wir hier eine zu (12) äquivalente RWA der Dimension n+5 durch

$$(13)\qquad \begin{aligned} & F'^*v + \frac{1}{2}F''^*[\alpha p + \beta q + \varepsilon v]^2 + \frac{1}{\varepsilon^2}R = 0 \\ & v_2' = \alpha' = \beta' = 0 \\ & \mu_1' - p_1^T v_1 - p_2 v_2 = 0 \\ & \mu_2' - q_1^T v_1 - q_2 v_2 = 0 \\ & B[v_1] = 0, \ \alpha(a)^2 + \beta(a)^2 - 1 = 0, \ \mu_j(a) = \mu_j(b) = 0, \ j=1,2 \end{aligned}$$

Die Skalare v_2, α und β sind dabei als (konstante) Variable eingeführt worden. Es gilt nun folgender Existenzsatz, der das von Crandall & Rabinowitz [1] angegebene Resultat verallgemeinert und gleichzeitig einen Weg zur numerischen Behandlung weist.

SATZ 2

Es gelte (10) und

$$(14)\qquad \operatorname{codim} R(F'^{*}) = 1,\ R(F'^{*}) = \{y \in C_n[a,b] \mid \langle \psi, y\rangle = 0\},\ \|\psi\| = 1,$$

sowie

$$(15)\qquad \tau = a_1 a_3 - a_2^2 < 0$$

mit $a_1 = \langle \psi, f''^{*}pp\rangle$, $a_2 = \langle \psi, f''^{*}pq\rangle$, $a_3 = \langle \psi, f''^{*}qq\rangle$, $f''^{*} := f''(\lambda^{*}, u^{*})$.
Dann existieren reelle Zahlen $\varepsilon_1, \varepsilon_2 > 0$, so daß die RWA (13) für $|\varepsilon| < \varepsilon_i$, $i=1,2$, stetige Kurven von isolierten Lösungen

$$(v^i(\varepsilon), \alpha^i(\varepsilon), \beta^i(\varepsilon), \mu_1^i(\varepsilon), \mu_2^i(\varepsilon))$$

besitzt, aus denen man mittels (11) zwei stetige Lösungskurven von (1) konstruieren kann, die sich in (u^{*}, λ^{*}) schneiden.

BEWEIS

Für $\varepsilon \to 0$ vereinfacht sich (13) zu

$$(16)\qquad \begin{aligned}
&F'^{*}\mathring{v} + \tfrac{1}{2} F''^{*}[\mathring{\alpha}p + \mathring{\beta}q]^2 = 0\\
&\mathring{v}_2' = \mathring{\alpha}' = \mathring{\beta}' = 0\\
&\mathring{\mu}_1' - p_1^T\mathring{v}_1 - p_2\mathring{v}_2 = 0\\
&\mathring{\mu}_2' - q_1^T v_1 - q_2\mathring{v}_2 = 0\\
&B[\mathring{v}_1] = 0,\quad \mathring{\alpha}(a)^2 + \mathring{\beta}(a)^2 - 1 = 0,\quad \mathring{\mu}_j(a) = \mathring{\mu}_j(b) = 0,\quad j=1,2.
\end{aligned}$$

Notwendig für die Lösbarkeit von (16) ist nach (14)

$$\langle \psi, F''^{*}[\mathring{\alpha}p + \mathring{\beta}q]^2\rangle = -\ \langle \psi, f''^{*}[\mathring{\alpha}p + \mathring{\beta}q]^2\rangle = 0.$$

Daraus folgt zusammen mit der Normierungsbedingung für $\mathring{\alpha}$ und $\mathring{\beta}$ das nichtlineare Gleichungssystem

$$(17a)\qquad a_1\,\mathring{\alpha}^2 + 2a_2\,\mathring{\alpha}\,\mathring{\beta} + a_3\,\mathring{\beta}^2 = 0$$

$$(17b)\qquad \mathring{\alpha}^2 + \mathring{\beta}^2 - 1 = 0$$

für $\overset{o}{\alpha}$ und $\overset{o}{\beta}$. Nach der Theorie der Kegelschnitte erhält man genau im Fall $\tau = a_1 a_3 - a_2^2 < 0$, d.h. wenn (17a) indefinit ist, zwei sich im Nullpunkt schneidende Geraden als Lösungen von (17a). Die Lösungen $(\bar{\alpha}^i, \bar{\beta}^i)^T$, i-1,...,4, von (17) ergeben sich als Schnittpunkte der beiden Geraden mit dem Einheitskreis. Wir wählen zwei linear unabhängige davon aus und nennen sie $(\alpha^i, \beta^i)^T$, $i=1,2$.

Zur Vereinfachung nehmen wir nun eine Transformation von p und q vor.
O.B.d.A. sei $a_1 \neq 0$. Andernfalls vertauscht man p und q. Falls $a_1 = a_3 = 0$ ist, kann folgende Transformation unterbleiben. Wir transformieren (p,q) in (p',q') gemäß

$$p' = \gamma p + \delta q, \quad q' = \varrho p + \mu q, \quad \gamma\mu - \delta\varrho \neq 0$$

mit

$$\gamma = \frac{-a_2 + \sqrt{-\tau}}{a_1}, \quad \delta = 1, \quad \varrho = \frac{-a_2 - \sqrt{-\tau}}{a_1}, \quad \mu = 1.$$

Sei $a_1' = \langle \psi, f''^* p'p' \rangle$, etc., dann ist $\tau' = a_1' a_3' - a_2'^2 = -4\tau^2/a_1^2 \neq 0$, und man erhält

$$(18) \qquad a_1' = 0, \quad a_2' = 2\tau/a_1, \quad a_3' = 0.$$

Der Einfachheit halber bezeichnen wir die transformierten Größen wieder mit a_i, p, q, τ. Die Lösungen von (17) lauten nun

$$(19) \qquad \alpha^1 = 1, \ \beta^1 = 0, \ \alpha^2 = 0, \ \beta^2 = 1.$$

Zu $\overset{oi}{\alpha} = \alpha^i$, $\overset{oi}{\beta} = \beta^i$ sind $\overset{oi}{v}$, $\overset{oi}{\mu}_1$ und $\overset{oi}{\mu}_2$ durch (16) eindeutig bestimmt, i=1,2. Dies folgt aus der Orthogonalitätsbedingung an $\overset{o}{v}$.

Wir wollen nun in den beiden Punkten $(\overset{oi}{v}, \overset{oi}{\alpha}, \overset{oi}{\beta}, \overset{oi}{\mu}_1, \overset{oi}{\mu}_2)$, $i = 1,2$, das Theorem über implizite Funktionen anwenden. Falls die Linearisierung von (16) in diesen beiden Punkten regulär ist, so ist damit die Behauptung des Satzes bewiesen. Die Regularität der Linearisierung von (16) wird in Hilfssatz 1 gezeigt.

q.e.d.

HILFSSATZ 1

Die Voraussetzungen von Satz 2 seien erfüllt.

Dann sind die Lösungen

$$(\overset{oi}{v}, \overset{oi}{\alpha}, \overset{oi}{\beta}, \overset{oi}{\mu}_1, \overset{oi}{\mu}_2)$$

von (16) mit $\overset{oi}{\alpha} = \alpha^i$, $\overset{oi}{\beta} = \beta^i$, $i = 1,2$, isoliert.

BEWEIS

Wir betrachten die Linearisierung von (16) in den genannten Lösungen. Es muß gezeigt werden, daß

$$
(20)\qquad
\begin{aligned}
& F'^{*}\tilde{v} + \tilde{\alpha}\overset{oi}{\alpha}F''^{*}pp + \tilde{\alpha}\overset{oi}{\beta}F''^{*}pq + \tilde{\beta}\overset{oi}{\alpha}F''^{*}pq + \tilde{\beta}\overset{oi}{\beta}F''^{*}qq = 0\\
& \tilde{v}_2' = 0, \quad \tilde{\alpha}' = 0, \quad \tilde{\beta}' = 0\\
& \tilde{\mu}_1' - p_1^T\tilde{v}_1 - p_2\tilde{v}_2 = 0\\
& \tilde{\mu}_2' - q_1\tilde{v}_1 - q_2\tilde{v}_2 = 0\\
& B[\tilde{v}_1] = 0, \quad 2(\tilde{\alpha}\overset{oi}{\alpha} + \tilde{\beta}\overset{oi}{\beta}) = 0, \quad \tilde{\mu}_j(a) = \tilde{\mu}_j(b) = 0, \quad j=1,2
\end{aligned}
$$

nur die triviale Lösung $\tilde{v} \equiv 0$, $\tilde{\alpha} \equiv \tilde{\beta} \equiv \tilde{\mu}_1 \equiv \tilde{\mu}_2 \equiv 0$ besitzt.

Damit (20) lösbar ist, muß gelten

$$
\begin{aligned}
(\overset{oi}{\alpha}a_1 + \overset{oi}{\beta}a_2)\tilde{\alpha} + (\overset{oi}{\alpha}a_2 + \overset{oi}{\beta}a_3)\tilde{\beta} &= 0\\
\overset{oi}{\alpha}\tilde{\alpha} \quad + \quad \overset{oi}{\beta}\tilde{\beta} &= 0
\end{aligned}
$$

Aus (18) und (19) folgt $\tilde{\alpha} \equiv \tilde{\beta} \equiv 0$ für $i = 1,2$. Es bleibt

$$
\begin{aligned}
& F'^{*}\tilde{v} = 0, \quad \tilde{v}_2' = 0, \quad B[\tilde{v}_1] = 0\\
& \tilde{\mu}_1' - p_1^T\tilde{v}_1 - p_2\tilde{v}_2 = 0\\
& \tilde{\mu}_2' - q_1\tilde{v}_1 - q_2\tilde{v}_2 = 0, \quad \tilde{\mu}_j(a) = \tilde{\mu}_j(b) = 0, \quad j = 1,2.
\end{aligned}
$$

Wegen der Orthogonalitätsforderungen an $\tilde{v}$ folgt $\tilde{v} \equiv 0$, also auch $\tilde{\mu}_1 \equiv \tilde{\mu}_2 \equiv 0$.

q.e.d.

Zur numerischen Behandlung der RWA (13) benutzt man Standardmethoden für nichtlineare RWA'n, etwa Differenzen - oder Shooting - Verfahren. Man geht dabei für jeden Zweig jeweils von

$\varepsilon = 0$ aus und verwendet ε - Homotopien.

5. Bestimmung des Verzweigungspunktes

Wir setzen hier voraus, daß wenigstens eine der beiden sich in (u^*,λ^*) schneidenden Lösungskurven von (1) eine glatte Parametrisierung nach λ gestattet.

Dann können p und q in der speziellen Form

$$(21) \qquad p^* = (p_1^*,0),\ q^* = (q_1^*,1),\ \langle p_1^*,p_1^*\rangle = 1,\ \langle p_1^*,q_1^*\rangle = 0$$

angesetzt werden, wodurch sie bis auf Vorzeichen eindeutig bestimmt sind. Es ist nun klar, daß die gesuchten Größen u^*, λ^*, p_1^* und q_1^* Lösungen der folgenden, sie definierenden RWA sein müssen:

$$(22) \qquad \begin{array}{ll} Lu - f(\lambda,u) = 0, & B[u] = 0 \\ [L - f_u(\lambda,u)]p_1 = 0, & B[p_1] = 0 \\ [L - f_u(\lambda,u)]q_1 - f_\lambda(\lambda,u) = 0, & B[q_1] = 0 \\ \lambda' = 0 & \\ \mu_1' - p_1^T p_1 = 0, & \mu_1(a) = 0,\ \mu_1(b) = 1 \\ \mu_2' - q_1^T p_1 = 0, & \mu_2(a) = 0,\ \mu_2(b) = 0. \end{array}$$

Diese besteht aus N = 3n+3 Differentialgleichungen und 3n+4 Randbedingungen, ist von den Randbedingungen her "überbestimmt" und stellt daher keine Standardaufgabe dar.

Wir schreiben (22) zusammengefaßt als

$$(23) \qquad y' = h(t,y),\ a \le t \le b,\quad \bar{B}[y] = \bar{B}_a y(a) + \bar{B}_b y(b) = \eta$$

mit geeigneten $\bar{B}_a$, $\bar{B}_b \in \mathbb{R}^{N+1,N}$ und $\eta \in \mathbb{R}^{N+1}$.

SATZ 3

Für (1) gelte (2), (10), (14) und (15). Ferner sei mindestens eine Lösungskurve glatt durch λ parametrisierbar.

<u>Dann besitzt die homogene lineare RWA</u>

$$(24)\qquad w' - h_y(t,y^*(t))w = 0, \qquad \bar{B}[w] = 0$$

<u>nur die triviale Lösung. Dabei ist</u>

$$y^* = (u^*, \lambda^*, p_1^*, q_1^*, \mu_1^*, \mu_2^*)$$

<u>mit</u> $\mu_1^*(t) = \int_a^t p_1^*(s)^T p_1^*(s)ds$ <u>und</u> $\mu_2^*(t) = \int_a^t q_1^*(s)^T p_1^*(s)ds.$

<u>BEWEIS</u>

Wir schreiben (24) komponentenweise auf mit $w = (\tilde{u}, \tilde{\lambda}, \tilde{p}_1, \tilde{q}_1, \tilde{\mu}_1, \tilde{\mu}_2)$ und $L^* = L - f_u^*$

$$(25)\qquad \begin{array}{ll} L^*\tilde{u} - f^*\tilde{\lambda} = 0, & B[\tilde{u}] = 0 \\ L^*\tilde{p}_1 - f_{uu}^* p_1^* \tilde{u} - f_{u\lambda}^* p_1^* \tilde{\lambda} = 0, & B[\tilde{p}_1] = 0 \\ L^*\tilde{q}_1 - f_{uu}^* q_1^* \tilde{u} - f_{u\lambda}^* q_1^* \tilde{\lambda} - f_{u\lambda}^* \tilde{u} - f_{\lambda\lambda}^* \tilde{\lambda} = 0, & B[\tilde{q}_1] = 0 \\ \tilde{\lambda}' = 0 & \\ \tilde{\mu}_1' - 2\cdot p_1^{*T}\tilde{p}_1 = 0, & \tilde{\mu}_1(a) = \tilde{\mu}_1(b) = 0 \\ \tilde{\mu}_2' - q_1^{*T}\tilde{p}_1 - p_1^{*T}\tilde{q}_1 = 0, & \tilde{\mu}_2(a) = \tilde{\mu}_2(b) = 0. \end{array}$$

Aus der ersten Gleichung von (25) folgt

$$\tilde{u} = c_1 p_1^* + c_2 q_1^*, \quad \tilde{\lambda} = c_2, \quad c_1, c_2 \in \mathbb{R} \; .$$

Einsetzen in die zweite und dritte Gleichung liefert

$$(26)\qquad \begin{array}{l} L^*\tilde{p}_1 = c_1 f_{uu}^* p_1^* p_1^* + c_2(f_{uu}^* p_1^* q_1^* + f_{u\lambda}^* p_1^*) \\ L^*\tilde{q}_1 = c_1(f_{uu}^* p_1^* p_1^* + f_{u\lambda}^* p_1^*) + c_2(f_{uu}^* q_1^* q_1^* + 2f_{u\lambda}^* q_1^* + f_{\lambda\lambda}^*). \end{array}$$

a_1, a_2, a_3 aus (15) lauten hier

$$a_1 = \langle \psi, f_{uu}^* p_1^* p_1^* \rangle, \quad a_2 = \langle \psi, f_{uu}^* p_1^* q_1^* + f_{u\lambda}^* p_1^* \rangle,$$

$$a_3 = \langle \psi, f_{uu}^* q_1^* q_1^* + 2f_{u\lambda}^* q_1^* + f_{\lambda\lambda}^* \rangle \; .$$

Wegen $R(L^*) = R(F'^*)$ ist die Lösbarkeit von (26) äquivalent dazu, daß c_1 und c_2

$$a_1c_1 + a_2c_2 = 0$$
$$a_2c_1 + a_3c_2 = 0$$

erfüllen. Wegen (15): $a_1a_3 - a_2^2 < 0$ folgt $c_1 = c_2 = 0$, damit $\tilde{u} \equiv 0$, $\tilde{\lambda} \equiv 0$ und

$$L^*\tilde{p}_1 = 0, \; L^*\tilde{q}_1 = 0, \quad B[p_1] = B[q_1] = 0.$$

Somit ist $p_1 = dp_1^*$, $q_1 = ep_1^*$; $d,e \in \mathbb{R}$. Aus den beiden letzten Gleichungen von (25) folgt $d = e = 0$. Damit ist gezeigt: $w \equiv 0$.

q.e.d.

Zur numerischen Lösung der "überbestimmten" nichtlinearen RWA (22) kann man das Shooting - bzw. Multiple - Shooting - Verfahren in geeigneter Form verwenden. Wir beschreiben hier nur das einfache Shooting - Verfahren.

Man sucht eine Lösung des überbestimmten nichtlinearen Gleichungssystems

(27) $$G(s) = \bar{B}_a s + \bar{B}_b y(b;s) - \eta = 0, \; G: \mathbb{R}^N \to \mathbb{R}^{N+1},$$

wobei $y(t;s)$ Lösung der AWA $\frac{d}{dt}y(t;s) = h(t,y(t;s))$, $y(a;s) = s$ ist. Zur Lösung von (27) suchen wir ein globales Minimum des Funktionals

(28) $$g(s) = \frac{1}{2} G(s)^T G(s).$$

<u>SATZ 4</u>

<u>Seien die Voraussetzungen von Satz</u> 3 <u>erfüllt und sei</u> $s^* = y^*(a)$. <u>Dann ist das Funktional</u> g <u>aus</u> (28) <u>strikt konvex auf einer Umgebung</u> U <u>von</u> s^*; <u>insbesondere ist</u> $g''(s^*)$ <u>positiv definit</u>.

<u>BEWEIS</u>

Es ist $G'(s^*) = \bar{B}_a + \bar{B}_b Z(b;s^*)$, wobei $Z(t;s) \in C^1_{n\times n}[a,b]$ mit

$$\frac{d}{dt}Z(t;s) = h_y(t,y(t;s))Z(t;s), \; Z(a;s) = I.$$

Nach [3] hat der Nullraum des durch

$$w' - h_y(t,y^*(t))w \quad \text{und} \quad \bar{B}$$

definierten linearen Differentialoperators die gleiche Dimension wie der Nullraum der Matrix $\bar{B}_a + \bar{B}_b Z(b;s^*)$. Also hat $G'(s^*)$ nach Satz 3 den vollen Rang N und

$$g''(s^*) = G'(s^*)^T G'(s^*)$$

ist positiv definit. Damit existiert eine Umgebung U von s^*, auf der g strikt konvex ist.

q.e.d.

Zur Minimierung von g lassen sich Standardverfahren aus der Theorie der unrestringierten konvexen Optimierung verwenden. Bei der Bestimmung eines Verzweigungspunktes nach dem hier vorgeschlagenen Verfahren handelt es sich um die Lösung einer gut konditionierten Aufgabenstellung, im Gegensatz zu bisher bekannten Methoden. Dies folgt aus Satz 4. Der Schlüssel zum Erfolg der hier beschriebenen Vorgehensweise liegt in der in Satz 2 gegebenen Charakterisierung eines Verzweigungspunktes, speziell der Voraussetzung (15).

6. Ein Beispiel

Von Pimbley [4] stammt folgendes Beispiel einer Hammersteinschen Integralgleichung

(29) $$\lambda u(s) = \frac{2}{\pi}\int_0^{\pi}(3\sin t\sin s + 2\sin 2t\sin 2s)(u(t)+u(t)^3)dt, \quad 0 \leq s \leq \pi.$$

Neben der trivialen Lösung $u^0 = 0$ besitzt (29) die nichttrivialen Lösungen

$$u^i(\lambda;t) = \pm\frac{2}{\sqrt{3}}\sqrt{\frac{\lambda}{4-i} - 1}\;\sin(it), \quad i = 1,2$$

$$u_+^3(\lambda;t) = \frac{2}{3}\sqrt{\frac{2}{3}\lambda - 1}\;\sin t \pm \frac{2}{3}\sqrt{\frac{\lambda}{6} - 1}\;\sin 2t$$

$$u_-^3(\lambda;t) = -\frac{2}{3}\sqrt{\frac{2}{3}\lambda - 1}\;\sin t \pm \frac{2}{3}\sqrt{\frac{\lambda}{6} - 1}\;\sin 2t$$

u^1 verzweigt von $u^0 \equiv 0$ bei $\lambda = 3$, u^2 verzweigt von u^0 bei $\lambda = 2$, u_+^3 zweigt von u^1 bei $\lambda = 6$ ab. Wir interessieren uns für die sekundäre Verzweigung in $(u^*,\lambda^*) = (\frac{2}{\sqrt{3}}\sin t, 6)$.

(29) kann leicht in eine RWA der Dimension $n = 5$ überführt werden; u entspricht dann u_1. Sie lautet

$$(30)\quad \begin{aligned} & u_1' = \frac{6}{\pi\lambda}\cos t\,(u_2+u_3) + \frac{8}{\pi\lambda}\cos 2t\,(u_4+u_5) \\ & u_2' = (u_1+u_1^3)\sin t, \quad u_3' = -(u_1+u_1^3)\sin t \\ & u_4' = (u_1+u_1^3)\sin 2t, \quad u_5' = -(u_1+u_1^3)\sin 2t \\ & u_1(0) = u_2(0) = u_3(\pi) = u_4(0) = u_5(\pi) = 0. \end{aligned}$$

Die RWA (22) zur Bestimmung des Verzweigungspunkts besteht aus 18 Differentialgleichungen mit 19 Randbedingungen und soll wegen ihrer einfachen Struktur hier nicht wiedergegeben werden (s. [6]). Die RWA (13) lautet hier

$$(31)\quad \begin{aligned} v_1' = {} & \frac{6}{\pi\lambda^*}\cos t\,(v_2+v_3) + \frac{8}{\pi\lambda^*}\cos 2t\,(v_4+v_5) - \Big[\frac{6}{\pi\lambda^{*2}}\cos t\cdot \\ & \cdot(u_2^*+u_3^*) + \frac{8}{\pi\lambda^{*2}}\cos 2t\,(u_4^*+u_5^*)\Big]\, v_6 - \Big[\frac{6}{\pi\lambda^{*2}}\cos t\cdot \\ & \cdot\{v_7(p_1^2+p_1^3)+v_8(q_1^2+q_1^3)+\varepsilon(v_2+v_3)\} + \frac{8}{\pi\lambda^{*2}}\cos 2t\cdot \\ & \cdot\{v_7(p_1^4+p_1^5)+v_8(q_1^4+q_1^5)+\varepsilon(v_4+v_5)\}\Big]\cdot(v_7p_2^*+v_8q_2^*+\varepsilon v_6) \\ & + \Big[\frac{6}{\pi\lambda^{*3}}\cos t\,(u_2^*+u_3^*) + \frac{8}{\pi\lambda^{*3}}\cos 2t\,(u_4^*+u_5^*)\Big]\cdot \\ & \cdot(v_7p_2^*+v_8q_2^*+\varepsilon v_6)^2 + R(v_2,v_3,v_4,v_5,v_6;\varepsilon) \\ v_2' = {} & Q_1, \quad v_3' = -Q_1, \quad v_4' = Q_2, \quad v_5' = -Q_2, \quad v_6' = v_7' = v_8' = 0, \\ v_9' = {} & p_1^1v_1 + p_1^2v_2 + p_1^3v_3 + p_1^4v_4 + p_1^5v_5 + p_2^*v_6 \\ v_{10}' = {} & q_1^1v_1 + q_1^2v_2 + q_1^3v_3 + q_1^4v_4 + q_1^5v_5 + q_2^*v_6 \\ & v_1(0) = v_2(0) = v_3(\pi) = v_4(0) = v_5(\pi) = v_9(0) = v_9(\pi) = 0, \\ & v_{10}(0) = v_{10}(\pi) = 0, \quad v_7(0)^2 + v_8(0)^2 - 1 = 0 \end{aligned}$$

mit $Q_j = \sin jt\cdot\Big[(1+3u_1^{*2})v_1 + 3u_1^*\{v_7p_1^1 + v_8q_1^1 + \varepsilon v_1\}^2 +$

$$+\varepsilon\{v_7 p_1^1 + v_8 q_1^1 + \varepsilon v_1\}^3],\quad p_1^* = (p_1^1, p_1^2, p_1^3, p_1^4, p_1^5),$$
$$q_1^* = (q_1^1, q_1^2, q_1^3, q_1^4, q_1^5)$$

und einem geeigneten Restglied R.

In beiden Fällen wurde das Shooting - Verfahren, für (31) in Verbindung mit einer ε - Homotopie, bei (22) zusammen mit dem Levenberg - Marquardt - Algorithmus zur Minimierung des Funktionals g, benutzt. Die AWA'n wurden mit dem klassischen Runge - Kutta - Verfahren 4. Ordnung mit fester Schrittweite h integriert.

Bei der Bestimmung des Verzweigungspunktes ergaben sich für die Variable λ aus (22) folgende Ergebnisse:

	$h = \pi/50$	$h = \pi/100$	$h = \pi/200$
$\lambda = \lambda(0)$	5.9999800	5.9999987	6.0000000

Die Resultate für die übrigen Variablen waren von ähnlicher Genauigkeit.

Bei der Bestimmung beider Zweige durch den Verzweigungspunkt wählten wir $h = \pi/100$ unter Verwendung der oben mit $h = \pi/200$ erzielten Ergebnisse. ε - Intervalle: $[-0.5,+0.5]$; die Ergebnisse stimmten mit den wahren Lösungen auf 7 - 8 wesentliche Dezimalstellen überein, z.B. ergaben sich:

ε	0.01	0.2
$\lambda(\varepsilon)$	6.0099975	6.1991079
$u_1(\varepsilon;\pi/2)$	1.1566230	1.1924033
$u(\lambda(\varepsilon);\pi/2)$	1.1566230	1.1924033

Primäre Lösung (u^1)
u bezeichnet die wahre Lösung

ε	0.01	0.2
$\lambda(\varepsilon)$	6.0000218	6.0087484
$u_1(\varepsilon;\pi/2)$	1.1547033	1.1558224
$u(\lambda(\varepsilon);\pi/2)$	1.1547033	1.1558224

Sekundäre Lösung (u_+^3)

Die Rechnungen wurden mit einfacher Genauigkeit, ca. 8 Dezimalstellen, auf der HB 66/80 des Rechenzentrums der Johannes Gutenberg - Universität Mainz durchgeführt.

Literatur

1. Crandall, M.G., Rabinowitz, P.H.: Bifurcation from simple eigenvalues, J. Functional Anal. 8 (1971), 321-340

2. Keller, H.B.: Numerical solution of bifurcation and nonlinear eigenvalue problems, in: Rabinowitz, P.H. (Ed.): Applications of bifurcation theory, Proceedings of an advanced seminar conducted by the Mathematics Research Center, The University of Wisconsin at Madison, New York, Academic Press 1977

3. Langford, W.F.: Numerical solution of bifurcation problems for ordinary differential equations, Numer. Math. 28 (1977), 171 - 190

4. Pimbley, G.H.Jr.: Eigenfunction branches of nonlinear operators, and their bifurcation, Berlin, Springer, Lecture Notes in Mathematics 104, 1969

5. Scheurle, J.: Ein selektives Projektions - Iterationsverfahren und Anwendungen auf Verzweigungsprobleme, Numer. Math. 29 (1977), 11-35

6. Weber, H.: Numerische Behandlung von Verzweigungsproblemen bei Randwertaufgaben gewöhnlicher Differentialgleichungen, Dissertation, Mainz 1978

7. Weber, H.: Numerische Behandlung von Verzweigungsproblemen bei gewöhnlichen Differentialgleichungen, Numer. Math., to appear

8. Weiss, R.: Bifurcation in difference approximations to two - point boundary value problems, Math. Comp. 29 (1975), 746-760

Helmut Weber
Abteilung Mathematik
Universität Dortmund
Postfach 500 500
D-4600 Dortmund 50